FREEDOM AND CREATION
IN THREE TRADITIONS

Para Andrés

for a continued discussion

B Burrell

29. VI. 95.

Freedom and Creation
in Three Traditions

DAVID B. BURRELL, C.S.C.

University of Notre Dame Press
Notre Dame, Indiana 46556

Library of Congress Cataloging-in-Publication Data

Burrell, David B.
    Freedom and creation in three traditions / David B. Burrell.
        p.   cm.
    Includes bibliographical references and index.
    ISBN 0-268-00987-2 (alk. paper)
    1. Creation–Comparative studies.   2. Free will and
determinism–Comparative studies.   3. God–Omnipotence–
Comparative studies.   4. Freedom (Theology)–Comparative
studies.   5. Judaism–Doctrines.   6. Islam–Doctrines.
    I. Title.
BS652.B87   1993
291.2′4–dc20   92-53745
                                                                        CIP

⊗ *The paper used in this publication meets the minimum requirements*
of the American National Standard for Information Sciences–Permanence of Paper
for Printed Library Materials, ANSI Z39.48-1984.

In gratitude to
Georges C. Anawati, O.P.,
of
L'Institut Dominicain d'Etudes Orientales
Cairo,
whose encouragement and prodding
have assisted so many
and whose hospitality
helped to bring this study and so much else to birth

Contents

Preface

This study had its proximate origins in a colloquium held at the University of Notre Dame on September 8–9, 1989, to which colleagues knowledgeable about these matters were invited to learn from one another, under the aegis of the Theodore M. Hesburgh, C.S.C. Chair in the College of Arts and Letters. These included Avital Wohlman, Joseph Incandela, James Ross, Kathryn Tanner, Mark Jordan, Joseph Wawrykow, and Paul Griffiths; as well as Michael Loux, Frederick Crosson, Thomas Flint, and Kenneth Sayre, and Timothy O'Meara. The intent was to explore these questions in the largely hospitable environment of the departments of Philosophy and Theology at Notre Dame, inviting participants from Jerusalem, New Haven and Philadelphia as well. The model had been an earlier conference jointly sponsored by the department of Theology and the Center for the Philosophy of Religion at Notre Dame with the Institute for the Advanced Study of Religion of the Divinity School at the University of Chicago, where the participants explored Jewish, Christian, and Muslim elaborations of creation. That conference had in turn been inspired by a symposium at the Dumbarton Oaks Center in Washington in 1985, organized under the title of "Mysticism and Philosophy," where Jewish, Christian, and Muslim scholars engaged in serious conversation on issues affecting their beliefs and practices. If our colloquium lacked an explicitly Islamic dimension, that can be traced to matters of economy: the issues surrounding freedom and creation in that tradition are so rich and so contested that it was judged appropriate to remand their treatment to a later colloquium promised under the auspices of the Hesburgh Chair.

The advantages of such a comparative study of topics in philosophical theology will be displayed, I hope, rather than argued for here. This study follows on my earlier attempt to explore the interfaith, intercultural perspectives operative in the medieval doctrine of God as expounded by Ibn Sina, Maimonides, and Aquinas—*Knowing the Unknowable God* (Notre Dame, Ind.: University of Notre Dame Press, 1986). The interrelation of freedom and creation seemed a promising next step, and the fascinating contributions to the 1989 colloquium proved that to be the case. I am especially indebted to those who responded to the invitation of that gathering, for I invited people from whose perspectives I knew I would profit, and who would be sure to learn from one another. Among those who responded to my request for critical comments on an earlier draft of this work, I am grateful especially to Diogenes Allen, Paul Burrell, John Cavadini, Frederick Crosson, Seymour Feldman, Jamie Ferreira, Lenn Goodman, Paul Griffiths, Stanley Hauerwas, Joseph Incandela, Nicholas Lash, Barry Miller, Tom Morris, Carol Ochs, Jean Porter, Kathryn Tanner, and Joseph Wawrykow. Their comments improved my efforts in matters large and small, saving me from egregious errors and enlarging my horizon in a number of places. The reader will be grateful to them. Any inquiry is ideally collaborative, and comparative studies necessarily so, so the emerging community of inquirers engaged in the issues broached here would have heartened Charles Sanders Pierce and Bernard J. F. Lonergan, both of whom saw clearly the need for community in philosophical and theological inquiry.

Certain references frequently cited will be appropriately abbreviated: Thomas Aquinas, *Summa Theologiae* = *ST,* with parts, questions, articles, and responses listed in serial order: *ST* 1–2.3.6.7 = Part I of the Second Part, article 3, question 6, response to objection 7. Similarly, Moses Maimonides' *Guide of the Perplexed* (= *Guide*) will be cited by book and chapter: 2.57. Bernard Lonergan's *Grace and Freedom* = *GF,* and the new edition of the *Encyclopedia of Islam* = *EI²*, while the *Shorter Encyclopedia of Islam* = *SEI*.

My special gratitude to the University of Notre Dame Press, in the persons of its director, James Langford, and its editor, Ann Rice, who have consistently supported my forays into relatively uncharted waters, and in whose list in philosophical theology it is a privilege to participate. Gerard Jacobitz has graced the volume with a thorough index.

Introduction

This exploration into human and divine freedom in the three traditions which avow a free creation – Judaism, Christianity, and Islam – has many related goals. It is primarily an essay in philosophical theology, yet one carried out in comparative fashion. That means that we will be entering into two and even three liminal and hence contested regions. For comparative studies in religion have been a long time finding their feet, despite the obvious need to carry out inquiries in that fashion in our time. And philosophical theology arguably belongs to philosophy as a subsection of philosophy of religion, yet (I shall argue) is more properly a subdiscipline of theology, since it cannot hope to make any progress without attending to the religious traditions which animate its inquiry. And that contention introduces the third liminal feature of our inquiry, for anyone who begins with religious faith and practice is susceptible of being labeled a "fideist," since they have eschewed an approach to inherently religious questions which purports to be that of "pure reason." Yet such polarities – *fideism* or *pure reason* – have a curiously archaic ring to them today, as we become more sensitive to the role which tradition plays in any inquiry, religious or not. And especially so in a religious domain, where the faith and practice of a community forms the living context for inquiry. So I have been urged to be clear about my manner of argumentation, my ways of utilizing sources, and candid about the approaches which I find less than fruitful and to which I shall be offering constructive alternatives. But before addressing these multiple questions of method, let us consider the subject matter and its intrinsic importance.

"Divine freedom and human freedom in the context of creation" has been the working title of this inquiry for some time. The initial heuristic hypothesis stemmed from exasperation at the tendency of the modern West to pit these two freedoms against one another, so that God and human beings were presumed to be engaged in a "zero-sum game," in which one party's gain was inevitably the other's loss, and vice-versa. Indeed, much of the motivation for what Henri de Lubac depicted as the "drama of modern atheism" stems from just such a presumption. Christian theology suffered from the same cultural bias, so that baroque controversies regarding human freedom and divine grace were preoccupied with "reconciling" the two. My heuristic hypothesis contended that theologians and atheologians alike were guilty of mixing modes of inquiry: of taking the universe to be the given context for the divine-human encounter and then projecting that encounter in interpersonal terms. Such a starting point would be the expected one for natural scientists, for whom the universe is simply that: the given context for their inquiries. And if such inquirers happened also to be people of faith, it would be natural enough for them to speak of divine-human relations in interpersonal language. Yet such a One as God would inevitably so overshadow the human actor that the freedom of our response would then become problematic. But what if we were to focus on believers who also professed this God to be the free creator of all-that-is? Would we not then be able to finesse the "zero-sum" presumptions of any divine-human encounter by actively recalling that the two protagonists are of decidedly different orders: the one creator and the other creature? And if at first blush this explicit shift only served to magnify the original "problem," might not an explicit inquiry into the ways in which *creation* is elaborated by each of the three traditions which avows it to be the free action of God expose the confusing presumptions underlying the "zero-sum" picture? That is, the creator can hardly be considered as simply another "person" on the scene, nor need we presume creatures always to be subservient to their creator. It was here that a comparative inquiry suggested itself, focusing on the three traditions which avow a free creation: Judaism, Christianity, and Islam – the three "Abrahamic" faiths. That step would seem a natural enough one in any case, but the history of Christian theology calls for some explicit correctives in this regard. For despite the fact that Christians confess their faith in "one God, creator of heaven and earth," a set of factors have worked in a cumulative fashion over time to eclipse that faith in creation as the initial gift of God in favor of the divine self-gift in Jesus. Redemption, in short, has so overshadowed creation in the Christian sensibility that Christians generally have little difficulty adopting a naturalistic attitude toward the universe. Rather than approaching it and responding to it as a *gift*, they can easily treat it simply as a *given*. Three factors appear to have been decisive in fixing this stance: the liturgical shift from the sabbath to the "day of the Lord," connotative fallout from the medieval distinction of *supernatural* from *natural*, and the nineteenth-century cleavage of history from nature.

Doubtless the first had the most pervasive effect: as the sabbath celebrated creation by creating a space in which God's people explicitly refrained from any activities designed to improve God's creation, the fact that human beings are not involved in creating or sustaining the universe was regularly borne in upon them. All that slipped into umbrage once the regular celebration became that of the Lord's resurrection and our promised share in that transforming event. In the thirteenth century Philip the Chancellor introduced the conceptual distinction of *supernatural* from *natural* activity, so distinguishing the realms of grace and of nature. And since *grace* correlated with *supernatural*, a spontaneous implication could easily be drawn that what was natural was not in fact a gift, but rather a given. In this way, a conceptual device which was to prove immensely useful in opening traditional Augustinian theology to assimilate the analysis of Aristotle unwittingly augmented a tendency to "naturalize" the created universe and so further obscured the theological import of the Christian profession of faith in the creator. As an academic corollary, a division of labor emerged between philosophy and theology in which the one, creating God tended to be treated under the rubric of *philosophy* (or *natural theology*), while the triune, redeeming God became the proper subject of *theology*. Finally, the nineteenth-century separation of history from nature offered conceptual reinforcement to the earlier distinction, by now hardened into the "two-story universe" of baroque theology: the world of nature now belongs to natural science while the world of history to the "human sciences," and biblical theology focused its attention on the "God who acts" in "salvation history."

The corrective which comparative work with Jewish and Muslim traditions promises to bring to such a scenario stems from their focus on God as free creator of the universe, and the reluctance of either of these traditions to elaborate a distinct ontological "order" when treating of God's redeeming revelation and of our response to it. Yet it will soon become clear that each tradition's way of understanding and elaborating the doctrine of God's free creation of the universe will reflect their particular assimilation of the divine invitation addressed to them in the form of a revelation. And understandably enough, since no doctrine of creation allows for witnesses to the "event"! The conception of divine freedom operative in creation, then, will mirror a community's experience of a freely inviting God; and since each of these three communities structures the relatedness of human beings and God differently, appreciably different ways of elaborating creation will emerge. The intent of this work is not to find a "common denominator," but to allow each tradition to illuminate the other. While the author's tradition and standpoint is Christian, we shall not be preoccupied with domestic issues in Christian theology but rather with discovering how each of the traditions has sought for an appropriate philosophical scheme to articulate their grounding faith in God's freedom to create our universe.

That focus makes this a work in philosophical theology, while the comparative structure emphasizes the role which tradition plays in suggesting the conceptualities appropriate to such limiting questions as "the distinction" of God from the world, as well as the freedom of creation.[1] Negatively, this focus intends to rule out any confident recourse to "our intuitions" in such arcane matters, for whatever "intuitions" *we* may have will represent the residue of our particular traditions and often betray accents peculiar to specific theological traditions within the dominant faith group. It would be better, then, to trace those traditions in their parallel developments and so explicitly acknowledge that our inquiry in these matters is "tradition-directed."[2] That should allow us to put to rest *a priori* charges of "fideism" by challenging the availability of a "neutral" perspective on such matters. And similar observations obtain about the use of philosophy in theological inquiry: not only are certain philosophical strategies more consonant with one's faith perspective than others, but philosophical categories themselves may have to be adapted, expanded, and even transformed to do the job required of them in elaborating a doctrine of free creation of the universe. Such is certainly the history of the matter, and this essay relies as much as it does on Thomas Aquinas, precisely because his astute capacity to adapt and transform the Hellenic philosophical tradition transmitted to him through Avicenna and Averroës offers an outstanding working example of philosophical theology in the sense intended. Since creation is our focus, and a more mature understanding of freedom our goal, I shall be arguing against current proposals to utilize contemporary notions of "possible worlds" or of "libertarian" freedom to elaborate a metaphysics consonant with Jewish, Christian, and Muslim religious teaching of the free creation of the universe.

Creation and freedom are inherently related in the Jewish, Christian, and Muslim traditions because of their insistence that the act of creating is a gratuitous one on the part of divinity. Yet it would be temerarious to infer that the term *freedom* means the same thing when used of the creator of all and of rational creatures. So while the medieval controversies centered around the neoplatonic challenge of a necessary

emanation of the universe from "the One," our climate invites greater clarity about the freedom with which God creates and that whereby we respond to the explicit invitations
enshrined in the respective traditions.[3] What will emerge is
a notion of created freedom, or the freedom proper to creatures. Such a notion cannot function as a simple alternative
to the currently prevailing notions of freedom as "autonomy,"
since the context which it presumes is one of free creation
and response to an invitation – realities unavailable without
faith. Yet the kind of analysis required to elaborate such a notion, as well as the results obtained, may be compelling enough
to readers to make them question the relatively unexamined
notions of human freedom employed currently by philosophers. Indeed, some feedback of that sort ought to be the
fruit of a philosophical theology which allows itself to be directed by the traditions to which it is in fact beholden. For
traditions can offer unexpectedly fresh perspectives on peren-
nial human questions, especially when they represent the fruit
of reflection over centuries.

In summary, then, ours is a constructive proposal designed
to illustrate the worth of explicitly tradition-directed inquiry,
as well as the fruitfulness of comparative inquiries in philosophical theology. The world in which we live demands our
reaching out to understand other traditions, notably religious
ones, and our efforts to do so usually help us better to appreciate our own, largely because the pressure of comparative perspectives demands that we mine hitherto unsuspected
reaches of what we have thought we knew. It is in this fashion that traditional disciplines of philosophy and of theology
may each be enriched by the forays of such an inquiry. Many
questions remain unanswered and many more unaddressed.
In part, the essay represents a way of approaching these sub-
jects which hopes to inspire more incisive and better informed
efforts on the part of others.

1

The Context: Creation

The very notion of creation is notoriously difficult to clarify, for it contains scriptural as well as metaphysical elements and does so in a fashion in which they are quite impossible to disentangle. Nor need we separate them neatly, yet clarity demands that we identify the components of the notion which we shall need—a notion beholden to Hebrew and Christian scriptures, the Qur'an, and diverse philosophical legacies. The arresting note would seem to be: once there was nothing and then there was something; in short, an absolute beginning. That is how most people understand the biblical and Qur'anic notion of *creatio ex nihilo,* and those seemed to be the terms in which the medieval debate was posed: between an eternal emanation and a creation such that there was a beginning moment of time. Yet Thomas Aquinas, following the lead and the strategy of Moses Maimonides, argued that the notion of absolute beginning was a sign of the difference between believers in scripture and neoplatonist advocates of eternal emanation, rather than itself marking that difference. Both argued that it was possible to *conceive* creation in the manner required by revelation as an affair without a beginning but that the *apparent* insistence of Genesis on a point at which this temporal universe began made the utter dependence of creatures on a creator that much more evident. It also underscored the fact that the very existence of such a dependent universe did not belong to the nature of divinity but represented a free initiative on God's part, for if the universe were without beginning, it would be

more natural to think of it as the necessary concomitant of
its creator.

1.1 GRATUITOUS ORIGINATION

It is in the spirit and interest of our inquiry to begin with
these two medieval philosophical theologians, one operating
from a Jewish and one from a Christian tradition, yet both
beholden to an Islamic philosophical context. What one finds
so fascinating about them is their hermeneutic sophistication, however patronizing that observation may sound. They
clearly ground what they believe to be the essential elements
of a biblical notion of creation in the scriptures but are neither
misled by the initial verses of Genesis to identify *creatio ex nihilo* with an absolute beginning of time, nor do they need
to base their convictions on those verses alone. What they
find delivered by their respective traditions regards the nature of divinity even more than the nature of the created universe, while their respective treatments are clearly shaped by
their shared argument with the necessary emanation scheme
of neoplatonism – the principal contender to a revealed worldview. *Creation* means the free origination of all from the one
God, who gains nothing thereby. Moreover, what the notion of *free* primarily concerns is the lack of any constraint,
even a *natural* constraint; so it need not involve *choice,* as it
spontaneously tends to do for us, except quite secondarily.
That creating fills no need in God and so is an utterly spontaneous and gracious act: that is the cumulative message of
the scriptures appropriated by Maimonides and Aquinas. Everything else, including the apparent description in Genesis
of an initial moment for the created universe, is secondary
to that assertion. While they both believed that such was
indeed the case, and recommended it to the belief of their
respective communities, the situation would have been different had there been a persuasive and clear philosophical
proof to the contrary. Had Aristotle succeeded in demonstrating the "eternity" of the world, Maimonides noted that
he would have had no difficulty interpreting the scriptures

in that vein, but the absence of such a cogent demonstration allowed him to espouse the plain sense of Genesis in that regard.[1]

This very discussion, however, reveals that the temporal/ "eternal" issue was quite secondary, since what Maimonides would have found most damaging in such a demonstration was rather the *necessity* with which the universe emanated from the One, and the consequent necessity inscribed in the universe itself. For that would have left no room for God's revelation to Israel, and so would "necessarily be in opposition to the foundation of our religion" (*Guide* 2.25). This discussion makes it clear that "Aristotle" is really Ibn Sina (Avicenna), and the protagonist is the necessary emanation scheme of the Islamic philosophers (*falasifa*). So once again, it is the freedom of divinity to act, in creating and in revealing, which constitutes the nub of the notion of *creator* which both Maimonides and Aquinas consider to be the deliverance of the scriptures. And if that freedom means primarily that the act of creating is a spontaneous and gracious one, then the God who so creates is fulfilling no natural need and has nothing to gain thereby. This marks what Robert Sokolowski has called "the distinction" of God from the world and also sets up an utterly unique philosophico-linguistic situation. For it means that we cannot speak of God and the world as parallel entities, nor can we use merely contrastive language when speaking of God from the viewpoint of the world.[2] In short, we are thereby invited to a specific view of the transcendence of God, and the doctrine of creation, as espoused by Jews and Christians, as well as Muslims, addresses that defining feature of divinity as well.

Aquinas is more explicit than Maimonides regarding the internal conceptual connections between creation and the doctrine of God, yet the sense of God's all-sufficiency as the ground for the specific freedom involved in the act of creating is already present in Maimonides' notion of the *oneness* of God. For the rabbinic sense of God's oneness is not merely that the category *divinity* has but one member but, more radically, that to be this God *is* to be unique: the philosophical analogue of the stricture against idolatry. Aquinas expresses this "formal fact" in the prologues to questions 2 and 3 of the *Summa Theologiae,* where he fixes the reference of his extended inquiry as follows:

> the fundamental aim of holy teaching is to make God known, not only as he is in himself, but as the beginning and end of all things and of reasoning creatures especially (1.2)

and then in addressing what God is *in se,* reminds us:

> now we cannot know what God is, but only what he is not; we must therefore consider the ways in which God does not exist rather than the ways in which he does (1.3).

Putting the two statements together allows us to see how we can be led to God as God is *in se:* namely, by understanding how God is *not* one of those things whose beginning and end lie in God. If this be one of the consequences of the full-blooded sense of creation which both Aquinas and Maimonides adopt as consonant with their respective traditions, our discourse about divinity will have to be carried out by way of transcategorial or analogous expressions. That is, we will not be able to say things about God in the customary manner that presumes the spatio-temporal positioning normal to other substances.

Maimonides' ontology of language and of predication forbade him making any direct statements about God using human language, for he could not countenance any way of detaching the manner of signifying from what it is that we wish to say. As a result, anything said *of* a subject must be understood to inhere in that subject as an accident in a substratum, following the metaphysical semantics of Aristotle. Yet since such a characterization would turn God into a composite (and hence a creature), we must be doing something other than making statements when we say, for example, that God is merciful. Aquinas, on the other hand, invites us to recognize that we can be aware in such cases of *using* language in an improper yet illuminating sense, for when we assert that God is just, conscious of the fact that the One of whom we are speaking is in principle beyond the world of created things as its very source, then we will realize that the form of predication is *sui generis*. Aquinas offers a way of bringing that to consciousness: one recognizes that the adjectival (concrete) expression ['just'] will be inadequate and misleading when predicated of divinity, and must be complemented by the nominal (abstract) expression ['justice'] (*ST* 1.13.1.2). For as creator, God is not only characterized by perfections, as the adjective connotes, but is the source of them as well, as the abstract term expresses. Indeed, God can only be characterized by them *as* the source of them, so the astute speaker about God will recognize that both predicates will be necessary even if only one be expressed. Now we can see the connection between the two prologues cited: knowing that our God is "the beginning and end of all things" *is* to know that "we cannot know what God is," for the language which we can use to understand things because it reflects their (matter/form) structure in its very (subject/predicate) structure must be put to very special use in speaking of something which does not belong to the set of "all [created] things." Yet we *can* use our language, appropriately adapted, because this One is the "beginning and end of all [such] things": their source and the source of all their perfections. Such is the ontological linguistics (or linguistic ontology) of Aquinas, so it is no wonder that the celebrated German commentator Josef Pieper has insisted that creation is "the hidden element in the philosophy of St. Thomas."[3]

But perhaps we have moved too quickly into the heavily ontological semantics of Aquinas, for it may be difficult for those not versed in medieval speculative grammar to grasp the flow of his reasoning. The purpose was to indicate how spontaneously this Christian thinker, like his Jewish predecessor and guide in these matters, had recourse to philosophical tools to give sharper expression to "the distinction" of God the creator from the created world which each took to capture the biblical doctrine of creation. How are we to reconcile their spontaneous moves with contemporary complaints that *creatio ex nihilo* is not to be found in the biblical ac-

count?[4] By reminding ourselves, of course, that philosophical theologians like Maimonides and Aquinas did not pretend to be offering an exegesis of the opening chapters of
Genesis but rather a distillation of that account in relation
to the rest of the Bible and the subsequent tradition of Judaism and Christianity.[5] They are speaking of the creator as
one aspect of the God known to Jews or Christians in their
structured response to the original revelation, and what struck
them both was the sense of God as free originator of all there
is. Each then tried to develop the metaphysical implications
of such a claim, using and adapting the philosophical tools
available to them.

What these two philosophical theologians exhibit is the
manner in which revelational texts pose questions which will
require astute conceptual tools to negotiate. Correlatively, anyone using such tools to clarify questions posed by these texts
will want to demand that their use be semantically controlled
by the basic assertion of "the distinction" of the creator God
from all that is created, as this is taken to be the heart of the
revelatory texts. Such control will not only entail that the expressions we use will have to be "playing away from home,"
but the more radical caveat from both Maimonides and Aquinas that the very form of discourse will be misleading.[6] And
while that concern remains beholden to their specific semantics, those who operate from other metaphysical bases will
need to have some way of marking that the God about whom
they are speaking is the source and goal of all things, and not
simply the most excellent of those things. This is the ontological import of Sokolowski's "distinction," while the intentional import accents God's freedom: *not* primarily in the sense
that God might have created things differently and thus had
choices in the matter, but more radically in that God *need*
not have created at all, so the act of creating offers a kind of
paradigm for divine gratuity.

1.2 HOW CREATION IS A FAITH-ASSERTION

A famous eulogy for Maimonides claims that "from Moses to Moses there is no one like Moses." It was indeed the

figure of Moses, the traditional author of Genesis, who un-
settled the Hellenic presumption that the universe had always been there: a natural enough presumption since the universe forms the very context for all our inquiry and was either
thought to contain a privileged place for the gods or be itself
divine. In short, Genesis demands that the goal of inquiry
be reoriented, since the universe itself now needs to be explained rather than remain that in terms of which everything
else is explained. If the universe itself has always been, as the
presumed context of inquiry, then explaining any specific
thing amounts to finding its proper place within that whole,
generally speaking. But if it cannot be presumed always to
have been, then those sorts of explanations remain valid,
though the structure of explanation opens out onto something beyond the universe itself. Yet the manner in which
this new explanation is proposed makes all the difference, determining whether "the distinction" is marked or not. For
Aristotle had already argued that a privileged part of the universe, the "unmoved mover," was required to account for its
vitality, even if the universe itself did not require an accounting.[7] Plotinus, in the first half of the third century, linked
Aristotle's cosmological scheme with Plato's sense of the per-
vasiveness of "the good" to derive all that is from the One,
itself "beyond being." This bold and unifying pattern of explanation fascinated the Islamic philosophers, and al-Farabi
concocted a tenfold scheme of emanation which Ibn Sina
adopted with minor modifications. This seamless array of
necessary implications from the One, which we found Maimonides associating with Aristotle and which we classify as
"neoplatonism," represented the pagan response to Moses'
challenge – pagan in the sense that there can be no adequate
distinction between such a One and all that necessarily emanates from it. We shall see how this crucial lacuna tended to
alienate Islamic *falasifa* from the wider Muslim community.

The way in which the one God "explains" the world cannot run parallel to the way in which something's place *in* the
world explains that thing, for if it did, then creation would
no longer be a gratuitous act. (The plausibility of the emanation scheme came from its patterning on logical deduction;

its sufficiency turned on resolving all things to one principle.) So it cannot be that we are able to conclude directly from
the perceived " contingency" of the universe to the necessity
of One who assures its being unless we are antecedently convinced of the primacy of a necessary explanation, which would
seem to be the mindset that predisposes one to be a neoplatonist. But something makes us ask whether our characteristic explanatory modes can tell the whole story, and that
wonderment leads us to inquire what it is that has been left
out. I would contend that Aquinas' "five ways" proceed in
that fashion, as well as more recent endeavors like David
Braine's "project of proving God's existence" and Barry Miller's
From Existence to God.[8] That is, rather than propose an extension of our explanatory strategies to link all things to a single
principle, this approach challenges the completeness of those
very strategies, and so focuses on the lacuna between what
we can explain and what we cannot but nevertheless need
to. This second approach will alert us to the differences between the way in which a creator might "explain" and those
explanatory strategies with which we are familiar, and so alert
us to "the distinction" of God from the universe and its causal
interactions.

Whence comes this need to inquire further, this acute sense
of the contingency of things which will not be content simply to be contrasted with *necessity* and so brings with it a sense
of the incompleteness of our explanatory strategies to "tell
the whole story"? It probably has far less to do with an intellectual impulse to complete explanation than with a felt
sense of the precariousness of existence – of our own, and of
the universe itself. This extrapolation needs to be made plausible, however, since one's own sense of mortality, however
acute, need not entail anything at all about the universe. In
fact, a simple presumption that individual things come and
go while the entire context remains would seem equally plausible. To cast the question in terms familiar to Thomistic philosophers, we are faced here with the ongoing debate as to
whether the real distinction of *essence* from *existence* can be
recognized this side of acknowledging a transcendent source

of all existence.[9] In terms of our discussion there is an even prior question: Is some form of belief in a creator-of-all a practical prerequisite to giving intellectual warrant to that acute sense of contingency needed to fuel attempts to prove the existence of God? Put in this form, the question could be threatening to those philosophers who regard a rational proof of God's existence as a prerequisite for a warranted faith in God, but to spell out their concerns that clearly is to wonder who would ever make such a demand.

1.2.1 The Hebrew Contribution

Here is where the scriptures of the three traditions should prove relevant, articulating in the fashion proper to revelational documents that quality of concern which could impel people to a faith that would enlarge their perspectives beyond the presumedly ultimate context of the universe itself. And what is more, these writings will prove *not* to be in the mode which metaphysicians favor, so attempting to explicate their bearing on this question should make us more appreciative of the labyrinthine ways leading to that sense of contingency relevant to speaking of a creator-of-all. The most apposite place to begin would seem to be the Hebrew scriptures, as they form the base for both Jewish and Christian belief and provide the background for Qur'anic assertions as well. Recent discussions of Genesis 1, in particular, have challenged those who would find there a forthright assertion of *creatio ex nihilo*.[10] This challenge can be issued, of course, from various ideological presumptions about the relation between scripture and the tradition in which it is embodied yet which it also norms. Jews and Catholics are generally less worried about *grounding* their faith in the words of scripture, so it will simplify matters to follow that direction of inquiry and to see the challenge not as intending to undermine the use which subsequent thinkers in the traditions have made of Genesis 1 but rather to inquire into the specific sense of contingency which the text embodies, so preparing us to see how later tradition may have elaborated it. In short, *creatio ex nihilo*, in the dual sense of presupposing nothing at all and of the universe enjoying a beginning point, may be acknowledged to be the developed content of a biblical faith without having to find the lineaments of that faith in the very text of Genesis 1.

It is by now commonplace to remark that the Genesis account is imbedded in a liturgical setting, in which the sevenfold articulation of the beginnings culminates in God's resting from the labors of creation, which are nonetheless never related as laborious. So more than description is at stake, making the usual query whether one should "take Genesis literally" to be quite senseless. For "taking it literally" *is* to take it as a liturgico-poetic rendition designed to show those who believe in the God of Abraham, Isaac, and Jacob that their God sovereignly rules over all that is, as well as give them a way of relating to the initial moment of that God's display of divine power and solicitude. For those who believe in this God do so primarily in the wake of the actual parting of the waters in favor of God's people Israel over their powerful Egyptian oppressors. So the overarching theme of the creation story is the Lord's sovereignty over the negative powers of destruction and darkness, epitomized by the boundless sea and enveloping night. Indeed, the Genesis account clearly presupposes both: "there was darkness over the deep, and God's spirit hovered over the water" (Gn 1:2). Vestiges of the Babylonian origins myth, the *Enuma Elish,* long acknowledged to provide the background for many of the scriptural images, notably that of the powerful Leviathan, may be discerned here and in other portions of the text, so that the Jerusalem Bible note that "'darkness over the deep' and the 'waters' are images that attempt to express in virtue of their negative quality the idea of 'creation from nothing'" (Gn 1:2n) sounds quite jejune. It may well be that the Bible has other points to make which were perceived as even more relevant to the concerns of Israel than the metaphysical assertion of *creatio ex nihilo,* even though that doctrine may be seen as a legitimate development of Genesis and the rest of the Hebrew scriptures. And the best clue to the original sense of the text would be the form of Genesis 1, together with its allusions to other shaping portions of revelation.

The articulation of the origins-activity into a sevenfold process allows creation itself to be "mimetically reenacted by the worshiping community, the people of Israel" in such a way that "the annual renewal of the world has become a weekly event" (Levenson, 77). To what end? That this people might be privileged to participate in the founding activity of the universe as an integral part of its renewing its own response to the God who called it into being in the promise to Abraham and out of annihilation in the exodus deliverance, assuring them as well that "our god" is God. Yet since the form of response given them was that of a covenant, we would expect to see intimations of covenant in the Genesis story. And these emerge more perspicuously if we regard creation as Genesis clearly does: "a victory and an act of liberation — YHWH's defeat of the angry, roiling waters of chaos and his liberation of the lowly from their grasp" (106). The people so liberated, once they are constituted a people by the covenant at Sinai, can now participate in that act of liberation not only in the annual celebration of the Passover but in the weekly sabbath rest: "as creation is a continuing cipher for divine philanthropy, so is the Sabbath a regular and unending implementation of the philanthropic attitude within the domain of ordinary human affairs" (106).

The central blessing — the *Amidah* — of the sabbath eve service manifests this liturgical reenactment:

> You have sanctified the Seventh Day for Your Name, the goal of the creation of Heaven and earth; You blessed it above all the days and sanctified it above all seasons. . . . Our God and God of our fathers, take pleasure in our rest, hallow us by Your commandments, and grant our portion in Your Torah.[11]

If covenant itself cannot be enacted within an origins story, which is one of exclusive divine initiatives, the sevenfold form of that story nevertheless embodies the essentials of covenant by accentuating "the possibility of human access to the inner rhythm of creation itself: Israel can rest the rest of God"

(Levenson, 111). If "the priority of God and the lateness of the creation of human beings make the term 'cocreator' or 'partner in creation' inaccurate, . . . it is . . . still appropriate to speak of a certain subordinate role that humanity is to play in the cosmogonic process" (117). In fact, the lineaments of that role are spelled out in other mitzvot as well, notably the dietary laws, whose explicit justification "views Israel's own separation of fit from unfit foods as a continuation of the process of her own separation from the Gentiles so that even so humble an activity as eating replicates the ordering that is fundamental to God's world" (118), an ordering expressed in the manifold separations which stand as the only descriptive elements in the Genesis account. So the liturgical linkage of Torah observance with the origins story, as its reenactment in a way that is possible to all human creatures yet given to a particular people, represents a living commentary on the text itself.

So if the Genesis story cannot be counted on to render a teaching as ontological as *creatio ex nihilo,* it can nevertheless offer clear depiction of divine sovereignty over the powers of darkness and do so in such a way as to offer humanity – in the form of God's own people – a way of sharing in that power over the forces of destruction: "it is through obedience to the directives of the divine master that his good world comes into existence" (127). Yet that obedience cannot be said to be merely *heteronomous,* as the modern idiom would insist, for if the account of creation is so crafted as to permit human creatures to participate in it, the covenant story grounds God's commandments "in the history of redemption, [so] they are not the imposition of an alien force, but rather the revelation of a familiar, benevolent, and loving God," with the result that "the ethic is not one of pure heteronomy" (144). In fact, as we shall see, the polarity *autonomy/heteronomy* will prove quite inadequate for a Jewish, Christian, or Muslim view of the relations of human beings to God and especially inadequate in the measure that each of these traditions sees those relations to be grounded in creation. And what makes this Jewish reading of Genesis so striking is the way in which the scriptural account depicts creation as inherently linked with covenant, so that the "grounding" of the divine/human relation in creation reflects its actual enactment in the community of Israel. So the free assumption of the role of *servant* (or steward) allows human beings to express their participation in the founding activity of the "master of the universe." This same melding of perspectives will be reflected in the concatenation of Qur'anic references to creation, so that taking both together should help to undermine the propensity of post-patristic Christian theology to deal with creation and redemption as two moments or levels in God's relationship with creatures.

1.2.2 A Christian View

Since our presentation of a Christian perspective on creation will reveal striking parallels with the Jewish view just outlined, it is best to begin with two mainline witnesses: Thomas Aquinas and Karl Barth. In the course of assessing the doctrine of the trinity of divine persons, Aquinas has occasion (in responding to one of those medieval objections) to remind us how useful, indeed "necessary" such a revealed knowledge of God can be to us "for the right idea of creation: the fact of saying that God made all things by His Word excludes the error of those who say that God produced things by necessity. When we say that in Him there is a procession of love, we show that God produced creatures not because He needed them, nor because of any other extrinsic reason, but on account of the love of His own goodness" (*ST* 1.32.1.3). While Aquinas' response places the emphasis on the gratuity of the act of creating, Karl Barth would parse the initial phrase, "by His Word," as well as the concluding phrase, "the love of His own goodness," in the following way: "In the same freedom and love in which God is not alone in Himself but is the eternal begetter of the Son, who is the eternally begotten of the Father, He also turns as Creator *ad extra* in order that absolutely and outwardly He may not be alone but the One who loves in freedom."[12] So Barth explicates the note of gratuity by focusing on what sets creation apart from necessary emanation: "creation denotes the divine action which has a real analogy, a genuine point of comparison, only in the eternal begetting of the Son by the Father, and therefore only in the inner life of God Himself, and not at all in the life of the creature" (Barth, 14). This retrospective reading of Genesis from the perspective of the "inner life of God" reminds us how "creation and covenant belong to each other" (48); indeed, although "the distinctive element in creation consists in the fact that it comes first among God's works" (42), "it would be truer to say that creation follows the covenant of grace since it is its indispensable basis and presupposition" (44). What is first in intention is last in execution, Aristotle reminds us; so it is with the works of God.[13] Far from presenting a two-stage universe or a two-phase history, both Aquinas and Barth would direct us to God's liberating actions on behalf of God's own people as the way to understand the supreme freedom with which that same God creates the universe.

For that freedom refers not simply to the gratuity of the act of creation – that it corresponds to no *need* in divinity; it refers even more substantively to the spirit animating that gratuitous action: "the free love in which [God] accomplishes this willing and this positing in His own power and by His own independent resolve. It is in the same free love that He Himself is God, i.e., the Father in the Son and the Son in the Father by the Holy Spirit" (Barth, 230). So "the wisdom and omnipotence of God the Creator was not just any wisdom and omnipotence but that of His free love" (231), and that love finds expression in the covenant offered to God's own people, "which, as the goal appointed for creation and the creature, made creation necessary and possible, and determined and limited the creature" (231). "The Israelite who hears or reads about the Creator is to think at once of the One to whom he and his nation owe everything . . . this God is the God of creation" (234). Barth's development of this perspective from the shape of the biblical narrative, and especially as rooted in the image of human beings as man and woman, will serve us well later. For now it suffices to note that he is making a point utterly consonant with patristic renderings of creation, notably with their insistence that the universe was created *in* or *by* God's own Word.

While Barth's own *animus* against what he considered to be the pretensions of "natural theology" may have motivated his desire to distance a Christian understanding of the creation accounts from philosophical arguments to a "first cause," it is noteworthy that his actual outworking of the biblical narratives into his own theological narrative may be seen as a commentary on the opening observation of Aquinas regarding the "necessity" of having a full knowledge of the God revealed in Christ in order to gain the proper *philosophical* perspective on creation. While Aquinas, operating in a context and from an agenda quite different from that of Barth, does not hesitate to fix the reference of the One arrived at by each of the five ways as "what everyone understands by God," or "to which everyone gives the name 'God'," or "this we call 'God'" (*ST* 1.2.3), he does not thereby imply that any of these ways would by themselves yield the One whom Jews or Christians know as "the creator." So the "ways" come at the outset of the *Summa Theologiae* to acknowledge the intrinsic connection between that study—theology—and the exigencies of the human mind to understand how all things stand. Aquinas never proposed, however, that those intellectual exigencies could *ground* this study of God "as the beginning and end of all things" (1.2 Prol.), which is deemed at the outset to require something beyond philosophy, namely, revelation (1.1.1).

What Barth makes explicit and Aquinas presumes is that the scriptures supply a personal language with which to speak of God the creator, and this reinforces the point that the covenant is the inherent goal of the creative activity of God. What the biblical accounts presume (and as we shall see, the Qur'an makes explicit) is that the goal of bringing the universe into being is to relate that world, via its human microcosm, to the One who creates it. So those narratives are not concerned to detail a *natural* level of divine activity and human response

accessible to philosophy, which then forms the stage for a
supernatural intercourse accessible to faith, but rather to offer
an account of the origin of all which makes such convenantal
relationships possible. "Creation is not covenant," as Barth
insists (97); so the distinction of *natural* from *supernatural* will
not prove otiose, yet any implicit alignment of creation with
philosophy and redemption with theology misconstrues the
radical difference Genesis makes in our thinking about origins. And the fulfillment (from a Christian perspective) of
the covenant in Jesus makes the point even more forcefully:
the freedom of the act of creation stems from the inner life
of a God of love. It may sound strange to link reflections of
this sort with our intellectual exigence for complete understanding, for they press for a response quite different from
that exigence as we know it. In fact, the concern of the scriptures to establish "the distinction" of God from God's universe will assure us that the response will be inescapably "dialectical": an explanation which will not serve to explain in
the way we might expect. The alternative, we have seen, would
be some form of emanation scheme, threatening to the freedom of originator and originated alike. Yet again, remarks
like these seem commonplace, and need only release us from
distractions.

1.2.3 An Islamic View

The Qur'an does not offer an account of creation, although
it identifies God as the One "who created the heavens and
the earth, and what is between them, in six days" (25:59),
"creating the two kinds, male and female" (53.45). Moreover,
"God creates whatever He will" (24.45), so there is no constraint on the divine action, nor "is there any creator apart
from God who provides for you" (35.3). Indeed, the entire
tenor of the Qur'an celebrates God's bountiful gift—"God is
the creator of everything" (13:16)—and the fact that this activity bestows on God one of the ninety-nine canonical names:
"He is God, the Creator, the Maker, the Shaper" (59:24).
There is, as might be expected, special attention to the crea-

tion of humankind and insistence that creation reflects divine wisdom and purpose: "He created the heavens and the earth in truth" (16:3), "surely We have created everything in measure" (54:49); "nor have I created jinn and mankind except to serve Me" (51:56). So divine purpose and freedom dominate the perspective of the Qur'an, which is even less concerned than the Bible to probe more recondite philosophical questions like *creatio ex nihilo*.[14] Indeed, the accounts of the creation of human beings oscillate between sperm, clay, and dust as the material out of which God created man. Thomas O'Shaughnessy has collected the relevant texts, and finds some correlation between the time of their revelation and the material cited: the first Meccan period focusing on sperm, the second and third on clay, and the Medinan period identifying the material as dust (ch. 2). A reconciling text from the final group brings them all in: "Men! If you are in doubt about the Resurrection, [remember that] We have created you out of dust, then out of a drop [of semen], then out of a blood clot, then out of a fleshy cud . . . (22:5). This announcement also reminds us of the purpose of creation, which focuses on human destiny, culminating in the restoration of creation, whose purpose "is to requite the doers of good and evil" (O'Shaughnessy, 61).

Indeed, the dominant themes of the Meccan suras, focusing as they do on the appropriate warning and guidance for human beings who have gone astray, tend to emphasize the final judgment as the preponderant sign of God's power and our status as servants. So a firm promise of resurrection becomes "evidence" for the original creation, which itself shows that the very idea of resurrection is not preposterous: "It is He who originates the creation; then He will restore it, and it is most easy for Him to do" (30:27), for "when [the Creator of the heavens and the earth] decrees [the creation of] a thing, He merely says to it 'Be,' and it is" (2.111). This last assertion is the most metaphysical the Qur'an becomes, and it is not surprising to find it in a late Medinan sura. It is more characteristic of the Qur'an to focus on the command of God, linking it with the insistence that God "creates in truth": "It is He Who created the heavens and the earth in truth. On the day when He utters 'Be,' and it is, His utterance is the truth" (6:73).

The three names which the Qur'an uses for God as originator of "heaven and earth and all that is between them" are *al-Khāliq, al- Bārī,* and *al-Musawwir,* rendered above as 'the Creator', 'the Maker', and 'the Shaper', respectively. They have been incorporated into the canonical list of the "beautiful names of God" and may be seen as three separate ways of representing the manner in which God circumscribes all that is.[15] The commentaries were less concerned with metaphysical issues than with discrepancies in the slight accounts offered and with the nuances to be assigned to each name in accounting for the origin of all things. Another name, *Badī',* which has been rendered 'the Absolute Cause' or 'the Innovator', seems to gesture more toward God as the utter beginning of all things, while *Khāliq* is more associated with the creation of human beings.[16] What seems to be central to the Qur'an is what follows from affirming the oneness of God (*tawhīd*): that God has no competitor in originating the universe or in carrying out the divine purposes within it. Questions which we associate with *creatio ex nihilo* did not arise until later and, as we shall see, even then masked two distinct questions.

1.3 CREATOR: DEMIURGE OR CAUSE OF BEING?

When scholars rush to remind us that the scriptural texts cannot be invoked in support of *creatio ex nihilo,* they are making a point about the genre of those accounts and warning us from reading later conceptual refinements into those founding texts. Yet their insistence prompts us to ask how those later refinements may relate to the original accounts? What these scholars have helped us appreciate is that the relationship is not a straightforwardly logical one, as though the scriptural accounts *implied* the later developments. What we must do is ask what the truth of the narratives would presuppose about the One who functions in the narratives as agent. That is, even though the narrative, as narrative, will be unable to

describe the actions of a creator in a manner other than presupposing something to work with, need that fact about the
narrative imply that there must *be* something presupposed
to the act of creating? Clearly not, or we could never think
creator except as demiurge. But when would we be warranted
to insist that the truth of a narrative did not presuppose that
things in fact were as it describes them? What sets these accounts off as intrinsically inadequate? What tells us that they
are telling a story which cannot be told in story form? Where
does "the distinction" emerge in the texts themselves?

The answer to the last question would seem to be that it
does not, nor can it, since the One which "the distinction"
insists on keeping distinct from everything which originates
from it must nonetheless appear as the principal actor in the
narratives. So anyone who pretends to describe an utterly originating action will be pressing language beyond its ken, and
we can recognize that immediately. So it must be the community, as it seeks to understand these texts in relation to
the larger sweep of revelation, which insists that they are intending something which they cannot say.[17] For the respective communities came to realize that the divine action portrayed narratively must nonetheless be understood as that of
causing the very being of things and indeed of all that is. This
is what we mean by *creatio ex nihilo,* which intends to state
that nothing at all is presupposed to this activity of creating,
and has come to refer, more popularly, to an absolute beginning of time as well. Yet as Maimonides and Aquinas realized, these are distinct assertions: the origination need not
originate time as well; the universe could have utterly depended from its originator without a beginning point. While
that may boggle the imagination, it does not confront the
intellect with a contradiction. That it boggles the imagination, however, explains why the phrase *ex nihilo* can so easily
be read in a temporal sense, for (as Aquinas noted) an absolute temporal beginning makes the utter dependence that is
required much more evident to us. And the scholars are deny-
ing that the scriptural texts *state* either an absolute beginning
of (the more recondite) utter dependence. Yet the respective

traditions assert both and explicitly ground their faith in the texts of their scriptures.

What seems to have pressed them to realize that the truth of their respective narratives requires that the God in the narrative must *be* in such a way as not to presuppose whatever the stories describe as being there already, was their efforts to characterize this creator. And those efforts were aided, of course, by the rest of what they took to be the self-revelation of that God. So the accounts of creation can never stand alone, nor can they even be understood from the outset, even when they stand first in order. For neither their form nor their intent is to offer a philosophical account of origins but rather to introduce the most radical sort of beginning: one that is utterly free on the part of the originator and so cannot even be said to be received, so originating is it. So the accounts of creation turn out to be, rather, revelations of the creator, and that modification should keep us from thinking of them as explanations. We may rest content with their narrative structure once we understand that there is no better way to put what they intended to convey. And the fact that the traditions instinctively turned to philosophy to elucidate that intent need not be problematic; in fact, it will come to be a most natural development.

2

On Characterizing the Creator

Just as biblical scholars today will argue that ancient Israel's appropriation of its God as creator of the universe represents a later reflection on the character and status of the very one who liberated them from bondage in Egypt, so it was with explicit elaboration of creation within the faith communities with which we are concerned. Their preoccupations with the God who calls forth and so redeems a people only slowly gave way to the more cosmic implications of that fact. Yet when such reflections took place, there was no hesitation to affirm this One as both sovereign and free. And the reasons for insisting that this be the case with the creator would plausibly stem from what the experience of redemption had taught them. Maimonides offers the crucial witness to this mode of argumentation, for though he was steeped in the Islamic appropriation of Hellenic philosophy, he sensed aspects of the *falasifa*'s scheme to be at odds with revelation as he had received it and went on to propose a strategy for integrating that mode of reflection with faith, which Aquinas adopted as well. And more germane to our account, it was indeed the Genesis account of creation which set up the conflict, yet Maimonides was hardly wedded to a slavish reading of it.

2.1 MOSES MAIMONIDES: SECURING "THE DISTINCTION"

The *prima facie* issue for Moses ben Maimon was the eternity of the universe *versus* creation *de novo*, although, as we shall see, he was quite aware that this was not the crucial issue philosophically. On this point, however, he quite candidly asserts that "our shunning the affirmation of the eternity of the world is not due to a text figuring in the *Torah* according to which the world has been produced in time" (*Guide* 2.25). He notes how much more numerous are the texts "indicating that the deity has a body" and suggests that it would be even easier to interpret the creation texts "figuratively" than to "have given a figurative interpretation of those other texts and have denied that He, may He be exalted, is a body." Yet the very effort to discover the higher senses of biblical anthropomorphisms had consumed the initial forty-five chapters of the first book of the *Guide*. His justification for so reading the manifest sense of the scriptures had come both from philosophy and from the scriptures themselves: "That the deity is not a body has [not only] been demonstrated . . . but is [also] intended by the [biblical] text." So regarding the origins of the universe, he takes pains to show (2.13–25) that what people thought "Aristotle" (whom Maimonides often conflated with Avicenna) had demonstrated cannot be shown from the relevant writings of the philosopher; indeed, the philosopher's resort to persuasive language suggests that he himself was aware that his arguments fell short of being demonstrative (2.16–18).

Yet demonstrative or not, what decides Maimonides against accepting what Aristotle was said to have taught regarding the origins of the universe is the philosopher's contention that "the world exists in virtue of necessity, that no nature changes at all, and that the customary course of events cannot be modified with recourse to anything"–a position markedly closer to Avicenna than to Aristotle. And what offends him about such a contention is that it "destroys the Law in its principle, necessarily gives the lie to every miracle, and reduces to inanity all the hopes and threats that the Law held out" (2.25). So Maimonides' preference for a view of creation which he is willing to call (for dialectical purposes) "the opinion of all who believe in the law of Moses" (2.13) rests on his concern to preserve intact the very possibility of di-

vine revelation to a people, along with the special providence
("miracles") which that entails. Creation must be of such a
sort as to subserve redemption. The presumption is that the
scriptures themselves are not decisive in this matter – they could
be interpreted in a less straightforward manner if need be –
but that failing a demonstration of the opposing necessitarian view, the believer in Torah is faced with a range of opinions (or "theories") and so is free to espouse the one most
consonant with the plain sense of the biblical text.

By linking his position on creation with the earlier exposition of the incorporeality of God, however, Maimonides may
be making more than an exegetical parallel. Indeed, the context does suggest more, for the real contrast is not between
a creation without beginning and one which initiates time itself, but rather between a universe which "proceeded obliga-
torily and of necessity from the deity [and one which] came
about in virtue of the purpose of one who purposed" to bring
it about (2.19). Incorporeality as such would hardly decide
between these two, especially since the paradigm of necessity
at work "is somewhat like the necessity of the derivation of
an intellectum from an intellect" (2.20), and Maimonides'
philosophical climate certainly regarded the intellect as im-
material, while he himself identified it with the image of God
within us (1.1). Yet what the defining feature of immaterial-
ity summarizes for Maimonides is relevant to the distinction,
as he concludes his elucidation of biblical language (1.1–45)
by insisting that "the guidance contained in all these figurative senses [which would otherwise presume a corporeal di-
vinity] is intended to establish in us the belief that there is
an existent who is living, is the agent who produces everything other than He, and in addition apprehends His own
act" (1.46). And we know this because, besides the bodily
allusions, scripture speaks of God acting in ways which "according to us constitute a perfection [so as to] indicate that
He is perfect in various manners of perfection." By interpreting the bodily expressions figuratively, Maimonides clears the
way for us to recognize that this One of whom scripture speaks
is not only incorporeal like the intellect, but unlike intellect,

which is caused, "we say that He . . . is eternal, the meaning being that He has no cause that has brought Him into existence" (1.58).[1] And if that be the case, then must we not insist that "His existence is identical with His essence and His true reality, and His essence is His existence," and that such a one "which has no cause for its existence [is uniquely] God" (1.57)?

From the fact that all originates with God, then, which can be considered to be a datum of scripture, Maimonides is led to affirm in a more technical philosophical idiom what must be said of the One from whom all comes: that its very nature must be to exist, since nothing brought it into existence. Moreover, the rest of scripture, and notably the giving of the Law, assures him that the manner of bestowing existence must not be one of impersonal necessity but of personal purpose. So his employ of Avicenna's distinction between *essence* and *existence* offers a way of parsing the claim that "His existence is necessary always" (1.57) as but another way of saying that it "has no cause for its existence."[2] In Avicenna's way of speaking, God's existence "is not something that may come suddenly to Him nor an accident that may attain Him." So one sees how spontaneously Maimonides adopted a philosophical manner of speaking to make a point about the God who gave his people the Torah. As one feature of divinity modifies the other, each is reinforced: it is *because* this God acts on behalf of this people that the origination of the world must be a free creation and not a necessary emanation. We are reminded of the reason Aquinas gave for our needing to know that God is triune: "it was needed for the right idea of creation; the fact of saying that God made all things by His Word excludes the error of those who say that God produced things by necessity" (*ST* 1.32.1.3). What revelation gives to each community is some insight into the character of God, and hence it sets some parameters for our understanding of the act of creation. In more contemporary language, then, we will not be misled into thinking that the scriptural accounts intend an *explanation* of the origins of the universe, something which the emanation scheme did attempt in the idiom proper to its time.[3]

Yet it remains necessary to offer a way of characterizing the creator which secures "the distinction" of God from all else that is, and this seems to require some philosophical precision. The reason, again, is articulated by Maimonides: if the origin of all cannot be itself originated, then we must say that "He exists, but not through an existence other than His essence; and similarly He lives, but not through life, . . . He knows, but not through knowledge" (1.57). The nature of this free first principle must be displayed in the very form of our discourse about it, since there is no other way to depict divinity. God is not simply incorporeal, and so indescribable, but uncreated and so not amenable to the very form of discourse apposite for things which receive their existence from another. Again, the way of putting the matter derives from Avicenna, yet we have seen how Maimonides detaches his Islamic mentor's formula for "necessary being" from the detailed mechanics of the emanation scheme to excise any necessitarian consequences about the world from the characterization of the One who originates it. In so doing, we might see Maimonides as more faithful to Avicenna's original impulse toward distinguishing *existence* from *essence,* but that would represent a retrospective view.[4]

2.2 THOMAS AQUINAS: *EXISTING* AS *ACT*

What Moses ben Maimon began, Aquinas completed in his severe treatment of the grammar of divinity in the initial questions of the *Summa Theologiae.*[5] If we can see the attempt to characterize "the ways in which God does not exist" (*ST* 1.3 Prol.) in questions 3 to 11 as an appropriation of Maimonides' strategy from the *Guide* as well as Avicenna's celebrated distinction (thoroughly reworked by Aquinas in his *De ente et essentia*), then we will be able to appreciate the need for so purely formal a treatment. For Aquinas completed what the others had begun by establishing a way of uniquely fixing

the reference for God the creator without trying to characterize such a One in terms appropriate to creatures. What fixes
the reference is a set of "formal features"–simpleness, goodness, limitlessness, and unchangeableness–culminating in a
characterization of God as *one,* which responds to the rabbis'
exaltation of this feature by removing it entirely from the nu-
merical, as though we needed to be informed that there was
only one divinity. Yet Aquinas also distanced his treatment
from Plotinus' unconditioned One by having recourse to his
own version of Avicenna's distinction, for what clinches divine simpleness (and so intrinsic unity) is the identification
of the divine nature with existence.[6]

   This very identification opens Aquinas' severely formal treatment to the theme which W. Norris Clarke has identified as
central to his metaphysics: action as the self-revelation of being.[7] For Aquinas' recasting of Avicenna's distinction had succeeded in removing any allusion to *existence* as an "accident"
by employing the Latin infinitive *esse,* which accentuates the
active force of 'be-ing' and may even be translated "act of existing."[8] The justification for this grammatical use was his recasting of Aristotle's metaphysics of *potency/act,* whereby "the
quiddity or form . . . must be potential with regard to the
being [*esse*] it receives from God, and this being is received
as an actuality" (*De ente* 4 ¶8), yet the fittingness of this expression stems from Aquinas' own metaphysical convictions
regarding "the natural connection between being and its overflow into action: . . . to be, in the strong sense of to be real
or actually existing, is seen to be ambiguous, incomplete,
empty of evidential grounding, unless it includes, as natural
corollary, *active presence,* that which *presents* itself positively to
others through some mode of action. To be is to be co-present
to the community of existents . . ." (Clarke, 65). So Aquinas' presentation of *existing* as an *act* introduces an analogical
use of 'act' which is at once grounded in a pattern of discourse
whose meanings can legitimately be so extended (Aristotle's
scheme of *potency/act*) and offers illuminating metaphorical
resonances as well.[9] If "action [is] the natural outflow of existential being," in the words of Norris Clarke, then the ac-

tions proper to a thing will suggest something of their source in that same thing's nature. This represents what I have called the "metaphorical resonance" of 'act' as applied to something's existing, and it also recalls Aristotle's telling instructions to help us come to a knowledge of something's nature: notice how it interacts with the world about it. In one fell swoop, then, Aquinas keeps us from regarding the nature of a thing as some inaccessible substratum and also directs us to the existing nature as the source of a thing's power to act.

Aquinas' alterations of the metaphysics he received from both Aristotle and Avicenna are all in the direction of securing a characterization of creator and of creatures: assuring that all things not only exist but operate in virtue of what they have received from the One who so exists as to be the source of existing for everything else. Rather than import a philosophical idiom into a scriptural domain, it is the exigencies of revelation that transformed the metaphysics Aquinas received into one properly his own.[10] This becomes most evident in his unabashed insistence on the primacy of *act* over *potency*, over against Avicenna's use of 'possibility'. Ibn Sina's division of all things into *possible* and *necessary* was an innovation over Aristotle, reflecting the force of the *essence/existence* distinction. One and only one being is *necessary* for Avicenna: God. All the rest are "possible of existence" but actually exist only in virtue of what they receive from the One. Yet the reception metaphor is a realistic one for him: possibles are *there*, as it were, to *receive* their existence. For before something is, it must be able to be, and possibles are "what are able to be."[11] But this sense of 'possible', Aquinas insists, ought not be confused with the intrinsic possibility of a power, for it is only said of "what might exist" in relation to the "active power of God" (*ST* 1.46.1.1). It is an equivocation of the use of the term 'possible' to presume that there must indeed "be" *something* which "can be." And the confusion can carry one into deep waters, for such a possible being, then, must be able to be adequately, if not completely, characterized to serve as *what* might exist. Such an item would then be said to "exist in" a *possible world*, one which God would be said to "actualize."[12]

2.3 AN ALTERNATIVE TO AQUINAS:
AVICENNA *REDIVIVUS*

On such a strategy, Ibn Sina's picture of *existence* "coming to" possible essences is resurrected, but this time for the process of *actualizing,* while *existing* is extended to possibles as well. So much for potential terminological confusions; what is really at stake? That should be clear by now: the sense in which everything that is stems from the creator of all. And since presupposing prime matter or possible essences in either case turns the creator into a demiurge, it behooves a philosopher who is writing in any of the traditions which avers creation to search for a metaphysics coherent enough to display that fundamental fact of God and of the universe.[13] One attempt to preserve Avicenna's vision of possibles presupposed to actual existing things is to have recourse to a form of "exemplarism" in which the essences of things are contained in the mind of God as the pattern which God follows in bringing certain of them into being. This would seem to acknowledge the primacy of the creator, since everything–possible and actual–would emanate from the divinity, and furthermore, such a picture offers us a way of conceiving God's freedom in creating as well: as though God chose among possible scenarios to bring one of them into being.

Yet it is worth asking why Aquinas, who had a plethora of such neoplatonic schemes at his disposal, did not make use of so obviously mediating a notion.[14] Again, the answer must be that he judged the primacy of *esse* over possible essences better to express the relation of creator to creatures, so that the so-called "divine ideas" are to be understood on the model of practical and not of speculative reason. That is, since God acts intelligently, God must use an intellectual (and indeed only an intellectual) instrument in acting, *ad extra,* to convey the divine intentions. It is not as though God knows all there is to know about an individual (and for some, even a "possible" one) by inspecting, as it were, God's own idea of that individual, but rather that God knows the individuals whom God brings into existence, since "God's knowledge extends as far as God's causality" (*ST* 1.14.11). "In this way, the divine essence makes (*facit*) a proper knowledge of each thing, insofar as it is the proper *ratio* of each one" (*De ver* 2.4.2), so that God's knowledge of individuals is in line with God's creating of them. Not derivative from them, certainly, but not of a speculative sort either: alternative designs remain a penumbra, a virtual component of an artist's creative act of making. On this analogy, Aquinas can say of those things which God in no way intends to make that "God has a certain actual knowledge [of them], but only virtually and not actually practised knowledge" (*De ver* 3.3). And what he means by that he spells out: that God's "knowledge of things to-be-made (*operabilis*) by God includes the manner in which some are not to be made" (ibid.). A mere penumbra, no more.[15]

So Aquinas' insistence on the primacy of *esse,* which we have been viewing as a debate with Avicenna, enters in the very center of a current discussion in philosophical theology. It intends far more than giving primacy to the "actual world." In that sense, it is not adequately characterized as a "strong actualism" if *actuality* remains in function of possibilities. What Aquinas is insisting, as a philosophical corollary of his understanding of the revelation concerning creation, is that there is no prior reference field (like that of "all possible worlds") to which God necessarily belongs. So the sense in which God is *necessary* is not a logical but an ontological one. That is, in the sense of 'necessary' which Aquinas adopts from Avicenna, all of being is divided into the One which is necessary and everything else which is possible *of existence,* so Avicenna's "distinction" of the One from the world is in function of his Muslim faith in a creator and employs the distinction of *existence* from *essence* as its conceptual vehicle. If Aquinas will have difficulty with his Islamic predecessor's contention that "possibles" must nonetheless *be* in order to receive their existence, he does so in the spirit of al-Ghazali, who saw this dimension of Ibn Sina's thought as a failure of nerve, a concession to Hellenic logic in the face of the Qur'an's clear avowals.[16]

For the only way to secure that the One, whose essence

is simply to exist, is thereby understood to be the source of everything else that is, is to regard all that is as *participating in* the existence of that One. What might be, then, is *possible* not in itself but in relation to the originating power of God, as we have noted, so that nothing at all is presupposed to God's creative action. And to characterize each thing's coming to be as a *participation* is to invoke the emanation scheme, but to employ it as a metaphor rather than an analogy. That is, the outflowing is no longer patterned on formal inference so that formal resemblances might be so explained; the participation is, rather, existential: "this is how things receiving existence from God resemble him: . . . precisely as things possessing existence they resemble the primary and universal source of all existence [*esse*]" (*ST* 1.4.3). Formal structures are then parsed as the *manner* in which God knows the divine essence to be imitable as this creature (*ST* 1.15.2), yet the actual "imitation" is the creature's existing.[17] And since that imitation is the result of a free act of God, rather than being a necessary feature of a scheme of which the One remains a part as well as its source, there can be nothing presupposed to the creative activity of God. Not that formal structures can be said to be themselves created, but that their presence as the *manner* in which creation may obtain is directly beholden to the activity of creating—another feature of what we have identified as the primacy of *esse*. Yet if the language of "participation" be misleading, we can say rather that all that is, by the fact that it exists, depends on the sustaining, originating One. How does it depend? Existentially, first of all, while the manner in which it exists will reflect the wisdom of the One who so allows itself to be depended upon. We shall look more closely at "existential dependence" in the following chapter but can simply note here that the life course of individual things is not a matter of their structure but of their history, or of the destiny they have forged by their actions. Any talk of "individual essences," then, will be quite different in a metaphysical context dominated by the act of existing, itself directly dependent upon the One whose essence is simply to exist, than in one in which things can be said to "be" even if they are not or never will be "actualized."

We shall consider these thorny issues of metaphysical alternatives at greater length in chapter 7. For the moment it should suffice to note how closely Aquinas' metaphysical moves are calibrated to a strategy which adopts the best of his philosophical predecessors yet amends their treatment, and even alters their basic categories, in the interest of theological concerns regarding the relation of God to the world which God freely creates. And in developing this strategy, he was initially guided by that of his Jewish predecessor, whose central dialectical work offered him a model for the interaction of faith and reason in such foundational inquiries as the nature of divinity and its relation to the universe. Like Maimonides, he realized that certain philosophical presumptions could undermine the faith he had received, yet he was equally unwilling to let that fact create a formal opposition between theological and philosophical inquiry. For there was an alternative: expand their categories in the directions indicated by revelation to make them over into useful intellectual tools for probing such transcendent reaches. Moreover, the more we come to appreciate this strategy which both medieval figures shared, the less impressed we will be by caricatures of either as "rationalist" or uncritically "Hellenic" in their pursuit of issues central to philosophical theology.

3

On Characterizing Creation

What is this relation of all-that-is to the source of all-that-is? Can one dispense with the very idea of a source-of-all by simply remarking that the cause of everything is the cause of nothing in particular?[1] Not unless we have decided that 'cause' must be so restricted. But the force of such a remark ought to be to remind anyone that we have to be using 'cause' in a different way in speaking of the source-of-all, and that reminder will help us to characterize this relation. Aquinas' way of putting it, beholden as he was to Aristotle's analysis of change, also served to cut the implication that *something* must be presupposed to the action of a cause, for Aquinas insisted that there is no motion involved in the coming-to-be which is creation. So it does not represent a change but is a completely new existence. It is this newness which the Arabic word for creation, *hudūth,* accentuates. The initial objection offers a salutary reminder that once we have the universe before us, the source-of-all seems able simply to be factored out, like a universal constant, yet we have been claiming all along—with the Jewish, Christian, and Muslim thinkers whom we have reviewed—that it makes *all* the difference. How can we reconcile these two perspectives? By a metaphysics which can do justice to both observations.

3.1 A METAPHYSICS OF ACT

If the relation of dependence-in-being were itself marked by a specific feature in the creature, then we would have to remark it and could not simply "factor it out." But if there be no such feature, if 'existing' does not function like ordinary predicates to express a feature *of* a thing, then we are either saying nothing about a thing when we say that it exists or something so basic that it cannot be typed as a feature *of* a thing. And since it literally makes all the difference whether something exists or not, we cannot be saying nothing, so we must be articulating something more basic than a feature of the thing.[2] Absent a creator, that would be all that we could say about the matter, which might offer some insight into the fact that Aristotle did not draw many inferences from the fact which he did notice: "that what human nature is and the fact that man exists are not the same thing" (*Post. an.* 92b8). For him, this followed from the fact that 'what is it?' and 'is it?' are two different questions, but his orientation to the actual world as the presumed background for all discourse led him to focus on *statements* as the unit of discourse and of logic.[3] So things could be presumed to exist, just as the universe was presumed as a given context for our inquiries. The distinction of *existing* from *essence,* then, seems to have awaited the advent of a creator, which in practical terms meant a revelation.

That has indeed been our thesis, yet to affirm it does not yet help us characterize *existing,* except perhaps in reminding us that no characterization will be forthcoming that is commensurate with our normal ways of characterizing things—as features *of* something.[4] For if we could do so, we would then be able to offer a positive characterization of the activity of creating and of the likeness of the creature to the creator. Yet we have seen that the best way of securing the difference between an act of creation, which presumes nothing at all, and an ordinary making—at least on Aristotle's analysis of comings-to-be—is to remind one that there is no motion (or change) involved in the activity of creating. And if no alternation is involved, there is no way of our grasping the activity since literally nothing is "going on." So while the affirmation of an act of creation highlights the distinction of *existing* from *essence,* it also assures us that we cannot come up with a categorial description of *existing*. How then might we attempt to characterize this dependence-in-being? It is here that Aquinas reaches for analogies with Aristotle's introduction of the notion of *act* (or *actuality*) in *Metaphysics* 9.6 (1048a25–b36), proposing that if *existing* may not be a feature of things, it may be understood as their most fundamental *act*—prior to and presupposed as the cause of any *activity* on the part of the thing itself. Aristotle himself offers the clue when he insists that "actuality is the existence of a thing" (1048a32) and can only be arrived at "by induction from individual cases," for what is presupposed to all consideration cannot itself be de- fined, since everything is defined in terms of it. It is for this reason that "we should not seek a definition of everything" (1048a36).

We could follow Aristotle's lead by suggesting pairings like the following: conception/assertion, proposition/statement, language/use (or language/discourse [*langue/parôle*]), anticipation/action, scenario/history, and finally Kant's one hundred possible/real thalers. What distinguishes the right member from the left is what we want to identify without attempting to separate it from the relationship, since it is always, for example, a proposition which is stated. In fact, any attempt to isolate the second member by that very fact reduces it to something like the first, since the first member represents the notional content, and to focus on something by itself requires us to treat it notionally. (Think how quickly *existing* becomes an "essence" in existential*ism*!) So the two items turn out to be intrinsically relational, with the right-hand member assuming the valence of *act*. This sort of analysis implies that we will be unable to isolate or independently characterize the *existing* which is the proper effect of the creator. Nor can we gainsay it either. The movement of thought here is not unlike the strategy which Aquinas adopts in his "five ways" for showing how our ways of analysis should lead us to affirming the existence of one whom "everyone gives the name 'God'" (*ST* 1.2.3). For those ways take some explanatory schemes and proceed to show how the very patterns of analysis invoked leave something out—something which they themselves would ordinarily call for, and hence something we sense to be missing. Their logic may not amount to a demonstration, but it can lead us to recognize the insufficiency of our explanatory schemes. Aristotle's pattern of analogies is not so demanding; it is rather designed to remind us of the context of existing things and actual practices which so forms the warp and woof of our lives that we could easily miss it. When Aquinas invokes this same pattern to offer a more coherent rendition of Avicenna's distinction of *existing* from *essence,* suggesting that we understand *existing* not as an "accident" but on the analogy of *act,* he is trying to locate that dimension of existing things which cannot be identified as a feature of things but which we can nonetheless sense to be there. In fact, as Kant reminded us in the example of the thalers, it makes *all* the difference.

This is the point where a constructive philosophical theology will let its categories be expanded to embrace the new context which revelation brings: *existing* will be given a positive characterization by employing the traditional philosophical pattern of *potency/act,* but giving it a new reach. The *act* which *existing* brings to each thing will not be directly characterizable but may be understood by analogy with *act* more generally. And what we can readily acknowledge but cannot otherwise characterize will be identified with that which is freely bestowed by the one source of all as its "proper effect." It is this employ of philosophical patterns of analysis which distinguished Aquinas from the Averroists and also separated Ghazali from both Ibn Sina and Ibn Rushd (Averroës). The crucial difference is whether one insists that a community's appropriation of revelation must be tailored to a current philosophical scheme or whether one may be licensed to extend philosophical patterns of analysis to allow the ensuing tradition its proper voice. If the latter is the case, can the result continue to be called "philosophy" or must we insist that it has now become "theology"? I offer the descriptive title "philosophical theology" in preference to "philosophy of religion" in an effort to acknowledge that we are indeed now doing *theology,* although we are being urged there by some issues which arise in the course of philosophical inquiry. Yet it is revelation which makes us aware of the new philosophical moves which we must make, so we cannot expect everyone to follow us across the threshold, even if we can hope that the philosophical arguments are cogent enough to lead them all to such a liminal position.

3.2 A COROLLARY REGARDING POSSIBILITY AND ACTUALITY

There is a corollary to the proposal that *existing* be presented as the *act* most basic to a thing, which ought to suggest a preference for that metaphysical proposal which best serves the free creation of the universe. It has to do with the primacy one accords to *actuality* or to *possibility*–positions sometimes identified as "actualism" or "possibilism."[5] In the medieval world, as we have seen, the demarcation between Avicenna and Aquinas can be drawn here. As Georges Anawati, the translator of Avicenna's Metaphysics: *al-Shifa,* puts it: "because he begins with essence, Avicenna is brought inevitably to consider the *esse* which affects it as an accident; by contrast, St. Thomas begins with the existing being and makes *esse* what is most intimate and profound in that being (*ST* 1.8.21)."[6] As we saw in the case of Avicenna, "beginning with essence" entailed his being unable to conceive a creation in which nothing at all was presupposed. A similar difficulty attends those who speak of creation as God's choosing which possible world to actualize. One need not accept the picture which those words invoke, of course; for philosophers can accommodate themselves to many manners of speaking. Alert to this infelicity, some will propose that the "possible worlds" envisaged simply represent God's knowing what God *would* do in diverse situations and so offer a way of formulating the freedom attending the divine act of creating. Here everything turns, however, on the way of presenting individuals and especially (as we shall consider in detail later) free individuals.

Can one speak of individuals constitued *before* they exist; is it coherent to speak in this sense of "individual essences?"[7]

Again, one need not picture them over against the creator; in fact, one may consider them to be "in the mind of God," thereby preserving, it seems, the primacy of the One from whom everything comes. Yet the questionable metaphysical point does not lie in the picturing, but in the assertion that "they" are what they are *before* their coming into existence.[8] And since "coming-into-existence" does not represent a change in *them,* any more than the act of creating involves motion, we quickly realize that any talk of "individual essences," or of "exemplars" of individuals in the mind of God, makes the act of creating into that of a demiurge. And it makes little difference whether the demiurge is gleaning, as it were, from its own intellectual constructs, because what is at stake is the role which *existing* plays (or not) in individuating and, as a result, the primacy of *this* world as God's creation. For if we can speak of individuals as fully constituted short of "their" coming into existence, then *existing* is indeed an "accident" (or in the undifferentiated discourse of contemporary meta-physicians, a *property*), for it is something which "happens to" the already constituted individual: namely, its "actualization."[9] Yet such an actualizing cannot be a simple verbal substitute for the "coming-to-be" which we usually associate with *existing,* because the individual already is the individual which it is before the divine decision that it will indeed *be.* Or to put the matter another way, if "coming-to-be" is to be given such an interpretation, one will be confronted with the curious picture of a fully constituted individual "emerging into reality."

It is difficult to adjudicate between these rival metaphysical schemes, for they represent strict alternatives, appropriately symbolized by the characteristic contrast between Aquinas and Scotus.[10] The most comprehensive defence of the primacy of *esse* as alone capable of constituting individuals is presented by James Ross in two recent essays.[11] His arguments defend the key assertion that "nothing but actual being can supply the determinacy that is logically required for individuals with respect to an infinity of predicates and with respect to difference from everything else, while allowing the things to have been otherwise than as they are" (Audi-Wainwright,

324). In other words, to propose that we think of the other ways in which *this* thing could have been as yet other "possible things," even though such possibilities be presumed to be "located" in the mind of God, only makes sense if we can presuppose *this* thing in our consideration; "for real ability to change cannot belong to a merely possible thing" (325). So transferring the existential valence of *existing* to "actuality" has the logical effect of reducing our ordinary sense of 'existing' to that of "self-identity" and so picturing the act of creation as one of adding existence to already constituted individuals. That is why I suggested that it effectively turns the creator into a demiurge, and centers the action in will rather than in intellect, thus offering a voluntarist rendition of the divine wisdom manifested in creation.

For it is no secret that one motivation of those who have adapted such a metaphysics to creation has been to offer a characterization of God's free agency, adopting the contemporary presumption that freedom is enshrined in choosing. Hence the picture of God's choosing among "possible worlds" to bring *this world* into being. But if freedom were not primarily exemplified in choosing, then the picture would lose its *prima facie* plausibility. And we have seen that it can also represent an embarrassment for those who are drawn to it. So it should offer a conceptual advance if we were able to characterize freedom in terms other than choice, however much its exercise may *involve* making choices or decisions. While that is a matter for a later chapter, we are now in a position to see that such a move would return the consideration of God's wisdom in creating to the domain of divine practical knowing, whereby the world as it exists represents not one choice among many, but rather the result of God's free intellectual activity, which may indeed be *described* retrospectively as involving what Aquinas calls *electio* (not altogether different from what we call 'choice'), but need not be pictured as a choice *among* "possible alternatives," but may be accommodated to that alternative design which always remains a penumbra or virtual horizon of an artist's creative act of making.[12] On such an account, the divine wisdom manifested in this creation does not lie behind an act of will understood as an act of choosing, but indeed constitutes and is constituted by the very creative act itself. Subsequent chapters will extend and bear out this analysis.

What is significant at this point, however, is the manner in which alternative metaphysical schemes offer different ways of characterizing creation. And since the concatenation of assertions regarding the free creation of the universe can never be a purely philosophical matter but rather reflects the ways in which each of the three faith-traditions has developed its revelational sources, one's preference for a metaphysical scheme will be in function of its better elucidating a particular tradition of understanding, as well as its internal consistency. But consistency is a relatively weak criterion; intelligibility is more often invoked. And here what is usually at issue is the congruence of a particular metaphysical scheme with current modes of understanding. So, for example, if one were simply to presume current notions of *existence* as "an on/off property: either you're there or you're not" as normative, then the metaphysics of act which we have sketched out would be "on the face of it unintelligible."[13] Yet if one were equally concerned to characterize the One from whom all-that-is freely comes, one might with a different sort of plausibility be pressed to adopt another and richer understanding of *existence*, as an explicit alternative to a presumedly contemporary one. Such is the way in which philosophical theology is constrained to operate, when traditions of faith offer complementary avenues for elucidation.

4

On Characterizing the Relation:
Jews, Christians, and Muslims

If existing makes all the difference and if we may not reduce it to the "actualizing" of one among many "possible
worlds," each of which is purportedly determinate prior to
its actualization, then it is crucial that this relation be a *transcendent* one – that is, that the difference which *existing* makes
not be characterizable as a *feature* of the object in question.
Of course, part of what has been meant by insisting that 'exists' is not a predicate is that it differs so much from ordinary
attributive predication that it is more illuminating to deny
it that status than to pretend to ask what it attributes to the
item in question.[1] This curious feature of the predicate 'exists' also explains why those philosophers whose metaphysics
accentuates *properties* and who are usually dubbed "platonists"
(with apologies to Plato) have little difficulty characterizing
actualization as "instantiation" and find it perfectly plausible
to think of "possible worlds" as quite determinate. For all deter-
mination represents what is characterizable as a feature and
thus lies in the realm of essence. What could *existing* possibly
add to the thing so conceived? Nothing, of course, if *what*
one is looking for must be a feature. Everything, if one thinks
to contrast a history with a mere scenario. The determina-
tions which follow from one's interaction with other things
constitute one's history; the result has a certain intelligibility,
to be sure, but the kind rendered by a story rather than by
its place in a theory. One may wish to speak of what results

as an "individual essence," yet in doing so *one* needs to realize that the intelligibility endemic to a narrative account does not ordinarily qualify for an essential explanation, but in fact quite the opposite: it is a way of bringing us to some understanding of contingent affairs by finding an intelligibility in what is precisely "nonessential," out of what "happens to something," or is (classically) *accidental* to it. So one's "individual essence" would not be available before one had lived one's life to the point in question. Wonderments like "what would I have been like if I had been born and raised in East Timor?" are just that: wonderments.

Now if existing constitutes an individual able to engage in the sort of interaction which yields a history, and if that capacity cannot be identified as yet another feature of the thing in question, since what it brings is not a *feature,* then *existing* itself will not be directly characterizable. That very inability to locate *existing* among attributive or even formal predicates will suggest to philosophical theologians that a fruitful way to characterize the relation of creator to creature would be to locate it in the bestowal of existence, since there could not then be any recognizable "similitude" between creator and creature.[2] That is, if the creation-relation terminates in the creature in a way which is itself not characterizable, yet which brings everything which can make the individual the very individual it is, then one has indicated what the creator *does* without thereby pretending to capture that *doing* in a particular effect in the creature. In that sense, *existing* "leaves everything as it is" yet also accounts for each thing's being the particular thing it is. As we shall see later, such a metaphysics will also leave creatures *free* while allowing us to acknowledge that everything comes from the creator. So it is understandable that thinkers in the three traditions which avow creation—Jewish, Christian, and Muslim—would gravitate toward a metaphysics which reached for some such formulation of *existing*.

It will prove strategic to begin with Islamic reflection on such matters, for while Islam represents the latest of the three religious traditions, its early encounter with Hellenic thought meant that its thinkers would convey to Jewish and to Christian philosophical theologians some crucial ways of recasting the world-shaping metaphysical questions in the face of a creator, as well as adapting the Greek responses to such questions to characterize the new relationship which would emerge: that of creature to its creator. In this sense, for example, both Moses Maimonides and Thomas Aquinas are explicitly beholden to Ibn Sina (Avicenna), however much each may have found it necessary to adapt their Muslim predecessor's thought on these matters. Moreover, the directions in which they would adapt it often follow contours already proposed by another Islamic thinker, al-Ghazali, even though neither explicitly acknowledges his debt to this thinker. Thus, the Islamic tradition contains two identifiable strains, both of which will reappear in Jewish and Christian philosophical inquiries into the relation of creatures to their creator. Hence it behooves us to elaborate that tradition first, lest the very notions employed later seem adventitious.

4.1 ISLAMIC STRATEGIES: INDIGENOUS AND APPROPRIATED

The Qur'an presents itself as a warning and a guidance – to Arabs initially, to be sure, but potentially to all of humankind who have lost their way, who wander ignorant of their origins and their destiny. And what is worse, that same ignorance renders us unconscious of our waywardness, so that nothing short of God's own work can recall us to our senses. The heartening fact is that the better part of mankind, on hearing the Qur'an, cannot but recognize its cogency: a clear testimony that the human heart does indeed come from the One who speaks to it and will recognize the voice of its maker. This cosmic coherence is also manifest in the principal teaching of the Qur'an – the *tawhīd* or unity of God, for nothing is more effective in releasing reason from the grip in which ignorance has held it than to remind us of the absurdity of worshiping many gods. So the power of the Qur'an to warn and to guide at once attracts the heart and persuades the mind,

thus leading human beings to recognize and to follow the
truth it proffers. And once they begin to do so, everything
falls into place, for the One whose word both warns and guides
is the same One who says "Be! and it is" (16:40): "the heavens and the earth and all that is between them"–that is, humankind. From that point on, everything created can become
a sign of the creator's presence and power.

The dialectic of ignorance and truth is a compelling one,
yet quite ineffectual so long as we remain in the grip of ignorance. For what can bring those unaware of their waywardness to seek the right path? Once revealed, truth cannot but
be persuasive, but failing to find such illumination, human
reason can hardly be expected to be able to extricate itself from
the maze of its own devices, for it cannot even acknowledge
its plight. Yet rather than dwell on the powerlessness of reason left to itself, we are invited to give praise and thanks to
the God whose Qur'an directs us in the right way and so en-
lists human reason in an adventure of understanding which
embraces the entire cosmos and penetrates into the recesses
of the human heart: grasping both poles of Socratic inquiry.
Such is at once the pessimism and the boldness of the dialectic of truth and ignorance which Islam elicits: reason in
the grip of ignorance cannot even recognize its plight, but
once freed it will pursue the truth wholeheartedly by following the multiple signs (or traces: *ayat*) to which it has been
alerted. The mediating factor is the human heart, which cannot be satisfied by idolatry and which is spontaneously attracted to the truth of the Qur'an. We shall see how this diag-
nostic of human bondage and liberation, itself unveiled only
by God's gracious bestowing of a Qur'an on a wayward humanity, will shape the way the Islamic tradition will characterize the relation of creator to creatures.

4.1.1 The Indigenous Strategies of the *Mutakallimūn*

The earliest attempts of Muslims to formulate the "heavens and the earth" in relation to the One who called them
into being–in short, a *true* cosmic picture–were carried out

in relative ignorance of the systematic metaphysical inquiries of the Greeks but within a broadly Hellenistic environment which called forth cosmological questions. So while their forms of thought were largely indigenous, they found themselves framing responses which we associate with metaphysical inquiry. These early thinkers carried out a form of intellectual inquiry called *kalām*, which were usually associated with apologetic pursuits yet which sought to formulate the way this world should be seen in relation to its originator. Western thinkers were made aware of this mode of argument through Maimonides' portrayal in the *Guide of the Perplexed* and more directly by the critique of "the philosophers" which al-Ghazali carried out in his *Tahāfut al-falāsifa* (translated by Van den Bergh as "The Incoherence of the Philosophers.")[3]

Let us call this group, then, theologians, in recognition of the fact that their overriding concern is the elaboration of a faith and practice grounded in the word of God, the Qur'an. If students of Christian history find their manner of reflection to be reminiscent of the Augustinian strain of theology from the eleventh to thirteenth centuries, that would be appropriate. The more systematic inquiry associated with Aquinas is not to be found here, for while the *kalam* exponents could mount robust arguments, their organization remained topical. More systematic developments in Islam were associated with "the philosophers," notably al-Kindi, al-Farabi, Ibn Sina (Avicenna), and Ibn Rushd (Averroës), who tended to extend the norm of reason to embrace even the dictates of the Qur'an. In short, a bridging figure of the stature of Aquinas did not emerge in Islam, so that 'theology' and 'philosophy' tended to be understood in opposition to one another, forcing the kind of standoff illustrated by the title of Ghazali's work.[4] Yet he himself, as well as a later theologian, Fakhr al-Din al Rāzī, showed remarkable philosophical acumen in forging a meeting between Qur'anic perspective and human understanding, recognizing that the criteria of acceptance must never be simply one-sided, but that each must in some fashion subject itself to the other.[5]

The theologians themselves divide into two groups: the

Mu'tazilites, literally "those set apart" (eighth and ninth Christian centuries), superceded by the Ash'arites, or followers of al-Ash'arī. While sharing a metaphysics designed to give primacy to God's creating action in the world, they divided crucially in their understanding of human action. Those differences will emerge in chapter 6; for now our concern is rather what unites the two groups: their insistence that God's power touches to the core of the being of each creature and that there be nothing in the creature which would impede or otherwise alter that action. This led the theologians to distrust a scheme of natures with inherent causal powers, preferring rather a version of atomism which seemed to leave creatures more malleable to the actions of the creator. The result is known to us as "Islamic occasionalism" and considered to be of one piece with an extreme fatalism by which everything which occurs is a direct result of divine decree. The world must be transparent to the action of God so that whatever takes place within it will function, for the believer, as a sign of divine wisdom and favor.

It should be evident that metaphysics would be quite secondary in such a perspective, yet the atomism which some of them would vigorously defend was to be discarded by later thinkers like Ghazali as an inconvenient hypothesis. What will prove central, however, is an aversion to causal connection in nature, precisely as an impediment to divine activity in the world. For Ash'ari and for Ghazali, God alone will properly be called *agent,* and what we take to be causal activity will be explained as customary connections established by the divine will.[6] This very insistence had the curious effect of dispensing early *kalam* writers from offering a closer analysis of *divine* action, since any action we experience would *ipso facto* be God's. Ghazali, writing under the influence of later philosophers, will identify God's action with the granting of *existence* and all that follows upon it, and in doing so will be articulating the working presumption of *kalam* thinkers. For, as we shall see in chapter 6, their working paradigm for action was creation—a fact made explicit in the controversy between Mu'tazilites and Ash'arites over human acts and their origin.

Ghazali will further insist that the only *bona fide* agent is an intentional one who acts for an end. The polemic here is with the philosophers, who present the universe as the necessary emanation from a single principle whose plenitude assures its being and whose unity accounts for its order. Yet Ghazali insists that the scheme which they adopted as the one most apt to explain the universe – that of logical deduction – effectively denies any freedom to the One, and by that same logical necessity elides "the distinction" of God from the world. However much one may exalt "the One," its connection with the universe which emanates from it according to the model of logical derivation makes it the first in a series.

4.1.2 The Appropriated Strategies of "the Philosophers"

If Ghazali proved critical of the strategies which certain influential Islamic thinkers adopted from Greek philosophy, that should not keep us from appreciating the lure of that system. The thinkers in question were notably three: al-Kindi (c. 800–870), al-Farabi (875–930), and Ibn Sina (980–1037). There were indeed a host of others, concentrated in Baghdad, who were attracted by the challenge of assimilating the received philosophy to the new and powerful revelation of Islam.[7] In isolating these three figures, we are acceding to the usual demand for a canon. Yet the main lines of this enterprise can be found in their writings, so the canon serves its purpose. Their efforts were concentrated on finding Arabic equivalents for the key notions of the philosophy they encountered and in using that system of thought to show the origins of the universe in one supreme being.

The translators commissioned to render Aristotle and Plato into Arabic were largely Syriac Christians, so the choice of some key terms may be explained by showing how Syriac provided a bridge between Greek and Arabic.[8] The work of al-Kindi, especially, offers us a view of this struggle to appropriate a working vocabulary and shows how creative that effort can be.[9] It is al-Farabi, however, who is properly credited with the scheme which historians of philosophy will identify as Islamic.[10] Taking his cue from the heavenly spheres of Aris-

totle, al-Farabi will postulate nine such between the One and
the lunar sphere which transmits successive influences to the
earth. And the One provides far more than Aristotle's prime
mover, for in the spirit of Plotinus and Proclus, the movement from unity to multiplicity is at once one of logic and
of vitality: what is communicated is a participation in what
the One possesses by nature—existence and all that flows
from it.[11]

So the philosophy which these thinkers adopted and
adapted was an amalgam of Plato, Aristotle, and Plotinus in
which the considerable differences between the first two masters were conciliated by a work transmitted as the "Theology
of Aristotle" but in reality was a version of the *Enneads* of
Plotinus.[12] This happenstance gave considerable impetus to
the Islamic disciples to adapt Hellenic philosophy as their own,
since it carried one inescapably to the One–God. One might
even speak of a "mystical dimension" to their thought, yet
if so, it remains the "intellectual mysticism" of neoplatonism.[13]
And it was this very penchant to transform the message of
Islam into a philosophical ladder modeled on logical deduction which gave considerable purchase to Ghazali's criticism
in his *Tahāfut al-Falāsifa*.[14] While his explicit objections to
the cumulative systematic work of "the philosophers" envisaged the precise points where that work clashed with the faith-
consensus of the Muslim community, his central argument
countered the way in which logical necessity reigned over
the universe, encompassing creator and creature alike. For
this contention directly counters the clear command of the
Qur'an, which gives mankind its goal and dignity: to acknowledge God as lord of "heaven and earth and all that is between
them."

Nothing, then, can encompass the "lord of heaven and
earth," least of all a logical system. It is this concern which
led Ghazali to restrict the full-blooded sense of *agent* to intentional agents and to restore to the One the freedom to
create or to refrain from creating a universe. His own arguments, to be sure, are vulnerable to considerable objections,
as Ibn Rushd (Averroës) makes clear in his trenchant response:

Tahāfut al-Tahāfut.[15] Ghazali was often more intent on his goal than on careful construction of arguments. Yet Ibn Rushd was no more prepared to defend Ibn Sina; his goal was to show the futility of both disputants when faced with an authentic Aristotle, whose genuine works alone offered philosophical training in the arduous path to truth. He would not enlist philosophy to illuminate Qur'anic faith, as Ibn Sina had pretended to do, nor did he respect what he regarded as Ghazali's weak arguments in defense of that faith. He was concerned, rather, with the integrity of philosophical argument, which he sought to return to the secure base provided by Aristotle. The dictates of faith were of another order, which any philosopher of merit could clearly recognize. Indeed, the severe demands of philosophical inquiry made it both fitting and necessary that humankind be led to recognize the truths essential to salvation by yet another means, and none is more apt than the Qur'an.[16]

This intellectual strategy of Averroës, however piously conceived, proved inimical to the spirit of Islam, on account of the straightforward hegemony which it granted to philosophy, with thinly veiled allusions to philosophers as an elite corps among searchers for truth. Indeed, this manner of arrogating unquestioned superiority to the conclusions of intellectual inquiry would carry over more into Western controversies than it would prevail in the Islamic world. There, in fact, the very manner of Ibn Rushd's refutation rather tended to confirm Ghazali's critique and to fix an unbridgeable gulf between the deliverances of faith and of reason. It could even be said that Averroës' manner of resolving the issue has proved in practice to acknowledge Ghazali's central point: a comprehensive explanatory philosophy is inimical to Islamic faith, so one must be careful to guard a dimension of the self where the believer can remain at home, acknowledging the creator as lord of heaven and earth.

The result of this is that a paragraph on Averroës' treatment of creation offers but a footnote to intellectual completeness to this section, for there is no real room to maneuver between the One from which all-that-is emanates after a model of logical necessity and the free creator of all-that-is. Averroës had to be faithful to Aristotle's limited picture of a prime mover as the source of motion in a universe taken to be everlasting, nor could he avail himself of Avicenna's distinction of *existence* from *essence* to construe Aristotle's prime mover as the source of being, as Aquinas would do. The result was inevitable: his position on creation is an equivocal one, with historians of philosophy contesting what he intended to say.[17]

4.2 JEWISH CONCERNS:
A CREATOR FREE TO GIVE THE TORAH

Jewish thinkers throughout the medieval period functioned within the intellectual and cultural parameters of the Islamicate. So much so, indeed, that one may well class them as Islamic philosophers without in any way implying that they were Muslim. It is Moses Maimonides, indeed, who sharpens the point of Ghazali's critique of the philosophers by proceeding to undermine the prevailing presumption that Aristotle had proved the "eternity of the world." By a close reading of Aristotle's texts, he shows that the arguments are not convincing and moreover are not even presented as demonstrations (*Guide* 2.19–20). This strategy allows him to create a space in which faithful followers of the Torah may indeed decide for the "theory of Moses" without ceasing to be resolute philosophical inquirers.[18] Should Aristotle or any other philosopher succeed in demonstrating the world's everlasting character, he avers, one could otherwise interpret the opening chapters of Genesis (2.25), as Maimonides himself had already done with various biblical expressions in the opening chapters of the *Guide* (1.1–49). But given Aristotle's expressed inability to achieve demonstration in such matters, it is preferable, he argues, to break with the necessity which is an inevitable corollary of an everlasting world and to acknowledge the absolute beginning of the universe by the sole power of a free agent able with equal freedom to grant the Torah to Moses: the God of Abraham, Isaac, and Jacob (2.25).

In what we have seen to be characteristic Jewish fashion, Maimonides' argument for a free creator in the face of the necessity which both he and Ghazali found to be embodied in the notion of an everlasting origination of the universe, turns more on Exodus than on Genesis. What leads him to recommend the "theory [or opinion] of Moses" as preferable to Plato's demiurge or to "Aristotle's" (that is, al-Farabi and Ibn Sina's) everlasting emanation, is precisely the concern to safeguard the possibility of "prophecy"–the generic Islamic expression for divine revelation (*Guide* 2.25). (To be sure, there has been considerable debate regarding Maimonides' "real position" on these matters, evoked by his own explicitly equivocal manner of exposition, but for our purposes it suffices to underscore his concern to leave room for divine free initiative in granting the Torah.[19] We shall see how a similar concern on the part of Aquinas will lead him to follow Maimonides' lead in these matters.) So while Maimonides presents the text of Genesis dialectically as one of three "theories" (or "opinions"), indeed that of Moses, its weight in his eyes is considerably greater than that of a theory or opinion, since the God in the creation account is the very one who reveals the divine name to Moses.

Other Jewish philosophers, it is true, will not find it necessary so to link God's freedom to create the universe and to bestow the Torah with an absolute beginning for the world. Narboni, Maimonides' Averroist commentator (d. 1362), and Hasdai Crescas (d. 1412) both contended that God is a voluntary agent who nonetheless creates the universe without a beginning.[20] Both Maimonides and Ghazali, however, identified an everlasting universe with its necessary emanation from the One, each finding that nothing short of an absolute beginning would offer sufficient "evidence" for distinguishing a free origination from a necessary one.[21] (If Aquinas will argue for the logical compatibility of everlasting or free origination, he will nonetheless acknowledge that an absolute beginning makes the freedom far more evident [*Summa contra Gentiles* 2.38 *ad fin*].) Many Jewish thinkers, however, do not share the conviction of Isaac Abravanel (1437–1509) that the

fact of a beginning of time entails *creatio ex nihilo*. This ambiguity may well remind us of Levenson's presentation of the
biblical picture; it also helps to explain diverse interpretations
of Maimonides as well.[22] In short, a universe which has an
initial point may well presuppose "something," so the beginning may not be an absolute beginning. Unless one has an
explicitly metaphysical rendering of the creator, such a conception does seem compatible with the quality of freedom
which Jewish thinkers require on the part of the creator.

Maimonides has a final suggestion which he proposes in
another context in the *Guide* and which he leaves as a suggestion, but which we shall find useful in offering an analogy
for divine action in the world. In treating God's providence,
where he argues that the knowledge we attribute to God must
be of an order utterly different from our own, Maimonides
lets himself be guided by the biblical imagery of *making*, to
suggest that we would not be misled were we to conceive of
God's knowing on the model of artisans' knowing what they
are doing (3.21). By recommending that we shift to Aristotle's
pattern for *practical* (as distinguished from *speculative*) knowing, Maimonides can contrast God's knowing to ours in two
ways. First, by reversing in the case of God his clear predilection for speculative knowing, in evidence from the opening
chapters of the *Guide,* we are forcefully reminded of the
difference between divine and human knowing. Secondly,
by suggesting that we consider divine knowing on the model
of practical knowing, he aligns himself with Ibn Sina, who
had already marked the difference by noting that our knowledge depends on things, while things themselves depend on
the divine knower.[23] So if we want to characterize the relationship, we should think of that kind of knowing whereby
things depend upon a maker, that which artisans have of their
artifacts.

Perhaps the reason Maimonides left this as a recommendation can be traced to his fear that a model so easy to imagine could, in the context of creation, lend weight to the various *kalam* arguments purporting to show the necessity for
an absolute beginning of the universe. It was Maimonides'

initial desire to distance himself from such pretended demonstrations that led him to adopt the indirect strategy he did. He was unwilling to recommend poor arguments to his interlocutor, Joseph, in his attempt to reconcile philosophical inquiry with the practice of the Torah. What he found to be wanting, above all, in such arguments was their inability to rise above the imagination in proposing to talk of the origin of all things (1.74, 2.16). For imagination cannot but proceed within a given context, so one must rely on logic rather than images when moving in metaphysical regions. Once having established that point, however, if we want or need—and we always do—an image to guide our deliberations on the relation of creator to creatures, there is no better one than the biblical anthropomorphism of *fashioning,* since the knowledge of artisans, transmitted through their hands, shapes what they bring into being. Absent the material connotations, the image offers the proper vector of dependence: that of creatures on their creator.

Another implication of the artisan model is that it issues in a particular result, by contrast with speculative knowing, which only attains the individual by way of propositional formulae. It was indeed Maimonides' insistence that the creator's providence extend to each human being—past, present, and future—which led him so radically to separate divine from human knowing. For if God's knowing were to be conceived on a speculative model, then future contingents known by such a One would no longer be free, yet everything about the Torah presupposes human freedom (3.20). Hence he opts for a radical agnosticism with regard to this and all other divine attributes.[24] So it is within that context of agnosticism regarding the mode of divine knowledge that the alternative model of practical knowing is offered; hence it is clearly no more than a model, though expressly recommended as one which will "lead to correct views"—albeit in a domain where we cannot be expected to understand adequately. His fourteenth-century commentator, Gersonides, however, finds such intellectual gymnastics quite unnecessary. He proposes, rather, what he takes to be an analogical scheme for the attributes, returning to Avicenna's speculative emanation model and allowing that God knows what is "ordered and defined" in each individual.[25] It should be clear from what we have said that Gersonides would be no more welcome in his community than Ibn Sina was in his, for nothing is more sacred to Jewish consciousness than the people's covenant with its God, yet that covenant would be a dead letter without the capacity for a free response of each individual member. Thus a God whose knowledge does not reach to individuals is intolerable. Including Gersonides here is not unlike mentioning Averroës earlier; yet since we shall later be examining philosophical proposals not unlike that of Gersonides, the paradigm should prove useful.

4.3 A CHRISTIAN PERSPECTIVE: A CREATOR FREE ENOUGH TO PARTICIPATE IN THE CREATED

If Jewish thinkers were concerned to stress God's difference from the world, albeit within a relationship of covenant, and Islamic thinkers were intent on establishing divine hegemony throughout creation, Christian theologians were confronted directly with another conundrum, yet one whose unraveling would provide them with unparalleled conceptual tools for characterizing the relation of creator to creatures. For the difficulty has been and continues to be: how to acknowledge the consistency of the creature, and especially the free creature, without compromising an all-pervasive divine hegemony? More succinctly, how can there be two agents, each of whom is authentically an agent, especially where one so mightily outclasses the other? Despite warnings not to construe divinity over against or parallel to the universe, one finds that way of imagining things to be a recurrent temptation. So the conundrum posed by the presence of the most high in our midst, in Jesus, brought the creator/creature relation to a precise, indeed a personal focus.

Moreover, attempting to fix the reference of our discourse about Jesus, including the community's prayers *to* him, would also force open the available metaphysical conceptions of the

One from whom all comes. For if Jesus *is* divine yet speaks to God as his "father," then the oneness of God is put in jeopardy, and Jews who profess such beliefs would be guilty of idolatry. So the need for clear formulae was a pressing one: we cannot say *tout court* that Jesus is God, since Jesus prays to God; and does the faith-assertion that God became man mean that God changes?[26] The struggle took three centuries to reach an initial formulation at Nicaea (325 A.D.) and another century more to attain the precisions of Chalcedon (451 A.D.): "We teach . . . that one and the same Christ, the Son, the Lord, the Only-Begotten is to be recognized in two natures without mixture, without transformation, without division, without separation; the difference of the natures being in no way abrogated through the unification; the properties of each nature remaining, rather, preserved" (Denzinger, 148). And while it is also fair to say that Christian theologians have never ceased to debate *how* such a formulation might be understood, the grammar of the matter is clear: two natures—creator and created—in one person, yet without confusing the modes of agency.

The actor, to be sure, is the person of the Word, according to a principle which will be enshrined in the scholastic adage: *actiones sunt suppositorum*—"actions belong to the existing subject." Yet inasmuch as that person is also human in Jesus, that very person—the Word of God—can suffer.[27] The reduplicative device—*inasmuch as* (or *qua*)—will prove a crucial conceptual tool for Aquinas' elaboration of Chalcedon, yet what interests us here is the very possibility of so characterizing the creator/creature relationship. It is not a possibility which could be envisioned by anyone who affirms the free origination of the universe, for none but the creator could, with equal freedom, overcome the very "distinction" which assured space to that freedom and do so without negating the "distinction" itself. There is no room for *avatars*, in other words, in a cosmology of free creation, nor can God's becoming man be so understood.

We have seen already how Aquinas will exploit this achievement, by way of a metaphysics of *act*, to assure that creatures, acting with participated *esse,* are themselves properly agents and causes. Moreover, they are able to be so without any hint of competition with the "universal cause of all being" (*ST* 1.45.2), precisely because God and creature are not to be thought of as two *beings* in parallel or over against each other. That rule is established by the metaphysical formulation of that One who is the "source and goal of all things" (*ST* 1.2. Prol.)—creator, in the widest sense of the term—as the One whose essence is to exist. For such a One is not, therefore, *a* being: a handy way of stating that the source of all is not contained within that totality; as Aquinas puts it, "does not belong to the genus of substance" (*ST* 1.3.5.1). The formulation of creator/creature, then, which Aquinas makes available to us, precludes competition between the two, yet allows for the integrity of the creature, parallel to the way in which the created nature of Jesus is not a contender for space in the person of the Word incarnate. This remains, of course, to be spelled out (in chapter 6) in the domain specific to free creatures, yet the point of this section has been to show how the manner of characterizing the creator/creature relation, in each of the three traditions, will inescapably reflect the particular way in which God is revealed in each of them.

4.4 A THEOLOGICAL RETROSPECT

A useful way of illustrating this contention—that the creator/creature relation can be recovered only in the fully theological context of revelation—turns on the age-old question: is God obliged to do good (and refrain from evil)? Socrates managed to raise the question even in the Greek context, where the gods were *ex professo* part of nature, whereby exhibiting himself as a liminal figure in that culture—a fact which never ceased to amaze the Christian philosopher Søren Kierkegaard.[28] Note that if the usual scenario prevails whereby God is taken to be over against the world, the question amounts to asking whether this One is bound by the rules of the world? So an affirmative answer places God within the world (as one of the gods, if you will), while a negative answer is a way of placing

God above the world. So anyone operating within the scenario yet anxious to affirm divine transcendence will deny that God is obliged to do good or refrain from evil. (We shall see that this is a fair representation of the Ash'arite position in Islam, which will consequently eschew, like later Christian voluntarists, making *good* or *evil* features of the created universe.)

If we resist the parallel scenario, however, to profess consistently One who is creator and hence the source of all worth, then we will have to distinguish the question: initially, as it were, there can be no obligation to create anything at all; nothing to which such a One need be true that would eventuate in a created universe. Yet once that One freely creates, then we may conceive that action in two distinct ways. On one pattern, the universe which ensues will reflect its source in its structure by *imitating*—or "participating in"—the divine essence, so that God's action with regard to it will reflect those same realities. *Not* because God is so *obliged*, but because God acts as befits the One who is source of all worth—even though God need not actively *be* such a source, since creating is itself utterly free. On the other pattern, one conceives of the divine freedom paradigmatically as one of *choice*, suppressing all suggestion of participation or imitation in the being of God, so that in God's creating, as in everything else, "God can do whatever God wants."[29]

One may put this difference metaphysically, as Roger Arnaldez does, by saying that the first pattern acknowledges divine ideas as exemplars of creation while the second eschews any such, and along with that negation comes the denial of natures and laws of nature—a prime contention, we shall see, of Ash'arite Islamic thought. Another difficulty lurks here, however, in the guise of a platonist form of "exemplarism" which would have individual essences present to God *before* *they* exist individually, thus using a particular formulation of "divine ideas" to subserve the same paradigm of divine freedom as *choice,* this time among "possible worlds" to create.[30] There is a way of avoiding such a picture, of course, and it is the way which Aquinas employs: "divine ideas" represent the *manner* in which things imitate, or participate in, the divine essence, hence are a way of speaking about that very participation which is at issue.[31] And the very point of this theological retrospect is to show that these metaphysical differences can be traced to a religious and theological background. In short, the way in which one is led to conceive the creator/creature relation, along with the metaphysics one finds appropriate, will be a function of that tradition's reception of its founding revelation, so the chronology of revelations reasserts itself.

The central fact for Jews is, of course, the covenant in which God freely engages with the people whom God selects out of all humanity. Christians can expressly presuppose this very God, whom they assert "became man" in Jesus, taking on a human nature in such a way as to invite and to lead all of humankind to union with God's very self. Muslims affirm that God bestows the Qur'an to an errant humanity so that humankind may be shown the "right way" and be rewarded for following it, as well as punished for not doing so. What is striking in this characterization is that the first two patterns imply reciprocity between God and humans, while the last need not, though such a gift must be freely received.

Each tradition will consequently find itself drawn to a certain metaphysics to articulate a cosmology fitting to that revelation. The Jewish intellectual tradition seems least in need of doing so, as we have seen, since the very pattern of Torah observance can be taken to be the performative expression of a cosmology, so offering an operative substitute for a metaphysical scheme. Yet that very fact finds itself reflected in Philo's contention that the creator implants in the world certain laws of causality, and in Maimonides' presumption that the One-who-is freely shares that existence according to certain patterns.[32] Christians could sensibly adopt a position like that of Philo and Maimonides, yet go on to insist that all who so share in God's existence as intentional creatures are further called to share in God's freedom as well: in the inner activity out of which God acts in creating, a dimension manifested to us in Jesus. For Muslims, God directs (*hada*) and orchestrates (*wafaqa*) creation, but without granting participation in divinity to what God brings into being. And since the conception of creation modeled on the bestowing of the Qur'an need imply no sharing in or imitation of divine being, there will be no reason to presume God-given structures. As a result, the tradition will be drawn to a metaphysics which presumes no such structures, be it in the atomism of *kalam*-thinkers, or the "occasionalism" of Ghazali. In fact, given the scenario of a Qur'an offered to an errant humanity, we can presume nothing, errant as we are, and so can but follow the way as it is given. If the pattern for creation imitates the pattern of revelation, a Muslim will have no prior ground on which to stand, while a Jew or Christian can presuppose a pattern revealed in a covenant granted.

These notable differences will be blurred somewhat, notably in the Muslim thinker al-Ghazali, whose explicitly occasionalist metaphysics is effectively mediated by his espousal of the *hadith* asserting that God creates humanity in God's own image. That assertion introduces an implicit metaphysics of participation, as we have seen, and so removes him from the camp of those for whom "God can do whatever God wants." In fact, as we shall see, Ghazali may be said to have developed, out of and for the Muslim tradition, a "metaphysics of love," which would suggest a cosmology much closer to that of Aquinas than the differences we have just noted.[33] With that qualifier registered, however, our central contention remains that it is the reception of the community of its revelation and of the God so revealed which shapes the story of creation and predisposes the community to a metaphysics adapted to articulate a cosmology appropriate to the story.

5

God's Acting in the World God Creates

It is a commonplace to say that the God of the Hebrews is a God who acts.[1] Maimonides' way of resolving the question of divine attributes may well reflect this perspective, insisting that such expressions do not refer to developed capacities in God, as they do in us, but rather signify discernible features of divine action (1.60). This strategy allowed him to use the attributes with respect to God's revealing deeds – the "face of God" we can see – while remaining appropriately agnostic about the One who executes them. The Qur'an, too, directs us constantly to God's actions on our behalf, fulfilled or promised, attaching one or another of the celebrated "names of God" to those activities.[2] The New Testament, as well, relates Jesus' acts of healing and of inspired teaching as reflecting the active presence of God in our midst. Yet the ontological affirmation that this God-who-acts is the creator of all compels us to look critically at the structure of narratives recounting divine action.

Narratives of divine action oscillate between two poles. In one series God is asserted (1) to be the real author of all that happens, be it good or evil, and to be so despite the appearances of genuine human agency. The other set places God within the narrative, carrying out specific actions, either (2.1) directly or (2.2) through human actors. The second set may veer close to the first, depending on the texture of human agency woven into the narrative, but the distinction lies in the author's identifying a specific action within the narrative as God's action, or making a global assertion about the agency in the narrative. Moreover, all three modes of narrative will have to be parsed in the light of what we know about divine activity in regard to the world if we are to avoid facile descriptions of God's action as, for example, "intervention." Not that narrative accounts are ever dispensable in the face of theorems of philosophical theology but rather that each story functions in a broader context of biblical or Qur'anic affirmations regarding the primary agent, God, and these must needs affect the way we accept the clues each narrative provides for its proper reading.

What do we know? At once very little yet a great deal. Aquinas offers us a handy formula: there is no difference between God's conserving activity and God's creating, other than the proviso that creating presumes nothing at all to be already present (*ST* 1.104.1). In other words, all of God's activity partakes of creating: all that God can do is to create; God does not "fiddle" or "micro-manage." If we add to this Thomas' theorem that the "proper effect of the universal cause of all things is things' existing" (*ST* 1.45.5), then God's activity in the world is ever an instance of or a consequence of bestowing existing (*esse*). Again, one would misconstrue matters if one thought of *existing* as a floor provided by the creator upon which and by virtue of which we then accomplished what is ours to do. That is a common enough picture, not unlike the prevailing deist conception of creation as "getting things rolling," a description which eliminates conservation altogether. Again, if *existing* were the mere positing in actuality, this picture would be a cogent one, but such a conception of existence—itself generally accepted—effectively denies the perspective of *creatio ex nihilo,* for it must logically presume a fully articulated "possible world" simply put into action.

So the perspective of creation extends to the current conservation of each existing thing, and does so in such a way as to animate its activities. That is, just as creation without conservation would no longer be creation, so "mere conservation" would not truly be conservation.[3] Aquinas' way of putting this is that God not only causes each thing to be, and thus makes it able to act, but God also acts in its acting by causing it to be the cause that it is (*ST* 1.105.5). The picture which such assertions inevitably elicit is one of "occasionalism," wherein God is the real actor with the creature providing but the occasion for the action to occur. Yet the picture only arises when we have pictured God parallel to the universe and presumed a univocal notion of *acting*. And while these two ways of thinking cohere nicely with each other, they both run counter to a creation perspective. So assertions like Aquinas' need not land us in "occasionalism," but may alert us to the truth which that position misconstrues.[4]

Occasionalism misconstrues God's omnipresent activity in large part because it presumes a univocal notion of *acting*, as in assertions like al-Ash'ari's that God alone can be called 'agent'.[5] Such statements are at least pragmatically incoherent, since we cannot make them without a stable notion of *agent*, and the working paradigms which we have of agents, intentional or not, are deemed *not* to be instances of agency.[6] And however friendly or adverse one may be to recognizing analogous uses of language, it is quite impossible, I should think, to deny that 'acting' must be so construed. Aristotle's introduction of the notion by way of a concatenation of examples is classic: there can be no general formula covering all instances of "being in act," yet we have no difficulty recognizing them as they are called to our attention.[7] So if any expression at all is analogous, 'action' or 'acting' is. And a creation perspective explicitly demands that it be so, as reflected in Aquinas' succinct observation that "creating is not a change" (*ST* 1.45.2.2).

So the truth which occasionalism misconstrues is that God's activity is indeed required to effect changes in the world of creatures, but that activity need not–indeed, must not–be construed as a change. So we would be correct in altering Ash'ari to read: only God's activity can enter into the actions of creatures in such a way as to make them actions. No creature's activity can do that. (We shall see how Ash'ari himself introduces a cognate distinction between the activity proper to God and that proper to creatures, in the context of assessing God's part in creatures' sinning.) What is at stake here, of course, is the capacity to distinguish creating from all other actions, and then to bear constantly in mind that conserving and creating are the same activity, so that God's acting will always be understood on the model of creating, while that of creatures will not. A corollary of this theorem is, of course, that God will never be said to "intervene," since creating cannot be represented as another vector added to the configuration of forces in the universe.

It should go without saying that analogies taken from current philosophical accounts of *person,* or adaptations of "action theory" to God's acting are quite beside the point. Appeals to such accounts or paradigms on the part of philosophers of religion only display their penchant for conceiving divinity parallel to the world, with divine person(s) construed by analogy with humans.[8] Yet the creator of all is not *a* being, nor *a* person either; and if the context is Christian trinitarian expression, the use of 'persons' here is expressly and notoriously analogous, as are the names 'Father' and 'Son'. All but certain specified implications are explicitly cut.[9] One must indeed acknowledge that one cannot conceive *how* God acts if one is obliged to consider all such acting as partaking in the paradigmatic bestowing of *esse* which is creation. But those are the rules of this game, and the recourse to three diverse religious traditions, with their distinct experiences of revelation, has been our attempt to cast some light, albeit obliquely, on this act which is the source of all activity.

In the face of our inability to conceive directly the creator/ creature relation, then, the insistence that any divine action will bring this very relation into play means that we must construct a set of rules for the proper use of language here, for straightforward descriptive use will inevitably misconstrue God's acting as though one were speaking of an agent in the world. (That is, of course, coherent with Aquinas' insistence that creating is not a change—itself a statement with rulelike implications for our use of creation language.) And that is indeed what we have been doing, in noting that divine activity will ever be "nonviolent," never be an "intervention," since the "universal cause of all being" (*ST* 1.45.1) already acts in every agent. Aquinas has a specific metaphor for his activity: "applying causes to their effects" (*ST* 1.105.5.3). It is hardly a felicitous one, since one may think of teachers' applying children's brushes to paper by taking their hands. Bernard Lonergan's detailed discussion of Thomas' treatment of this issue is somewhat more felicitous: he speaks of Aquinas' "theorem of universal instrumentality."[10] Only somewhat more so, however, for if we can appreciate the use of 'theorem' and of 'universal', we tend to balk at the suggestion of 'instrumentality'. For we can distinguish an agent from an instrument, and to say that *all* agents are instruments to God veers close to Ash'ari's dictum that only God can properly be called an agent. Lonergan, to be sure, is keenly aware of this implication, and intends both 'theorem' and 'universal' to restrict the sense of 'instrumentality' thus: it is only at the level of theory (or rule) and not of description that one may speak of what is unmistakably an agent functioning as an instrument. Furthermore, such a transposition is only operative in the widest possible context: that of the efficacy of divine providence.

We shall consider (in chapter 6) how this can be said of free creatures especially, and (in chapter 7) how the relation of divine to human freedom is sharpened in the face of God's action being inherently eternal. At this point it behooves us to add a model to the set of interlocking rules, if only to give us some idea of the import of expressions crafted according to them. That is the one already commended by Maimonides: practical knowing. For the assertion regarding the efficacy of providence, which may be considered a corollary to the full-blooded sense of *conserving* which we have been urging, inevitably raises questions of divine knowing. We may anticipate the later treatment of the eternal character of divine action just enough to finesse questions of "foreknowledge" at this point, as Aquinas reminded us that we speak of divine *pro*vidence, not '*pre*vidence' (*De ver.* 2.12). Yet for all that, we have great difficulty, with the slightest hint of a verb cognate to 'know', of thinking other than proposition-ally: they know *that* something is the case. Part of the reason, indeed, is that activities which involve practical knowing—like crafting, designing, arranging, administering, punishing, planning—seldom overtly use a cognate of 'know'. Therefore practical knowing is only grudgingly accorded the status of *knowing,* and then by dint of trying to assimilate it to 'knowing that . . .'.

How can the recommendation of Maimonides help us to clarify anything about divine agency if we keep losing our grip on practical knowing itself? The answer is, of course, that we ought to be able to improve our grasp of how we know when we know *what* we are doing, as contrasted with knowing *that* something is the case. So the prevailing lacuna in our philosophical practice is a corrigible one, and one which may have implications well beyond this topic.[11] And that it does promise a fruitful strategy in exploring the elusive domain of the creator/creature relation can be gleaned from the way Aquinas uses this very model to break through Avicenna's conceptualism regarding God's knowledge of creatures. Guided by the emanation scheme—itself modeled expressly on the central speculative activity of logical deduction—Avicenna concluded that divine knowledge envisaged the species which flowed from it, while individuals, imbedded in matter, remained *ipso facto* unknowable.[12] (We also saw how Levi ben Gershon [Gersonides] would defend Avicenna's conclusion by insisting that God thereby knew everything knowable about each individual thing—the manner in which it was "ordered and defined," so there was literally nothing else to *know* about it.) Aquinas, in concert with Maimonides, found such a philosophical ploy repugnant to faith in a living God and so detached Avicenna's axiom (regarding the directionality of divine knowing as constitutive of things) from the speculative emanation scheme to insist, quite simply, that "God's knowing reaches as far as God's causality" (*ST* 1.14.11). And since nothing (except evil) escapes the creator's doing, nothing will escape God's knowing. Without possessing a conception of *how* such is possible, Aquinas nonetheless invokes the model of practical knowing to insist that whatever God brings about God knows, for God must know what God is doing. Too neat a solution? Perhaps; yet on inspection, what more can be said? What more need be said? The proper use of models *in divinis,* like the adherence to proper grammar, seems to be the mark of thinkers worthy of following into such domains.

6

Creatures Acting in a Created World

The French Catholic philosopher who played such a key role in presenting the thought of Thomas Aquinas to our century, Jacques Maritain, devoted a treatise to resolving the longstanding dispute between Jesuits and Dominicans regarding grace and human freedom.[1] It is a quite technical opus crafted in the very terms of the *de auxiliis* dispute, and as a result not very useful beyond those walls. Yet in the preface of the English edition, written toward the end of his life, he estimates that his work on this question may well amount to his most lasting contribution to "Catholic philosophy." Such an assessment would astound any reader acquainted with his fertile mind, notably with his creative work in mapping the realms of political action as well as of art and our judgment of beauty. Yet his is the perspective of a person of faith sensitive to the negative resonances of Christianity among people of intelligence and painfully aware that this question—the impact of belief in the God of Abraham, Isaac, Jacob, and Jesus on one's sense of personal freedom—posed the most vexing obstacles to faith for his contemporaries. And so it has ever been, it seems, though more acutely so since the emergence of "the individual" in recent centuries.[2] Yet while it is especially true that we who so regard ourselves will inevitably conceive human freedom as "autonomy," we shall also remark a longstanding concern, in the face of a creator of all, that there be sufficient "room" for human freedom. So there are two philosophical issues at play, and often in function one of another: the complex of questions surrounding di-

75

vine action and another respecting human freedom. We have been occupied so far with the first and shall see how the articulations of divine action identified with the respective religious traditions will come to an acute focus in relation to the free actions of creatures. For the analysis of human freedom itself we will be able to build on the precisions of the creator/creature relation already achieved, to proffer an articulation of creaturely freedom as a cogent alternative to "libertarian" *autonomy*.

6.1 THE MUSLIM CONTRIBUTION: *"EN SH'ALLAH"*

The persistent Muslim response to hopes, projects, or simple plans to meet again is *"en sh'Allah"* – "God willing." A Western reaction oscillates between finding confirmation for the stereotype of "Islamic fatalism" and being confronted with a poignant reminder of the utter contingency attending "the future" – in short, a sign of religious particularism or a reminder of the fragile human condition. Yet the perspective we have been developing urges us to ask: why not both? Indeed, how might Islamic thought bring some special illumination to this question? How might the spontaneous *"en sh'Allah"* help find us a way out of the zero-sum impasse which tends to dog Western conceptions of freedom-as-autonomy in the face of a creator? Our inquiry will take us through an intra-Islamic controversy stemming from the origins of Muslim reflection on these matters and as yet unresolved – a controversy whose resonances have contributed to the stereotype of "Islamic fatalism."

The Qur'an, as we have seen, offers splendid relief to an errant humanity and extends the offer in the form of a choice: here is the right way; follow it and you shall find life, ignore it and you will face a harrowing judgment. The terms are every bit as stark as Moses' warning at the end of Deuteronomy: "today I set before you life and prosperity, death and disaster. If you obey the commandments of the Lord your God . . . , you will live and increase; . . . but if you refuse to listen, . . . you will most certainly perish" (Dt 30:15–18). Yet Moses' direct reference is to the people's life in the land, while the Qur'anic consequences are everlasting and even presented without the bilateral sustenance of an explicit covenant, yet nonetheless sustained by God's living word in the Holy Qur'an. Each person, however, holds the key to his or her salvation, for the *choice* is ours. These defining terms of the relationship of creature to creator require, as their indispensable prerequisite, human freedom. So whence the specter of "fatalism" which presumes a divine decree arranging it all? The tension arises, no doubt, from the unilateral character of the revelation, unmediated by an explicit covenant, resting on the ineffable word of God uttered in the Qur'an. Students of Islam find the Qur'an itself—as a warning and a guide—more supportive of human freedom, while the traditions attributed to the prophet (*hadith*'s) are more redolent of an air of "divine decree."[3] Yet Muslims are no more willing in practice than are Jews to drive a wedge between the written and oral traditions—however exalted their esteem for the Qur'an itself as God's uncreated word. So the tension remains, yet it is hardly surprising that the earliest religious thinkers (the *mutakallimūn*) were fierce defenders of human freedom.

6.1.1 Mu'tazilites: Making Room for Human Freedom

Our principal source for the school which came to be called Mu'tazilite is the *al-Mughnī* of 'Abd al-Jabbār (d. 978).[4] Their concern to defend human freedom was grounded, no doubt, in the Qur'anic background which we have enunciated, which presupposes free human choice in the face of a startling offer. Yet, more systematically, it reflects less a modern perspective of autonomy than a penchant for metaphysical rather than psychological analysis, coupled with a theological attachment to promoting divine justice. Not only does God pledge to reward good and punish evil, as the Qur'an everywhere attests, but the divine perfection makes it impossible that God "perform, whether directly or indirectly . . . , any act which is not ethically good."[5] Divine justice, then, demands both that human beings be the authors of their acts so that they can properly receive reward or punishment and that no evil act whatsoever be able to be attributed to God. (Jacques Maritain calls the latter dimension "the divine innocence," yet it is illuminating to bring both concerns under the rubric of divine justice.)[6]

The issue of praise or blame invariably turns on imputability, and this legal notion presupposes a strong sense of origination: put colloquially, "the buck stops here." To hold someone responsible for an action is to credit that person with the power to originate the action, however myriad the influences on him or her may be. It is this garden variety notion so integral to jurisprudence which structures the Mu'tazilite insistence on human freedom. As Richard Frank puts it, "their . . . actions are events whose occurrence we explain by saying 'so-and-so did it'."[7] So the discussion takes place within an intentional order, which can be presupposed as fundamental to the experience of any participant in the discussion. And since the key expression—*originator*—can be used of God as originator of the universe and of human agents as originators of their voluntary actions, 'Abd al-Jabbār and the Mu'tazilites more generally were forced to conclude that human beings and *not* God are the originators of human acts.[8] And if we recall their concern to dispense God from all responsibility for evil actions, we can better appreciate their desire to remove this domain from the creator's reach.

But one needs only to enunciate the results of their impeccable logic to realize that such a position could not prevail in Islam. For if the point of the Qur'an is to bring human beings to realize their dignity by freely acknowledging God as their lord, then exempting a significant segment of creation in principle from divine sovereignty cannot but strike one as bizarre. Making room for human freedom at God's expense may find ready acceptance among moderns accustomed to thinking of themselves as "autonomous individuals," but such an inverse logical connection between creator and creature could not long characterize Islamic religious reflection (or "theology").[9] It remained for an ardent disciple of the masters of the school of Basra, al-Ash'ari (d. 935), to renounce his allegiance to the *qadarite* thesis (derived from the Arabic term *qadar* for 'power') that rational creatures are the originators of their actions by a power created by God. Espousing the same presumption that acting freely implies originating something, he will insist that only God may be said truly to be an agent, since God is the creator of all that is.[10]

6.1.2 Ash'arites: Appropriating Acts as One's Own

From al-Ash'ari's radical beginning, which identified genuine activity with creating and so reserved it for God alone, subsequent thinkers will propose ways of allowing the human actor to participate in the formation of an action, but the principal intent is preserved and comes to be identified as the Sunni position on the matter: all initiative must come from the creator. What role, then, does the created actor play? If the action emanates from God, it must nonetheless be appropriated by the creature if that one is to be praised or blamed for it. But in what does such *appropriation* consist? That question, we shall see, will never quite be answered, even though successive generations of thinkers will make a try at it. The generic term 'appropriation' merely defines the task: to make something one's own. The specific notion which Ash'ari confirmed and others developed has the sanction of the Qur'an, where it reflects, however, its origins in business dealings and points to a *gain* one may have realized for life hereafter.[11] The Arabic expression is *kasb* (or in another form, *iktisāb*); it refers to the human contribution and is usually rendered lexically as 'acquisition'. An early formula uses the term precisely to signal the difference between the human contribution and God's: "God creates the act, man acquires it;" in other words, "the act is the act of God insofar as God creates it (*halaqahu*) and is the act of man insofar as one acquires it (*iktasabahu*)."[12] So the most one can say about the expression, from its initial introduction to its confirmation in Ash'ari's *al-Luma*, is that it offers a contrast term to 'create' (or 'bring into existence') without specifying *what* that contrast might be.

Richard Frank suggests that we render the term function-
ally rather than lexically, as 'performance'.[13] The English language allows us to make pointed reference to the performance
of an act in a way that romance languages, for example, do
not: 'l'actuation de l'acte' would be utterly redundant. Is this
a mere accident of two linguistic strains in English, or are we
really attending to something distinct when we speak so? Does
it convey anything more than the reduplicative 'in the act of '
used on formal occasions, as in "the picture catches the presi-
dent in the act of signing the bill into law?" The act of signing the bill, however, amounts to nothing more than signing
it. It would certainly be redundant to say that a pitcher is
performing his wind-up. Yet one may certainly say that Lawrence Olivier is performing Hamlet, where Hamlet is the central role in the play in which Olivier is performing. What seems
difficult to find, however, is a middle ground between 'perform' as an honorific for 'acting' or 'doing'–as in 'he usually
performs his duties with care'–and the use restricted to stage
or screen. Hence to say that a colleague was 'performing as
dean' would either sound pretentious or carry the connotation that he was not firmly established in the office; that he
was *not* in fact 'serving as dean' but only acting the part. So
Frank's proposal, designed to render *kasb* somewhat more
plausible, seems to falter on inspection, or else demand that
we explicate Ash'arite doctrine as attempting to turn the metaphor "all the world's a stage" into a literal description of creation in the face of its creator. Yet the author/character (or play-
wright/role) analogy is just that: an *analogy* for the relation
of creator to creature, and showing whether one finds it promising or not will require a distinct inquiry.[14] Daniel Gimaret
proposes that we simply acknowledge from the outset that
we are dealing with an ordinary expression put to technical
use and if it could have been rendered more plausibly, someone would have.[15]

Ash'ari himself never tells us what the term means, other
than to contrast *kasb* with *halq* (creation), as his predecessors
had done.[16] Successors have attempted to apportion the act
between components attributable to God and human beings,

respectively. But since an act has no material parts, some, like Baqillani, have tried to parse the description of an action, such as writing a letter to a friend, noting that it "contains" a genus (movement?) and several subspecies. But a metaphysics which requires different agents or causes for each logical part of anything would be strange indeed, as theirs turns out to be.[17] A later respected commentator of the Qur'an, Fakhr al-Din al-Razi, identified *kasb* with what gives ethical qualification to an act, as if to tailor what the human actor supplies to that very dimension which attends moral responsibility.[18] Yet the same critique can be made of his maneuver: by what strange ontology can we so distinguish the moral dimension of an act from the act itself? What these attempts seem to confirm is that any effort to restrict the meaning of *agent* to God alone will create an unstable situation, especially when the paradigms of agents remain ourselves as acting for motives which we can identify. For one deliberately renounces using the very paradigm which delivers the notion of *agent* in the first place.

I have already argued that 'acting' is an analogous term if any expression is. Any attempt to limit it to God alone, as al-Ash'ari does, will require us to look for another term to perform the role for which we need 'acting', yet also demand that we insist it does not describe an action. It would seem preferable to acknowledge candidly the inherently analogous character of 'action', and ask how it can be that created things truly *act* when all that they are (and so all that they *do*) is derived from the *act* of the One who creates them? That would at least put the question in terms which respect human language. And put in such terms, we do find a treatment of Ash'ari which amounts to distinguishing divine from human actions, despite his verbal restrictions. The context is the vexing issue of evil actions, which we saw offered the primary motivation for the Mut'azilites' removing the field of human actions from God's reach. Ash'ari does not shrink from admitting that if everything which exists comes from God, so must evil acts. But "these are created as the evil of another, not of God." That is, "God wills them to be as they are"; not, that is, as God's act but as the act of those who commit them.[19]

Introduced no doubt as a device, Ash'ari's contention will sound less like "double-talk" if we take it to be a way of characterizing what is unique to the action of a creator. Rather than being the sole authentic agent, God is an agent unlike any we know in that God alone can create an act which is not God's act but belongs to (*iktisāb*) another. Only the power to *create* can give that "distance" to an agent. This observation allows us to acknowledge we are dealing with an analogous term: there is an *agency* proper to humans, whose free actions are *ipso facto* their own; and an *agency* proper to God, who can also create actions which properly belong to God's creatures, since creating is the act which is the source of all activity. Were we to develop that difference in a way which respected the analogy of action between creature and creator, we would not be constrained to come up with a strange quasi-technical term like *kasb* to identify what makes our actions our own; it would simply be that we performed them, that is, *did* them. The creator's "part" in this would remain to be specified, but it would not involve an action like ours nor entail partitioning the act itself. We could accept al-Ash'ari's device as a prescient initial approximation to articulating the realities involved: the "distance" required, in a creation-ontology, for our actions to be our own derives directly from the specificity of the act of creation itself. God can do what none of us could do: create something *as* the act of another. What Ash'ari concocted (perhaps quite *ad hoc*) in the face of evil acts would extend to all creatures' actions: although created, they are genuinely their own actions.

Such an adaptation of Ash'ari to our purposes, of course, returns us to the radical unlikeness of creation in the face of actions we know: "creating is not a change," in Aquinas' challenging phrase. Yet while we cannot properly understand the act of creation by fitting it into categories proper to its result, the created universe, we ought to be able to find traces of it. And we do: ontologically, in the essence/existence distinction, as we have indicated; and intentionally, in an analysis of created willing. That will perforce carry us into Christian philosophy, which was pushed beyond the starkly metaphysical character of Islamic analyses by the need to clarify the person and actions of Jesus, as we saw, as well as the cognate demand to elaborate an analogy for the triunity of God, where the most accessible one turned out to be the intentional activities of knowing and willing. But before plunging into that analysis to offer an articulation of creaturely freedom, it will be well to assess the contribution of Judaism to this question. It appears to be meager indeed, but therein may lie a hidden lesson.

6.2 JEWISH PERSPECTIVE:
THE TORAH AND FREEDOM

Maimonides finds himself utterly at odds with "the [Islamic] philosophers," who are themselves quite unable to conceive of God's knowing individuals (3.16), for "it is a fundamental principle of the Law of Moses our Master, peace be on him, and of all those who follow it that man has an absolute ability to act. . . . [I]t comes from His eternal volition . . . that man should have the ability to do whatever he wills or chooses among the things concerning which he has the ability to act. This is a fundamental principle about which –praise be to God!–no disagreement has ever been heard within our religious community" (3.17). The religious contrast group for Maimonides is "the Ash'ariyya," whom he characterizes elsewhere as saying "that there is no act of a man but that there may be an acquisition [*iktisāb*] of an act by him" (1.51). It is equally fundamental to "the Law of Moses our Master that it is in no way possible that He, may He be exalted, should be unjust, and that all the calamities that befall men and the good things that come to men . . . are all of them determined according to the deserts of the men concerned . . . ; but we are ignorant of the various modes of deserts" (3.17). The last qualification, countering the egregious presumptions of Job's friends, is here directed at the strict retribution theories of the Islamic Mu'tazilites.

The origin of this unanimity is clearly the Torah itself, given to a people whose response forms them into God's own people, whose freedom is at once presumed and reinforced by fidelity to this God-given way of life. No heteronomy/autonomy dilemma here, for the One who singles out this people for a covenantal relationship is the very One who creates all that is and so wills that humankind be capable of freely responding to goods offered to us. A contemporary witness may be found in Robert Alter's literary analysis of biblical narrative.[20] The Joseph story (Genesis chs. 37 to 48) offers a handy paradigm for his analysis and for our comparative discussion, since the Qur'an also recounts it in Sura 12 (*Yūsuf*). Alter's general point is that narrative offers a way "to make sense of the intersection of incompatibles – the relative and the absolute, human imperfection and divine perfection, the brawling chaos of historical experience and God's promise to fulfill a design in history" (154). What is more, biblical narrative has a special poignancy, to which Alter surmises the biblical authors were impelled "at least in part because of the kind of knowledge it could make possible" (157): one in which the flesh-and-blood contingency of human beings is ever respected by an omniscient and all-powerful divinity. This pointed character of biblical narrative stands in contrast to midrashic commentary and to the *targumim* (popular renditions of the text for oral transmission), which by "concentrating on the present moment in the text and on underscoring a moral point, must make things more explicit than the biblical writer intended" (12). In the Joseph story, for example, Jacob's ignorance of his son's whereabouts is integral to the suspense character of the biblical narrative, whereas the Genesis *targum* and the Qur'an (which parallels it on several points) could not abide a patriarch being left in the dark!

Alter's focus on "biblical narrative as a fictional experiment in knowledge" (159) shows us "how the pleasurable play of fiction in the Bible brings us into an inner zone of complex knowledge about human nature, divine intentions, and the strong but sometimes confusing threads that bind the two" (176). The insinuation throughout is that "the consummate artistry of the story" offers the best vehicle we have "to make sense of human reality in the radically new light of the mono-

theistic revelation" (176). And the force of his case is cumulative, for it does not rely on generalizations about *narrative*
but on attention to the detailed structure of biblical stories
themselves, where the omnipresence of the divine actor in
no way suppresses but rather enhances the poignancy of human initiatives and failures. The God who can be party to
such a narrative need not "intervene," since the divine presence does not manipulate human agency so much as it calls
it forth. Such would be the effect of the covenantal context
of Israelite religion on the actions of its protagonists; and the
"realism" of biblical narrative does not disappoint us.[21] Moreover, the biblical text stands here in contrast to later attempts
in the Judaic tradition to highlight God's presence at the expense of the integrity of human actors, as the Joseph story
in the Genesis *targum* attests.[22] Finally, Alter's attention to
the peculiar genius of biblical narrative helps readers familiar
with the Bible to understand their consternation on first meeting the Qur'anic text. For the Qur'an employs narrative frag-
ments as the *midrash* or a preacher would, at the service of
paranesis or exhortation, so that the human actors who are
present or referred to lack the consistency of biblical charac-
ters—even when, as in the case of the Joseph story, they share
their name. That initial affront can lead readers accustomed
to biblical narrative to underestimate the dramatic impact of
Qur'anic texts, especially in recitation, finding there instead
the roots of "Islamic fatalism." Yet closer attention to the aural
reception of the Qur'an, as well as the drama inherent in paranetic use of narrative, can help one appreciate how Islamic
life and practice do incorporate a veritable dialogue with the
word of God.[23]

What stands out in the Jewish tradition, however, is an
untrammeled insistence on men and women as freely responding—positively or negatively—to the gift of Torah, for that divine invitation to a response constitutes this tradition. What
the Bible enshrines is flesh-and-blood stories of the quali-
ties of response, including refusal, which go on to shape that
living tradition, thereby inviting the current generation to
continue shaping it by their creative response in turn. The

presumption is that the One who extends to a people a covenant, and so invites individuals to forge a community by their
responses, is the very One who constitutes them free "in the
beginning," so that philosophical discussions of human freedom in relation to divine freedom are implicitly decided by
the very structure of Israelite religion enshrined in biblical narrative. Here again, the experience with revelation shapes a particular understanding of creation–in this case not so much
a conceptual articulation as the grammar for one: the creator's constitution and commerce with that portion of creation which bears the divine image will always be such as to
respect the freedom of response inscribed in the individuals
who constitute it. No wonder Maimonides found no dissent-
ing voices in Judaism to the contention "that man should
have the ability to do whatever he wills or chooses among
the things concerning which he has the ability to act" (3.17),
and that other Jewish philosophers will maintain human
freedom as well, however much they may have been influ-
enced by conceptual formulations veering toward subtle forms
of determinism.[24]

6.3 CHRISTIANITY:
CREATED NATURES ORIENTED TO THE GOOD

Freedom is no less a concern for Christianity than it is for
Judaism, for the repeated call of the New Testament is for
individuals freely to respond to Jesus' invitation to follow him.
Jesus' single-minded devotion to the "will of the Father" is
meant to be catching: "whoever does the will of my Father
in heaven, he is my brother and sister and mother" (Mt 12:50).
The will in question is, of course, the "will of God" (Mk 3.35,
Lk 8:21)–the very One who creates the universe and sends
the Son, the eternal Word of God, to lead humankind back
to their origin and their true goal. The motif of creation is
integral to the mission of Jesus: lifting the issue of divorce
from a legal wrangle, he reminds them: "Have you not read
that the creator from the beginning *made them male and female* [Gn 1.27]? . . ." So even if "Moses allowed you to di-

vorce your wives, . . . it was not like this from the beginning" (Mt 19:5, 8). It is implied that fulfilling the "will of God" is not an alienating or heteronomous activity, but amounts to fulfilling one's nature—however one may *feel* about it: "Father, if you are willing, take this cup from me. Nevertheless, let your will be done, not mine" (Lk 22:42). One's proper good, then, lies in aligning one's own will with that of the One from whom we receive our very being; the neoplatonic emanation scheme is transformed into a return to one's source by way of the intellectual faculty which orients us to the good: the will. Augustine's *Confessions* displays this transformation in recounting the life of its author as an encounter with the pursuing initiative of God. The intellectual ascent of Plotinus plays a crucial role in weaning Augustine from a crude way of conceiving the One who is source of all, and it does so by substituting the potentially infinite field of operation of "the mind" for the spatio-temporal parameters of the material universe. Yet *mind* is not limited for Augustine to the capacities of demonstrative reason, nor is it even paradigmatically evidenced there. Mind is rather displayed in the life of a whole person, as the dialectic of vision and desire in the *Confessions* shows so well.[25]

There are, of course, other ways to develop a Christian conception of human freedom, yet the strategy elaborated here will be that of Augustine as it has been employed by Aquinas to "make explicit" what Aristotle left in umbrage: the inner dynamics of voluntary human action. For Aquinas found the means/end scheme of Aristotle utterly appropriate to express the domain of created freedom, where *means* are matters of deliberation and choice, yet while *ends* are integral to the goal-seeking creature endowed with freedom, they are not *as such* the object of choice. Aristotle's conception of natures as sources of activity calibrated *naturally* with certain goals also provided Aquinas with a ready-made vehicle for the "intentions" of the creator. Unencumbered by the emanation scheme, with its necessitating corollaries, the Aristotle whom Aquinas discovered proved more plastic to the free activity of a creator than the neoplatonism which Muslim *kalam* writers had encountered (and which Maimonides often identified as "Aristotle"). Moreover, the means/end scheme offered ample room for the exercise of intellect both in discerning ends and deliberating about means, so there will be no hint of "voluntarism" in Aquinas' account of human freedom.[26] For the same reason, it would be procrustean to try to compress his account into the contemporary opposition between "libertarian" and "compatibilist" views of freedom, since these are predicated on a notion of *will* as an autonomous self-starter. As we shall see, their medieval parentage may be traced not to Aquinas but to Scotus, where *will* is postulated to be a self-starter, albeit in the wake of intellectual advice. The background for Aquinas is Aristotle's notion of *practical rationality*, together with Augustine's inner orientation to the good (or *will*), and his concern is to meld the two precisely in such a way that the will and intellect operate in concert, and the will's capacity to move is that of a moved rather than an unmoved or "autonomous" mover.[27]

The initial mover is none other than the creator, however, so that the initiative which we associate with voluntary action (or freedom) is not jeopardized but enhanced. It is the creature's orientation to its inbuilt end – the good in general – which allows the individual to escape from ends or goals conventionally proposed, as well as find itself faced with a choice of alternative ways to realize a goal which transcends particular aims or intentions. So while the means/end scheme parallels the intellect's pattern of principles and conclusions, so that the process of deliberation can even be assimilated by Aristotle to a "practical syllogism," no logical inevitability remains when "the good" is the inbuilt goal, since no determinate means will be adequate to it. And when Aquinas substitutes the God of Abraham, Isaac, Jacob, and Jesus for "the good," its transcendence is assured, as is also the grounding fact that this same God is the creator of the natures in question. In what, then, does freedom consist? Customarily, in our selecting means to the end which we discern to be for our good – a process triggered and sustained by the grounding orientation of our will to "the good," however deluded we may be in identifying it. Even more radically, however, we may also forego participating in that very process and so exhibit a freedom which is indeed that of "autonomy," yet destructively so. These two levels of operation are called by Aquinas *specification* and *exercise,* respectively (*ST* 1–2.10.2), and we shall see how they reflect the traces of the creator in free creatures.

The means/end scheme allows Aquinas to speak of *will* as a moved mover and so articulate from the outset its status as a created power, yet do so employing the outline of Aristotle's analysis. For its natural orientation to "the good" means that in following its natural bent the will *is activated* by its object. Moreover, when we are speaking of the "comprehensive good," we cannot be speaking of something which the intellect could apprehend and present to the will so as to *specify* it, for that is the normal way in which this power, like any other, is activated by its object. Thus, Thomas will argue, citing Aristotle's *Eudemian Ethics,* that the actual willing of "the good" must needs be incited by God (*ST* 1–2.105.4). The created tendency by itself is not enough, since the intellectual faculties of intellect and will are so correlated that the will can only move itself by virtue of a specification coming from the intellect: so it is always a moved mover. And normally speaking, *in medias res,* that specification will direct a will already actively desiring "the good." What distinguishes the putative first moment, then, is that something analogous to intellect must "specify" the will to that initial orientation to the "comprehensive good." But this good so outstrips the categories of created being that it cannot properly be apprehended by our intellect and so cannot be presented, properly speaking, by way of *specification.* Logic requires that the same creator who instilled such a power in us activate it in each creature: "God moves man's will as the universal mover to the universal object of will, which is the Good. And without this universal motion, man cannot will anything" (*ST* 1–2.9.6.3).

There is no hint of how such an activation takes place, except that it will not be forced, since it is in the line of the created tendency rather than opposed to it. The resulting situation will then be perfectly "natural," eliciting Aristotle's opening remark in the *Nicomachean Ethics* that "every action and pursuit is considered to aim at some good" (1094a1). So the need for divine activity at the outset of willing is not itself discernible but rather follows from the logic of the analysis, the grammar of the matter, once Aquinas had adopted Aristotle's means/end scheme with intellect and will correlated by way of *specification*.[28] The initial specification, however, will not appear, since "the good" defies categorization, so cannot be an ordinary "specification," and because the resulting activation of the will is what allows us to "determine ourselves by our reason to will this or that, which may be a true or an apparent good" (*ST* 1–2.9.6.3). In other words, we always *will* a particular good, though we can be made to realize that we are doing so by virtue of an orientation beyond that or any specific good.[29] In fact, freedom of choice stems from just that situation: in Yves Simon's terms, it is the "necessary adherence of the will to the comprehensive good [which] entails the indifference of the practical judgment" (Simon, 105). That is, our realization that no particular good can determine us to action leaves us a choice among them, and that realization reflects an inchoate awareness of our "living relation to the comprehensive good" (103).

What Aquinas has added to Aristotle is the immediate relation to a creator who not only inscribes the tendency in all rational creatures but activates it as well. That allows him to "explain" our self-determination in a way which relies not on autonomy but on the tendencies built into created natures and also identifies the initiator of willing with the free originator of all that is. This allows free creatures to be initiators in the realm proper to them—willing something, or willing this rather than that—but reserves the activating power to God. We might think of this as an elaboration of the doctrine of creation into the realm of willing, finding by analysis traces of the creator in creatures which would otherwise not appear. Aquinas meets the concern of objectors who sense that one who is so moved could not really be free, by recalling the founding relation of creature to creator: while "the very meaning of voluntary activity denotes an internal principle within the subject, this . . . does not have to be the utterly first principle, moving yet unmoved by all else. The proximate principle is internal, but the ultimately first moving principle is external, as indeed it is for natural movement, this being the cause setting nature in motion" (*ST* 1–2.9.4.1). And as if to offer commentary on the meaning of 'external' here, he acknowledges, in another context, that "to be moved voluntarily is to be moved of one's own accord, i.e., from a resource within. That inner resource, however, may derive from some other, outward source. In this sense there is no contradiction between being moved of one's own accord and being moved by another" (*ST* 1.105.4.2). Yet that "other" is limited to One: "God alone can really induce a change of this kind in the will" (*ST* 1.111.2). And since God is creator of all, bestowing the *esse* which is more interior to things than anything else, such a One can only be called "external" to the creature in a unique sense determined by the original "distinction" of creature from creator. Creatures are indeed capable of an utterly initiatory role, but it will not be one of acting but of failing to act, of "refusing" to enter into the process initiated by actively willing "the good."[30] In that sense, we can be "like unto God," but only in a self-destructive manner.

The key to Aquinas' presentation of human freedom lies in his adopting Aristotle's analysis of natures as goal-oriented powers: "to make clear [whether human beings have a free choice of their actions or make their choice of necessity] we must first realize that in human beings, just as in other things, there is an originating principle of their own actions" (*Q. D. de malo* 6). And what specifies human nature is that our principle of action is "intellect and will" (citing *De anima* 433a9). The inbuilt finality of our intellect and will to the true and the good offers the context for any discussion of free choice, with the significant philosophical result that neither *choice* nor *will* stand alone as defining human freedom. Will and intellect are always considered in relation to one another as complementary intellectual faculties, and choice is never offered as the paradigm for human freedom but as its most obvious result. So the mutual primacy of understanding or willing, parallel to the mutual implication of *true* and *good,* will characterize the dynamics of willing and of choosing among alternatives.[31] Moreover, alternatives only appear, as we have noted, in the measure that the overriding orientation to "the good" cannot be satisfied by any particular good that we may apprehend: "the will is in potentiality with regard to the universal good, so no good is more powerful than the power of the will so as to change it of necessity, except something that is good according to all ways of thinking about it. Only the complete good, i.e., well-being, is of this kind: the will cannot fail to want it, at least not in the sense of wanting its opposite" (*De malo* 6.7; also *ST* 1–2.10.2).

Yet while there is no *choice* with regard to the highest good, there does remain the capacity not to enter upon the activity, the radical freedom of *exercise*: the will "can, however, not actually be wanting it, as it can turn away the thought of well-being, since it changes the intellect toward its activity. So in this way not even well-being is necessarily wanted, just as people would not necessarily be heated if they could keep heat away from them when they wanted" (*De malo* 6.7). The analogy with natural process dominates the final example; the disanalogy we have already noted: *well-being* can hardly be compared with heat except in a case of extreme hypothermia, whereas to "turn away the thought of well-being" is self-destructive. So an analogy of human willing with creating, which dominated the Islamic discussion, is effectively diverted, since the only absolute beginning available to human willing is self-destructive. And even this absolute beginning will not be absolute, but the result of prior vices arising from a particular context. For human beings generally, sin is not so much an exercise of radical autonomy as it is wandering down treacherous paths with the wrong set of companions. So the exercise of autonomy, even of the self-destructive sort, is rare; the will is in fact much more moved than mover.[32]

A stark alternative in the Christian tradition to Aquinas'

picture of human freedom is that presented by John Duns
Scotus. Where Aquinas considers *will* in the line of nature,
Scotus opposes the freedom of will to the necessity of nature; where Aquinas expounds willing by analogy with reasoning and relies on the complementarity of these parallel
intellectual faculties to construct the dynamics of willing as
a moved movement, Scotus gives manifest priority to will as
an unmoved (or "autonomous") mover. (This summary statement would be contested immediately by Scotus scholars,
and I have tried to take their objections and nuances into
consideration in what follows, as a way of signaling my gratitude for their helping us trace the subtleties of the "subtle
doctor.")[33] It is true that one need not construe these considerable differences as polarizing these two thinkers on the
subject of human freedom, for they do indeed "agree on the
fundamental tenet that, ultimately, in a free choice it is an
act of will that settles which alternative will be pursued."[34]
What separates them, it seems, is a diverse set of preoccupations, proximate among which must be counted the condemnations of 1277, which arose in part because some were not
as careful as Aquinas in explicating the intellect's relation to
willing.[35] Yet they divide even more on their way of conceiving the relation of creature to its creator.

   With regard to our relation to God as our creator, Aquinas
had found Aristotle's conception of natures with inbuilt aims
a useful conceptual tool for elaborating the activity of intentional beings, now created in the image of their maker, whose
natures would be oriented to that same One as their goal,
yet that goal would only be realized through their free activity. (This activity, we shall see, becomes a *response* in the light
of divine grace.) Moreover, the Aristotelian principle, "whatever is in motion is moved by another," offered Aquinas a way
of showing how the dependence of such beings on the One
originating them could be incorporated into that very activity: the inbuilt orientation together with the initial "specification" of the will by that One to "the good" accounts for the
will's ability to originate activity, without however determining the outcome of any choice. For the "comprehensive good"

is not itself something chosen; whatever is chosen will be a means to this or lesser ends subordinate to it. And even in these choices, while the will may be specified (or "informed") by what one perceives to be best for one, the action itself flows from the action of the will: "for Aquinas as well as for Scotus, there are no *sufficient* conditions of the choice antecedent to the choice itself."[36]

Yet that activity will always be conceived, for Aquinas, as the activity of a creature in the manner we have sketched; whereas for Scotus it will be affirmed to be such, but conceived as the activity of a creature endowed with a capacity to originate activity, which enables it to "cooperate" with the divine will in a fully free act which would direct it to its true end.[37] Indeed, the notion of cooperation (or "concurrence") represents Scotus' mature position on the relation of intellect and will in producing a free act, with the intellect (as a "natural agent") subordinated to the inherently free activity of the will "to elicit an act."[38] And once the created agent is deemed to be autonomous, precisely to guarantee its capacity of initiation, then creature and creator will be conceived in parallel, the divine activity will be termed "concursus," and the stage is set for a zero-sum game in which one protagonist's gain is the other's loss. Theologically, the polarities observed in Islamic *kalam* cannot help but emerge: either creatures freely initiate their actions absent divine influence or they "acquire" (or "perform") actions created by God. Metaphysically, one will find oneself drawn to a "possibilism" in which such "agents" will be conceivable "before" they are created, so that the creator can envisage which "ones" it is fitting to cooperate with. The affinity with such a metaphysical position stems from the initial propensity to conceive creator and creatures in parallel or by way of simple contrast—which turn out to be the same thing. What such a perspective misses is the unique founding relation which is creation and which seems best elucidated by a metaphysics that can understand *act* analogously and so indicate how the originating activity of the creator continues to make the creature to be an agent in its own right. It is to that very relationship that we now turn.

7

On the Relations
between the Two Actors

It is time for explicit philosophical reflection on the crucial issues raised by each of the traditions which aver the free creation of the universe by the one God. The issues are crucial for our understanding of the faith of each, and so need to be approached in a manner proper to philosophical theology. Hence the relatively extensive canvassing of the ways in which each of these traditions has typically approached the questions which inevitably arise. Yet while each will confront the questions on its own terms, and even coin a technical vocabulary to meet them, the issues involved turn out to be sufficiently similar that the struggles for clarity of one tradition can illuminate another. That is particularly evident to us as we canvas them in turn and the more so as we eschew a putative overview but attempt to enter into each discussion on its own terms. We shall continue that approach in the two concluding chapters, which offer a glimpse of more exclusively theological topics, while this chapter will focus on the philosophical tools needed to explicate the unique relations obtaining between existents who are creatures and their creating source.

If the treatment gravitates toward Aquinas as the most credible spokesman for any of the traditions, that does not reflect any predilection for a Christian formulation of the conceptualities needed to develop a coherent theological framework. In fact, it may exhibit what was in fact the case: that Thomas incorporated into his synthesis the results of three centuries of prior labor by Muslim and Jewish thinkers on the very issues which confronted him.[1] He was simply positioned to do so. Yet it also suggests that because of his metaphysical acumen, perhaps also a function of his prior tutelage, he was able to transform the inherited Hellenic schemes in such a way as to exploit the implications of *creatio ex nihilo* and so create a specifically "Christian philosophy" that would also prove of considerable use to Jew or Muslim alike. For on these matters what Christianity adds, it seems, is not specificity so much as illumination. As he puts it in responding to a query as to what knowing divine triunity adds to our quest to know God by reason: we need such knowledge to have "the right idea of creation. The fact of saying that God made all things by His Word excludes the error of those who say that God produced things by necessity" (*ST* 1.32.1.3). Ghazali and Maimonides would readily concur, even though neither of them would be able to complete the brief for free creation by offering the reason which Aquinas did: "When we say that in Him there is a procession of love, we show that God produced creatures not because He needed them, nor because of any other extrinsic reason, but on account of the love of His own goodness." His conclusion, however, is shared by all three traditions, corroborating once again how "the distinction" of God from the universe may and may not be said to be a "Christian distinction."[2] For it will be presupposed to any account of free creation.

The issues relevant to this chapter are the ones which have recurred in our treatment so far: (1) causality: primary and secondary, the cause of being and causes of manners of being; (2) eternity and time as a corollary of creator/creature; (3) the efficacy of providence with respect to a world subject to failure; (4) the relative merits of a metaphysics which privileges the possible or the actual to explicate this unique relation, and (5) the pattern of love (or friendship) as an analogy for the interaction involved. The last presages the subject of the final two chapters, which will sketch how each of the traditions both images and acts out the relation which constitutes it. We shall also see that the imaging and performing involved may outstrip the capacity of any of them to articulate that "distinction" which can only be "glimpsed on the margin of reason" (Sokolowski, 39). But first to the conceptualities which could prove useful to formulate what lies "at the intersection of reason and faith": the relation of creator to creature.

7.1 CAUSALITY: PRIMARY AND SECONDARY

The very language of 'primary' and 'secondary' causation presumes a notion of *cause* or of *agent* which is analogous: that is, we can understand something to be an agent in distinct yet related senses. Moreover, there is an ordering intrinsic to the notion itself, so that the secondary agent or cause will function by leave of the primary one. For that is what 'secondary' and 'primary' meant in the context. This observation also reminds us how intimately the very notion of analogous usage of language presumes an ordering of the objects spoken of: we can justify our use of the same term functioning in radically different contexts in the measure that we can identify an ordering relation among the contexts themselves.[3] What this means is that 'primary' and 'secondary' do not indicate greater or less intensity of causing, or that a primary cause is *more* of a cause than a secondary one, for these assertions both presume a univocal genus, *cause*. The terms 'primary' and 'secondary', rather, come into play when we are faced with the situation where one thing is what it is by virtue of the other. So each can be said properly to be a cause, yet what makes one secondary is its intrinsic dependence on the one which is primary. This stipulation clearly distinguishes a secondary cause from an instrument, which is *not* a cause in its own right: it is not the hammer which drives the nails but the carpenter using it. Other examples, like a trained dog doing tricks, are less easily distinguished. What this distinction suggests is that whatever can function as a primary cause in a clear primary/secondary relationship will have to possess a unique ontological status.

We have spoken of primary and secondary causes in the context of the cause of being by contrast with causes of manners of being. Such a scheme introduces a paradigmatic notion of secondary causality that will be clearly distinguished from instrumental cause only in a metaphysical setting which can rise to affirming a primary cause as the source of all that is—and, arguably, only when that source is a free source, since the models of emanation make the intermediate causes to be instruments of the pervasive power of the first, for the connections must obtain with logical necessity if the model is to prove useful at all.[4] It follows that a philosophy whose model for origination involves some variety of necessary emanation will have to propose a "compatibilist" view of human freedom, whereby the ingredients essential to free action would be construed to be co-present with causally determining influences of the first. Similarly, a construal of the creator as less than totally originating, as some form of "demiurge," will have to find a way to constrict its power in order to leave room for human freedom, since such a "creator" would be sharing a world—if only a "possible" one—with its creatures. So the requirements of faith—Jewish, Christian, or Muslim—and of logic conspire to remind us that genuine agency on the part of creatures will be assured only if we can construe their connection with the creator in a way that assures no competition between the two.

That is not an easy task. We have seen how Islamic theologians, in their attempt to secure the provident sway of God as the free creator of all, were constrained to deny free creatures the origination of their actions. Some Jewish thinkers, notably the kabbalists, sensing this dilemma, proposed an imaginative "voluntary withdrawal" of divine influence and even of divine knowledge on God's part, precisely to assure human beings room to maneuver freely in God's universe— the celebrated doctrine of *tsimtsum*.[5] This proposal is imaginative in two senses: it is a creative extension of the voluntary dimension of creation, understanding that a free divine originator could indeed freely restrict the scope of divine activity; yet it also imagines a divine knower and actor as operating in the same domain as its creatures. So one finds, un-surprisingly, that kabbalist thought is proceeding according to the model of the Torah, in which God self-commits to act in a contractual fashion with a people who are thereby God's own, yet the form of discourse remains within the limitations of the narrative mode of the Hebrew scriptures. The next step would require recourse to a metaphysics, and one able to construe the originating and sustaining features of divine activity in such a way as not to interfere with but rather to enhance and assure human freedom. For such a metaphysics, a ruse like *tsimtsum* would be superfluous, for it could achieve the intended goal by incorporating a conception of God and of God's creatures which need not depend upon a distinct act of self-restriction on the part of the creator. Yet the prevailing intent of the kabbalists will have to be present as well: to show that God's care for all creatures is carried out in a personal manner which respects the intrinsic realities of each.

So the relation of primary to secondary cause must not only be such as to assure the primacy of the first along with the efficacy of the second but must be open to a personal reading as well. That is not an easy task in our climate of inquiry, which presumes causal language to be impersonal. Moreover, it will prove imperative that we proceed to the intentionality of the primary cause by way of its character as the "cause of being" rather than by analogies from human persons and their activity. That is, we will be constrained to think of the first (or "universal") cause of being in personal terms *not* because we are invited to think of God as "a person," but rather because in asserting that whatever exists is given existence by the One whose very being is to exist, we are gesturing at what is most intimate and individual about things. *Existing* cannot be a mere presupposition for a metaphysics which seeks to be faithful to creation; we must be speaking of what perfects things by bringing them about. And what brings about persons "must have as an aspect of its nature the formal character reflected in the existence of these effects, *viz.*, personal existence."[6] And this follows not from a general principle that effects are like their causes but from a closer examination of what the cause of being contributes to what it brings into being. If the proper effect of the creator's action, the *esse* of things, is what gives them their proper activity as well, then it is not hyperbole for Aquinas to insist that "existence is more intimately and profoundly interior to things than anything else" (*ST* 1.8.1). Here again we can discern the reciprocal relation between an affirmation of creation as the free participation in the very being of God and an understanding of creaturely existence as the activity founding each individual thing rather than a "maximally neutral" or "on/off property" of things.[7]

On such a metaphysics, God knows in a general fashion all that can participate in divine existence, and knows in a direct way whatever God desires to create.[8] The very notion of a free creator involves using intentional language to portray its activities, so we cannot escape regarding this causality in a personal fashion. And since the paradigm we have for such language is human persons, we cannot help but speak analogously about divine personal involvement in creation.[9] Yet that neither supposes nor licenses our moving "by analogy," as it were, from the activities of persons to a description of the *manner* of divine action. Analogous discourse *in divinis* does not function in so direct a manner but is governed by the *grammar* of divinity itself, which dictates the manner in which certain expressions—like 'knowing' and 'willing'—may be used in that domain. The fact that we must use such terms in reference to our experience of human knowing and willing reminds us of our practicing primary analogue, yet their application to God can never be by way of simple extrapolation but must be governed by the grammatical rules embodied in theorems like "[the creator] is the all-embracing cause of existence (*esse*) entire" (*ST* 1.45.2), and "God's knowledge stands to all created things as artists' to their products" (*ST* 1.14.8).[10] The first reminds us that a metaphysics must mediate all statements purporting to speak of God's activity in intentional terms, and the second advises us that God's relation to things as a knower will be the inverse of our own

–"we get our knowledge from natural things, of which God is the cause through [God's] knowledge"–so that "natural things will stand midway, as it were, between God's knowledge and ours" (*ST* 1.14.8.3). Both axioms block any simple inference from our modes of knowing to God's, yet the use of personal language is an inevitable consequence of the faith-assertion of a free creator.

If these strategies give the impression of being already in place and operative in Aquinas, we need only recall Ghazali's confrontation with the Muslim *falasifa* to see how difficult it can be to wrest a philosophical paradigm like *emanation* from an imperialistic attempt to preempt the intentional language of faith in favor of a model promising logical coherence.[11] So the effort will always be one of mediating the language of faith with demands for rational comprehension, and the mediating structures will perforce be metaphysical. Hence the need to find a metaphysical scheme which will not betray one or another source of our understanding in matters theological. I have been arguing that a scheme that privileges *existing* as *act* is indispensable to articulate the linkage which a free creation demands, without pitting two agents against one another. This contention will be severely tested as we move to a second feature of such a scheme: God's eternity. Here the need for an appropriate metaphysics will be imperative, for it seems that temporal parameters, inscribed as they are in the very tensed character of our discourse, are far more intractable than spatial ones–so much so indeed that contemporaries nearly despair of traditional assertions regarding divine eternity. Yet, as we shall see, the alternatives are no less inviting, and it will be possible to attain a tenuous grasp of God's eternal activity in relation to our temporal actions, but only by an appropriately *grammatical* strategy.[12]

7.2 ETERNITY AND TIME AS A COROLLARY OF CREATOR AND CREATURE

It seems that there is no more controverted feature of divinity today than that of eternity. And it represents a shift so dramatic that some of its detractors have dubbed the scheme which demands that God be eternal: "classical theism."[13] By that they intend to gesture toward a way of thinking which found change unworthy of divinity, privileging a timeless One; a scheme quite cognate to the neoplatonism that we have associated with everlasting emanation. Their contention has been that the interactive, reciprocal faith-world of the covenant was held hostage by a Hellenistic metaphysics which imposed a preconception of divinity, notably on Christian theologians. And once such a charge was leveled, it became difficult to disassociate insistence on God's eternity from a partisan conceptual scheme. (One is reminded of both Maimonides' and Ghazali's inability to conceive of a view of creation in which the universe had no beginning but was everlastingly derived from an eternal God. Since "the eternity of the world" was so intimately linked for them to schemes of necessary emanation, a free creation without an initial point of time was quite inconceivable.) Indeed, many discussions of God's "timelessness" turn on the inability to separate such a divinity from some form of neoplatonism, whereas the arguments of this work have been geared to show how theology in the three traditions which aver creation has explicitly disassociated itself from the scheme of necessary emanation. Thus detractors of eternity must argue that noxious vestiges remain.[14] Let us try to focus on the issue itself, for the case is difficult enough to elaborate without employing belittling labels.[15]

To be consonant with the faith-assertion of free creation, the corresponding doctrine of God must find a way of conceiving divinity which is neither parallel to nor in opposition to the universe.[16] The world and God cannot be correlatives if creating is to be the gracious gift of God, so the doctrine requires a metaphysics which can think divinity, not by contrast to the world, but *without* it. Even if it be utterly consonant for God to create the universe, the fact remains that God is not *part* of it. Fittingness does not impose necessity; divinity is not needy. (In fact, one may argue, the Christian paradigm of God-as-love is fulfilled better by a God who has no needs than by one who does, as one may show by analogy from a progressively selfless human love.)[17] The initial argument for God's eternity does not require a Hellenic metaphysics; it rather invokes "the distinction" consonant with a shared doctrine of creation: what could be without the world as we know it would simply have no reason to be *in* time. That One would be only because its nature is to-be; and what exists of itself in such a way as it is entirely present to itself exists eternally. That is simply what we mean by an eternal being: one for whom it would make no sense to say that it was "in time," since there is no reason to say anything temporal about it. There may be dimensions of the universe which can be expressed in timeless discourse, like mathematical relations, but God is not "timeless" in that sense, because God is not a dimension of the world. This seems straightforward enough, and it is hardly redolent of a Greek predilection for permanence over change. In fact, *eternity* cannot be expressed in temporal terms, whether of rest or of motion. So 'permanence' or 'duration' are as logically odd as 'fickle' or 'evanescent' in describing eternity.[18]

For Aquinas, *eternity* belongs to God alone, as the corollary of unchangeableness, which in the full-blooded sense can only be said of God (*ST* 1.10.3). And that sense harkens back to the creator's power to bring things out of nothing and so "preserve them in existence only by perpetually giving existence to them" in such a way as were God to withdraw it, they "would fall back into nothingness" (*ST* 1.9.2). Thus "no creature can be said to be absolutely necessary [or altogether unchangeable], for the preservation of a creature by God depends on the divine unchangeableness, not on natural necessity" (*De pot.* 3.17.3). So not only anything that changes but anything which comes into existence in any way at all—and that is everything but God—can be said to be 'changeable' in this sense of the term. It should be clear that divine immutability has nothing to do with "duration" or a "static God" but is itself a simple corollary of the manner of being of God: the One whose essence is to exist and from whose existence all existing things derive.[19] What "the divine unchangeableness" assures, then, is the continuance in existence of everything which is not God: this is the radical alteration in Aristotle's worldview wrought by creation and the metaphysics consonant with it. 'Eternal' and 'unchangeable' cannot be conceived by simple contrast with temporal or changing things, any more than God can be posed over against the world. In fact, they cannot be descriptive terms at all, but name "formal features" of divinity which will govern the imposition of any of the "divine names"–'merciful', 'wise', 'just', and the like. Such features are part of the grammar of a divinity which is "the beginning and end of all things" (*ST* 1.2 Prol.), so thinkers from Thomas Aquinas to David Braine will argue *to* such a One from the radical contingency which they find inscribed in our world, and it will be integral to their proof that this One be eternal, for nothing else could assure the world's continuance.[20]

The authors seem to divide on God's eternity according to whether they conceive divinity as the source of all, or by way of simple contrast to the world and hence (however implicitly) as *part* of it. The first group find *eternity* integral to their conception of divinity; the second are unable to comprehend it. The medieval debate between *creatio ex nihilo et de novo* and everlasting emanation presumed divinity to be eternal, which explains why those arguing from revelation for the novelty of creation had the harder time of it. At issue in that debate was the character of divinity: is it fully intentional or not? The contemporary discussion turns, rather, on the intelligibility of an eternal God, and more poignantly, on the relation of such a One to temporal realities. These are, of course, two sides of the same question, unless one so restricts *intelligibility* as to rule out anything which cannot be described in our temporal language.[21] We have so far seen how a God who creates *ex nihilo* cannot be itself temporal and so must be characterized as eternal, yet that God's eternity may not be reduced to mere *timelessness,* since such a One is the everlasting source of life.[22] So Boethius' definition of eternity as "the instantaneously whole [*tota simul*] and perfect possession of unending life" (*ST* 1.10.1) cannot escape temporal connotations in our tensed language, yet if we focus on 'life' we

will be able to parse *tota simul* as one must explicate *ex nihilo* –
as reaching for something which a language consonant with
a temporal context cannot directly express.

But how might we think of such a One being related to
the temporal realities it creates? Not impersonally to be sure,
as Plotinus' One, but intentionally and by analogy with artists to their products (*ST* 1.14.8). The strategy of taking divine knowing to be preeminently "practical" disarms many
objections concerning divine knowledge of temporal realities
by relating an eternal divinity to its temporal products, while
the disanalogy with ordinary *making* will allow us to head off
concerns about the integrity of created things. The account
runs like this: God, who knows eternally and who knows by
a practical knowing *what* God is doing, knows all and only
what *is,* that is, what God brings into being. Yet by that knowledge, like an artist, God also knows what could be, although
this knowing remains penumbral and general, since nonexis-
tent "things" are explicitly *not* constituted as entities.[23] By
definition, an eternal God does not know contingent events
before they happen; although God certainly knows all that may
or might happen, God does not know what *will* happen. God
knows all and only what *is* happening (and as a consequence,
what has happened). That is, God does not *already* know what
will happen, since what "will happen" has not yet happened
and so does not yet exist. God knows what God *is* bringing
about. Yet since our discourse is temporal, we must remind
ourselves not to read such a statement as saying that God is
now bringing about what *will* happen, even though what *will
have* happened *is* the result of God's action.

What these grammatical remarks underscore is the relent-
lessly *actual* character of God's presence to the world. The
eternity thesis has the primary advantage of releasing us from
so-called "counterfactuals of freedom," which amount to asking
what "Sally" would do in response to a particular invitation,
were she to be created. Besides being at a loss to know how
to answer such a question, that her name is in scare quotes
reminds us that the question itself is suspect. One cannot even
refer to a possible individual as anything more than one of

a kind, much less pretend to know how such a "one" would act freely, since such actions can only be predicated of existing persons. So to consider the statements themselves, asking whether the "counterfactuals of freedom" were true or false, would be to treat language without its mooring in reality, and thus represent an extreme "possibilism."[24] Yet those who find themselves pushed to such a position do so either because they are unable to conceive an eternal God or because the relation between an eternal creator and its creatures raises philosophical conundra which they prefer to avoid. It is incumbent upon us, then, to elucidate that relation in the clearest possible terms.

Did God know in 1900 that Auschwitz would occur? This question of Anthony Kenny poses several questions nicely: (1) it places the issue firmly in the actual world, (2) it inquires not into something which would ever be part of God's intent, but an evil action contrary to that intent, and (3) it asks about God's knowledge of future contingencies—a question which Aristotle faced and which Maimonides and others conceded would issue in determinism were God's knowledge at all like ours.[25] The answer we would want to be able to give would be *no,* since God's knowledge is not dated; nor by the same token would God have to wait to find out. Aquinas' treatment of God's knowing will help us construct that response. God knows individuals, he insists, because "God is the cause of things through his knowledge, [so that] God's knowledge has the same extension as his causality" (*ST* 1.14.11). The paradigm is clearly that of "practical knowing;" God's acting cannot be mindless. Yet God acts eternally in such a way as what is to be exists temporally, so if "*time* is properly the measure of motion, *eternity* is properly the measure of *existing* as such" (*ST* 1.10.4.3): whatever *is* is now. The *now* of time is of course double-edged, as Augustine reminded us poignantly in *Confessions* 10; in Aquinas' words: "for just as we become aware of time by becoming aware of the flowing instant, so we grasp the idea of eternity by grasping the idea of an abiding instant [*nunc stans*]" (*ST* 1.10.2.1, citing Boethius, *De Trin.* 4). Yet the grasp is tenuous, since we may not render *stans* as "standing still," without falling into a temporal language scheme. We can at best parse Aquinas' assertion that "eternity is the proper measure of *existing* as such" by returning to the creator-creature relation, insisting on the one hand that whatever *is* is now, and that God knows what God does. So whatever *is*, and hence soon *was*, as well as what *will have been*, God knows. Aquinas distinguishes this "knowledge of vision" from God's knowing what God might have produced, which he calls "knowledge of simple understanding," justifying the choice of labels by the fact that "whatever is seen by us has a separate existence over against the one who sees it" (*ST* 1.14.9).[26] So we are not implying that God is inspecting things but only that whatever is, was, or will have been, God knows. Let us review the grammar of these matters to see how we can assert that.

"Whatever *is* is now" asserts the primacy of actual existing. Yet our temporal 'now' is evanescent, so Augustine likens it to the dimensionless point separating past from future (*Confessions* 10.18); though Aquinas for his part will resist likening eternity to "the 'now' of time" (*ST* 1.10.4.3). Yet he too invokes that same *now* to give us whatever glimpse we might have of eternity "as the measure of *existing* as such," so returning us to the creator as the One who bestows *esse*. So God knows—in God's eternal *now*—what God does. About this *present* we can say nothing; that is, no attributions like 'lasting', 'permanent', or 'abiding' are appropriate, since our language for living, active things is inherently temporal. We can, however, offer grammatical rules: (a) we cannot identify that eternal present with any temporal *now*, even though each temporal now will only *be* in virtue of a relation of existential dependence on that eternal present; (b) we can only use present-tense verbs with God, and then only in such a way as to cut those implications (or presuppositions for their use) which reflect the imbeddedness of the present tense within a future/past scheme. Such a peculiar use will give the impression, certainly, of a "sort of duration," since together with (a), it implies that this "eternal present" comprehends all phases of time" (*ST* 1.10.2.4). Yet there remain substantive differences between what is, what was, and what will have been, so "all phases of time" is an inherently ambiguous phrase, since the three tenses are not in reality like species of a common genus. For if time is "the measure of motion" and thus comes to be only when changeable things come to be, then there would be no time "before" creation, and the extension of our time line into the future is but a projection as well. (This becomes especially clear in a creation-ontology perspective, so it might well be independent of an Aristotelian conception of time.) It could be that our accepting this projection as fact contributes to our picturing eternity as *duration*, along with thinking of the "what will have been" scenario as history not yet performed.

So what can be included in Aquinas' "whole of time [*totum tempus*]" (*ST* 1.14.13)? If it includes all and only what *is* and what *was*, then God is blind regarding what *will have been*, since God's action is not yet realized. But if it also includes what will have been, then we must have a way of distinguishing "what is not yet but will have been" from "whatever might happen." We have seen that Aquinas distinguishes them as two modes of God's knowledge: "knowledge of vision" and "knowledge of simple understanding." Molina's "middle knowledge" [*scientia media*] purports to accomplish this by means of a divine decision, yet the field of choice presupposes a determinacy regarding possibilities which those who give primacy to actual existence find incoherent—a determinacy likening the decision itself to a "divine decree."[27] Thus we need a way of formulating this difference as a function of divine eternity and without any connotation of a "divine decree (or plan)" that presumes a fixed future. Since conservation and creation are the same activity, let us return to the theorems governing creation. *God knows what God does:* the model is practical knowing, so the usual concerns about God knowing *that* something *will* take place are quietly finessed. Taking a cue from Aquinas' strategy regarding God's knowledge of singulars, we must say that divine knowledge extends as far as divine activity (for God does not work mindlessly) without having a more determinate model for divine knowing than that. *The effects of God's action are temporal.* The impact of understanding creation as bestowing *esse* is to assure that the eternity of the source does not diminish the temporality of the effect: created things are really temporal and temporally real.

Yet does not the fact that God acts and knows eternally put those things which will-have-been (by contrast to whatever might be) within the scope of God's "knowledge of vision"? Indeed, but according to the quite unimaginable modality of creation: the eternal act of bestowing temporal existence in such a way as to presuppose nothing at all. And as it belongs to God's eternal intention to create the universe, so that eternal intention includes each item in the universe being created such that it exists temporally by its proper created *esse.*[28] In this sense, then, "eternity takes in the whole of time [*ambit totum tempus*]" (*ST* 1.14.13), by way of God's creative intent working itself out temporally, and not by any impersonal image like a *duration* embracing all of time. So we can see that the activity of creation separates eternity from *timelessness* (or the oxymoron "timeless duration"), assuring that eternity belongs to God alone (*ST* 1.10.3), who always acts personally. The dynamics of the creating action of God returns us to the personal in God's activity, so that if "eternity embraces all of time" it does so in the divine intent. Yet this simply reminds us that a free creator acts not impersonally but personally (especially where *freedom* is understood more comprehensively than mere choice or trade-offs), and that *eternity* is a formal feature of such a One. So we will only understand God's eternity in the context of a One whose essence is to-exist and not as a property which we might be able to grasp otherwise, like *timelessness.*[29] *What will have been* is known as God's creating intent ("knowledge of vision"), while *what might be* is known only as such ("knowledge of simple understanding"), penumbral to the practical knowing which guides the divine creating and conserving action.

But what about human evil, which God cannot possibly intend—Kenny's astute question? Granted, God's acting and knowing cannot be dated, why does God not need to wait to see it happen? The key to answering this question is that no one – not even God – can have knowledge of what will have happened in such a way as it is all there *already*. So God's knowing eternally of evil which occurs will have to be a knowledge attendant upon the mode of action proper to divinity, that is, God's creating intent understood to be subject to human refusal. Here the fact that we have no model becomes particularly disconcerting, as we want to be able to *picture* such knowing *before*hand; otherwise we cannot but picture God as having to "wait and see" *until* it comes to pass.[30] Given that we cannot picture God's knowing of what-will-have-been, it is better to say that God does not *now* know what will-be and then correct the inevitable implications of that statement by insisting that God will not, however, be surprised by what in fact occurs, since what-will-have-been is part of God's eternal intent, either directly or inversely, as in evil actions (*ST* 1.10.10). It remains that we will try, inescapably, to picture such an intent as God "peering into *the future,*" so we must then insist that the entire point of calling God's knowledge of the "actual world" that of *vision* is to call attention to the "contemporaneity" of an eternal creator with all that emanates from it, whereby whatever is, is so in its being *present* *to* its creator (*ST* 1.14.13).[31] Yet the manner in which temporal realities are present to their eternal creative source is not available to us, so it is hardly surprising that we lack a model for God's knowing eternally what-will-have-happened. For that reason I would prefer the arresting picture of God not knowing "the future" (which is also literally true) to the one which seems invariably to accompany the assertion that God does eternally know what will-have-happened – namely, that God can do what no one else can: peer into "the future."[32] God knows eternally what God brings about temporally; but this assertion does not entail that God *now* knows what God *will* bring about. The hiatus between eternity and time presents another manifestation of "the distinction," so it is only plausible in the perspective of creation and never comprehensible.

7.3 THE NECESSITY FOR A METAPHYSICS PRIVILEGING THE *ACTUAL* OVER THE *POSSIBLE*

Divine eternity dramatizes the conceptual difficulties involved in thinking of God in terms other than that of a being-in-a-world, even that being which is present in any possible world. So we have seen how crucial it is to elucidate eternity as concomitant with what it means to be creator of all that is. Unlike *timelessness, eternity* is a formal feature of divinity as such and not something which might be said of certain sectors of the world, like numbers. To understand the nature of mathematical reality, whatever ontological status one proposes to grant to it, is to know that it is timeless. Yet that same feature also removes mathematicals from the causal interaction attendant upon temporal individuals. Divine eternity is of another order, however, for it attends God as the origin of all that is, the source of existence, and is seen to follow upon that description. Since such an agent is not (by definition) part of the world, we cannot have independent access to God's eternity. Hence my insistence that eternity is not a property, but a "formal feature" of divinity, and known to be so from our understanding of God as a free creator. Asserting the primacy of *act* in God and in God's world follows a similar pattern. If one has an independent notion of divinity as part of the world, indeed the principal part, then one may find oneself picturing creation itself as God's selection among a myriad of possible scenarios, like a jury in an architectural contest. Or one might, as Augustine did, elevate the entire process into the divine mind, where God will then canvass God's own ideas to make the world which most pleases God. The contention of this section is that a literal Augustinian picture does not in fact preserve "the distinction" of God from the world, but amounts to doing what was just suggested: projecting a pagan picture of a demiurge onto a Jewish-Christian-Muslim canvas of a creator. Yet what really jeopardizes the status of the creator is not the picture itself but the metaphysics which usually attends it. And that confusion makes these issues especially difficult to elucidate.

Moreover, metaphysical strategies are often adopted in function of perceived religious reasons, as one might expect in philosophical theology and as we have noted generally to be the case with regard to articulations of the creator-creature relationship: they will follow the contours of a tradition's experience with its proper revelation. Yet in this case, philosophical perspectives intrude to frame the problematic, as Molinists feel compelled to adopt a metaphysics supportive of "middle knowledge" because their view of human freedom in the face of divine freedom presumes a zero-sum game.[33] On our account, this presumption overlooks the unique relation of creator to creature, and that criticism would be corroborated were the supporting metaphysics to elide the difference between a creator and a demiurge. Yet is that not precisely what is effected by the scenario required for "counterfactuals of freedom" to be true? That is, if God (alone) is to know what a possible creature would freely do in any circumstance, that "creature" would have to "be" without God's having brought it into existence. So though such a God might be called a creator, it would in effect be a demiurge, since such possible individuals would "be" in a fashion independent of God's having creating them. Alternatively, God would know which counterfactuals would be true, without presupposing any "possible individuals" whose possible actions would make them to be true.[34] Yet while this strategy may at first appear less metaphysically implausible, it soon accumulates objections: what has become of the privileged status of existential individuals? Correlatively, what happened to the status of free action as attributable to this one's acting? Why does God's knowing the truth of such counterfactuals not determine their outcome? In other words, without the interposition of an individual freely acting, what can it mean to say that some "counterfactuals of freedom" are true and others false?

Were it not for the centrality of creation, this discussion might be thought abstruse, or a mere matter of metaphysical preference. So besides catering to a culture of pluralism, such a reading would also dispense us from undertaking taxing philosophical discriminations. Yet creation, we have seen, must be utterly central to any philosophical theology executed by Jews, Christians, or Muslims. So the fact that much philosophical discussion of these matters can simply overlook it, or can read Aquinas' treatment of these issues, in which the creator-creature relation figures crucially, as though that relation were not at work, challenges us to specify the philosophical difference which creation makes.[35] There is no direct way to do this, of course, since creation is not an event in the world, and so seems compatible with various pictures one might propose for it. And since these pictures will reflect diverse metaphysical commitments, how can we expect reference to the act of creating to adjudicate among them? By arguing for a metaphysics more consonant with a community's appropriation of revelation, much as Ghazali, Maimonides, and Aquinas confronted Avicenna's scheme of eternal emanation with *creatio de novo: not* contending that philosophical arguments alone could adjudicate the issue, but that faith favored the *de novo* reading in the absence of demonstrative proof to the contrary.

In a parallel vein, I will contend that a metaphysics which privileges the actual—as Aquinas does and Scotus does not—offers us a clearer rendition of the act of creation and of the relation of creature to creator, such that divine and human freedom can be related not extrinsically but intrinsically, thereby assuring an account of created causality that is at once dependent yet properly initiatory.[36] In other words, such an account of creation will set up a relation between creating and created actors which will allow us to use 'act' properly of each while affirming the complete dependence of the created actor on its creating source. This entails that created agency need not be characterized as "autonomous" to assure its genuinely initiatory role, nor need complete dependence imply "occasionalism." What will result is a coherent account of "secondary causality" which in no way derogates from the causal efficacy of the one called "secondary," but rather indicates its utter dependence on a creating "primary" cause. And what makes this possible is a metaphysics which links creator to creature in a way which presupposes nothing at all, so that all-that-is, and preeminently the existence itself of each thing, comes forth from the creator. By identifying the action of conserving in existence with that of creating, and insisting on the *ex nihilo* aspect of creation, we can begin to see how things so dependent can enjoy a proper initiative without losing a whit of their ultimate dependence.[37]

Everything turns, of course, on the ability to characterize the creator of all things as the cause of being, and to understand the capacity to act on the part of self-determining creatures to be a participation in existence freely granted by that primary cause. If, on the other hand, we think of the creator as surveying universes of fully determinate possible beings "before deciding" which one to create, we are at a loss to understand how such "creatures," possessed of at best "intelligible existence [*esse intelligibile*]," could be understood to be free actors and hence "fully determinate."[38] Hence the picture we have of God as creator will imply a specific metaphysics, and vice-versa. It may be that some who are independently persuaded of the validity of a metaphysics which "sees actuality as a subset of possibility" will positively promote the surveying picture of creation rather than simply find themselves mesmerized by a picture which others might regard as an uncritical extrapolation from human choosing.[39] Moreover, their predilection will be colored by a desire to safeguard human freedom in the face of an all-pervasive creator, yet I hope to show that this very anxiety results from the metaphysics chosen.[40]

For once one pretends to be able to conceive of fully determinate "possible worlds," so that there is no difference between a scenario and a history except that the history offers an *actual* description which one can simply move "on stage" without alteration, then the dependence of all such "worlds" on the creator is a matter of "simple understanding [*simplicis intelligentiae*]," to use Aquinas' terminology. What distinguishes the world in which we live is not a distinct form of knowledge on God's part ("knowledge of vision") but simply *will*. On such a metaphysics there can be no distinction in the creator's *knowledge* between what might be and what is, was, or will have been. The only thing which sets the real world apart is God's *choice,* so that 'real' does not add anything *intelligible* to 'determinate'. This means that the dependence of creatures on the creator will not be able to be thought in existential terms, but solely in terms of "simple understanding." It is then a simple step to presuming that such terms are adequate as well: there will be no problem, then, in "God['s] having the idea of an object prior to its becoming actual," because any created thing will be identified with its "individual qualitative essence [which will] include only purely conceptual properties."[41] Linda Zagzebski believes that the conceptual device of "individual [qualitative] essence allows there to be all the possibilities *de re* there could have been without forcing us to say that there *are* possible but nonactual individuals[:] there are no possible but nonactual individuals, but there are unexemplified IQEs" (143). But how can we distinguish an individual – the sort of thing we encounter, one of Aristotle's "primary substances" – from its "qualitative essence"? At best by something called "an haecceity that supervenes on an IQE" (142), where the curious term *haecceity* (Latin for 'thisness') adapts a neologism of Scotus to allude to what distinguishes the subsisting individual when one's metaphysical account is unable to identify any intelligible difference between what is and what might be.[42] All that Linda Zagzebski's "theory" has accomplished is to spell out what it looks like when there is no difference, with the hope that this elucidation will persuade us that the difference is negligible. Yet it can have just the opposite effect as well.

We can easily enlarge the context of this discussion by posing it in terms of Augustine's and Aquinas' treatment of "divine ideas."[43] We saw Roger Arnaldez associate an inveterate voluntarist strain in Islamic thought with "the negation of exemplary ideas in God: the divine essence is not participatible since nothing exists which resembles [God]"; whereas the complementary intellectualism of Christian medieval thought is reflected in God's possessing such *exemplars* of whatever God brings into being.[44] Yet everything turns on the way one conceives such "ideas" *in divinis.* Do they amount to "individual qualitative essences" which may or may not be "exemplified," or are they directly linked to the act of creating? And what difference could it possibly make? As James Ross has reminded us, Aquinas will carry his original distinction between the "simple understanding" which the creator has of what might be and the "knowledge of vision" attendant upon what is, was, or will have been into the divine ideas themselves, so differences are very important to him.[45]

Aquinas adapts a distinction he finds in Plato's treatment of *ideas* to modify the legacy he has received from Augustine of ideas in God's mind as the heavenly archetypes of things which we encounter. The distinction is between "ideas as principles of the knowledge of things and of their coming into existence," both of which functions are played by ideas "in the divine mind." When an idea functions as "a principle of the production of things it may be called an *exemplar,* and belongs to practical knowledge; [whereas] as a principle of knowing, it is properly called an *intelligible nature* [*ratio*], and can belong also to speculative knowledge" (*ST* 1.15.3). And these *rationes* are then explicitly "related to all the things God knows, even though they never come into existence; and to all the things he knows in the intelligible natures proper to each, and as known by him in a speculative way." So Aquinas takes pains to distinguish practical from speculative knowing in God, noting that speculative knowing takes in what is, was, or will have been as well as what might be, but in a manner different from practical knowing of those same things: for it only reaches to the "intelligible nature proper to each [*propria ratio*]." Those things, then, of which God has *exemplars* will be those individual things which correspond to the divine intent; of the rest God will have but *rationes,* "some idea," in our way of speaking.

Would these qualify as "individual qualitative essences" in the theories of Linda Zagzebski and others? Perhaps so, but with the crucial proviso that such knowing is for Aquinas *merely* speculative: what it takes to transform such a *ratio* into an *exemplar* is more than a simple choice: it is an application of practical knowing.[46] That is, the creator has a specific intentional relation to those things which the creator intends to create; a relation hardly clarified by 'choice' or 'exemplification'. The practical thrust of Aquinas' treatment of divine ideas is evident throughout, as he justifies their presence *not* as that "*by which* there is knowledge," for "it would be contrary to its simplicity were the divine intellect informed by a plurality of knowledge-likenesses [*species*]" (1.15.2), but on the analogy of an architect: if we think of "God acting as an intellectual agent, there must be in the divine mind a form, to the likeness of which the world is made—since the world is not made by chance" (1.15.1). And if God's intention to make something is not a mere choice, the *exemplar* will contain more than the simple *ratio*: it will embody "the direct object of [God's] creation: the order of the whole universe" (1.15.2). The "order of the universe" is what belongs essentially to the divine intent to create this world: it relates among themselves those things which God intends to participate in existence and so distinguishes history from a scenario, practical from speculative knowing, *exemplars* from *rationes*.

What we have been sketching out, of course, is a way of presenting creation which gives primacy to existing things and does so in such a way as to acknowledge that the actuality which is *existing* may not be detectable by us as a feature of things but is nevertheless intelligible in its divine origin. Moreover, such a primacy allows one to return everything to the creator, since possibilities represent modalities of existing things which have the valence they have because they are created by God and so participate by express intention in divine existence. Thus a metaphysics which privileges *act* over *possibility* serves to highlight the initiating and continuing presence of the creator in the universe. It is in that sense that I have argued for its peculiar congruence with faith in a free creation. One could, of course, argue for such a metaphysics without making direct reference to creation, as both James Ross and Barry Miller have done.[47] Discerning readers will recognize my indebtedness to both writers in my insistence that possible beings are not sufficiently determinate for successful reference and other such arguments. In the context of a work of philosophical theology, however, I have been intent on showing how some metaphysical strategies may be more congruent with one's faith commitments, and vice-versa, so I will leave the direct argumentation to Ross and to Miller. It is worth remarking, though, that their argumentation against "possibilism" is not unrelated to a view of the origins of the universe exemplified by the faith traditions operative here. Perhaps the strongest argument in favor of a metaphysics which privileges individual existing things over possibilities can be found in Aquinas' query whether creatures can be said to resemble God? The usual theorems of effect resembling cause lose their force in the face of the creator's transcendent causality. Yet one thread remains: "precisely as individual existing things [*entia*] they resemble the primary and universal source of all existence" (*ST* 1.4.3). That will not leave a discernible trace, of course, but it should suggest a metaphysics appropriate to elucidating this primary relation—one which begins with such things and focuses on what it is that sustains them in existence.

7.4 THE EFFICACY OF PROVIDENCE IN A WORLD SUBJECT TO FAILURE

Since conserving is the same divine activity as creating, one would expect divine providence to follow a similar pattern as one's treatment of creation. For providence but adds to conservation "the idea whereby all things are planned to an end" (*ST* 1.22.2). If God's action reaches to individuals, and that action is thoroughly intentional, they will all be ordered to an end. That is why Maimonides and Aquinas each castigate Ibn Sina for limiting God's knowledge, and by implication God's caring activity, to the species.[48] Yet at the same time, it seems bizarre to have the one creator concerned about the doings of every ant! The emanation scheme had the advantage of keeping divine efficacy at an appropriate remove, consigning the sub-lunar realm to the ample Aristotelian domain of chance. So some middle ground needs to be found. Maimonides offers a suggestion: "divine providence watches

only over the individuals belonging to the human species"
(*Guide* 3.17). He draws the line here by inference from the
examples used in scripture: "I never found in the book of a
prophet a text mentioning that God has a providence watching over one of the animal individuals, but only over a human individual."

Aquinas takes Maimonides expressly to task for this opinion, insisting that "everything that is real in any way whatsoever [*quae habent quocumque modo esse*] is bound to be directed by God to an end [because] the causality of God, as
the primary agent, extends itself to all existing things [as] the
source of their singularity" (*ST* 1.22.2). Logic is on Aquinas'
side, since the mode of causality proper to the origin of all
things makes each one to be and, as a thoroughly intentional
activity, will direct each to its end. Yet Aristotle's thesis that
the end of subhuman individuals is but the preservation of
the species allows Aquinas to return to the spirit of Maimonides' middle position: God provides for "mortal individuals
. . . only secondarily, like instruments for preserving the species" (*ST* 1.23.7). Moreover, the primary/secondary cause
scheme fully obtains only for "rational creatures [who] are
masters of their actions, . . . in that God ordains them to
act voluntarily and of themselves. Other creatures, however,
do not act except as acted upon by divine operation" (*ST*
1.19.12.4).

So both Maimonides and Aquinas effectively focus divine
providence on rational individuals, yet each does so in a fashion reflective of their respective traditions's experience with
revelation. Citing al-Farabi's lost commentary on Aristotle's
Ethics, Maimonides makes the degree of divine guidance to
be a function of an individual's alignment with the divine
intellect. Yet lest this be taken as utterly elitist, his cryptic
closing comments indicate that what the philosophers must
strive for is also available to anyone who faithfully observes
the Torah: "Consider this chapter as it ought to be considered;
for through it all the fundamental principles of the Law will
become safe for you and conformable to speculative philosophical opinions" (*Guide* 3.18). We shall see how he turns

such alignment into something far more intimate than mere observance, however, in the concluding chapter of the *Guide*. For now it should suffice to note the contrast with Aquinas, for whom God's providence over human beings amounts to something altogether distinct from that providence "whereby all things are planned to an end," since the end to which God has called each human being, in Christ, clearly "exceeds the proportion and ability of created nature, and this is eternal life, which . . . consists in the vision of God" (*ST* 1.23.1). The modality will be the same as providence; it will be a *ratio* pre-existing in God, but one to which creatures need "to be led by being carried by God [*quasi a Deo transmissa*]." Aquinas names this ordering "predestination," thereby distinguishing it from simple providence; yet as we shall see, the theorems which are operative in providence, deriving as they do from the conserving in being which cannot really be distinguished from creating, shall be operative here as well. What distinguishes predestination from providence, then, is not a distinct modality of God's activity but the divine intention to grant human beings a share in the very life of God and the human capacity to "withdraw oneself from the ordering of the divine intellect" (*ST* 1.17.1).[49] Grace and sin, then, form the new parameters announcing a new phase in the creator-creature relationship.[50]

7.4.1 The Efficacy of Providence Regarding Contingent Things

Although the end result is never in doubt, accounts of the efficacy of providence vary greatly from Muslim to Jewish to Christian thinkers. Islamic thought seems to have as its major concern the sovereignty of God, while Jewish thinkers are less worried about securing the sovereignty of God, apparently confident that the "master of the universe" will prevail. Ghazali's criticism of "the philosophers" stemmed at least in part from their willingness to delegate the divine activity to a series of intermediaries whose necessary interconnection assured that the world could never deviate from a logically invariant track. Maimonides also rejected an everlasting world conceived on the model of logical derivation because such a system would have prevented divine activity from spontaneously bestowing the Torah. Yet he did not feel constrained at the same time to deny causal linkage altogether, as did his Muslim counterpart, Ghazali. Why not? Because the laws of nature could well be inscribed in created things by the Lord, after the pattern of a torah which would not encounter in the rest of nature the recalcitrance it met in free creatures. So once again each community's experience with its mode of revelation will help to shape the way in which creation is structured. Mediacy does not pose the threat to God's pervasive action in a Jewish context that it might in Islam, where God's immediate presence seems required to assure the efficacy of the divine activity.

These differences are more clearly tendencies, of course, than discriminating marks, since Islamic and Jewish thinkers like Ibn Rushd and Isaac Albalag had little difficulty espousing an everlasting universe with necessitarian overtones. Yet the *kalam* tradition, which Ghazali had sought to bring into fruitful contact with "philosophy," had been adamant in insisting upon a world utterly open to divine creating action at each moment, and so quite devoid of causal interaction, while later kabbalist thinkers, as we have seen, sought to leave room for contingency and for freedom by picturing the "master of the universe" withdrawing the divine presence sufficiently to allow for random interaction. We may at least say that each of these traditions was prone to conceive the divine-human arena as a zero-sum encounter. Although the Christian picture is hardly homogeneous on this point, we can say that Aquinas does not so conceive things. While he is explicit in demanding that the divine creating (and conserving) power be immediate, he also insists that "God governs the lower through the higher, . . . from the abundance of his goodness imparting to creatures also the dignity of causing" (*ST* 1.22.3), in such a way that their existence and their causing reflect the divine activity. And since the creator is manifestly above the categories of necessary/contingent (*ST* 1.19.8), this action can sustain without determining (*ST* 1.22.4.3). What is startling about this view is that divine providence is said to be efficacious without even raising the specters of "determinism" or "occasionalism." How does he manage to assert such things? By relying once again on the nodal point of contact between creator and creature in "participated *esse.*" What allows Aquinas to assert what others might have wished to assert as well, but had not the conceptual tools to accomplish, are his complementary doctrines of God as the One in whom essence and existing are identical and of creatures as things in which the two are distinct.

As a result, since "necessary or contingent are corollaries to being as such, . . . the very mode of necessity or contingency falls under God's universal providence" (*ST* 1.22.4.3), so "what the plan of providence has arranged to result necessarily and without fail will come about so, what too it has arranged to result contingently will come about so" (*ST* 1.22.4.1). In short, God cannot fail even though creatures often do. What assures the efficacy of providence cannot itself be a part of created reality, for if it were, then the modality of the vehicle would either be *necessary* or *contingent,* and that would affect the results of providence, making them either necessary or contingent.[51] In this way the elaborate emanation scheme works against divine freedom, besides obscuring its proper mode of efficacy, by introducing a series of intermediaries whose necessary connection with the One assures providential efficacy at the price of reducing all events to a necessary plan. Divine action must effect its results immediately, yet not in such a way as to replace the created agents at work. The only possible candidate for such a cause is the cause of being itself, and even more precisely, the cause of each thing's existing. For only existing individuals can act, so that the One who empowers each thing to exist thereby empowers it to act. Yet if we persist in asking *how* this is done, we will be asking for a response in terms of created causes, which can only assure their results by necessitating them. Thus we are reminded once again that any account of divine causal activity must tailor itself to the paradigm of creation, which requires an activity without any attendant process; one which may be asserted but never tracked. And if the assertion of a free creation is already a faith-assertion, providence will be so as well. So the mode or manner of divine activity will ever escape us, yet we will be able to speak of it consistently, provided we keep referring any divine action to the constituting and originating activity of creation.

7.4.2 Predestination and Reprobation

We have seen how Maimonides insisted on a distinct providence for free creatures, avowing that God's individual care is reserved for them. Aquinas has an added incentive to distinguish providence at work among human beings in as much as the end to which all of us are actually ordained "consists in the vision of God, and surpasses the nature of any creature" (*ST* 1.23.1). So there is something added to providence, stemming from the orientation added to human nature by the incarnation of the Word of God, issuing in the death and resurrection of Jesus. Aquinas gives this added dimension the traditional name of "predestination." Yet the expression proves awkward in Aquinas' treatment, since the relation of an eternal creator to creatures removes any operative sense for the temporal prefix 'pre', as he had already remarked regarding the term 'providence': "God's knowledge of future things is more properly called 'providence' than 'pre-vidence'" (*De ver.* 2.12). So what preoccupies Aquinas in this domain is not the fact that God's intent will be achieved, for that follows from providence more generally, but rather the manner in which the actions of free creatures will contribute to that effect. And the actions which will give the most trouble, again, are not those whereby we act in concert with God's elevating impulse of *grace,* for these too will follow the pattern of creaturely acting more generally, but rather the behavior of human beings which stems from their "refusal" to collaborate with that divine initiative: sin. It is for this reason that 'predestination' is invariably linked with 'reprobation'.

Yet it is in the connection between these two that Aquinas'

treatment differs significantly from those who saw themselves as following the lead of Augustine, notably in the sixteenth century and later. As Bernard Lonergan puts it succinctly: for Aquinas "sin is a cause of punishment in a way in which merit is not a cause of glory" (*GF,* 114). If we retain the term 'predestination', which Augustine introduced, we can see how Aquinas' elaboration of God's providential care for individual human beings employs a metaphysics that allows him to be faithful to Augustine's intent in a way in which not even Augustine was able to be, and certainly not his later erstwhile followers. The account must be rendered in such a way as to remove any hint of responsibility for reprobation from God, and not merely in the limiting sense in which God owes creatures nothing, for that assertion, however it may underscore the transcendence of God, cannot but seem inhospitable in a Jewish or Christian context. The principle of covenant underlies these traditions, so that divine transcendence will not normally be articulated in a manner which makes one mindful of an arbitrary sovereign. A God who acted so would not be the God of Abraham, Isaac, Jacob, and Jesus.

So everything will turn on the asymmetry between good and evil, between collaborating with divine grace or that holding back from entering into the dynamics of free action which we have called "refusal." What is crucial for Aquinas' account here is his elaboration of free actions as "emerging from, and . . . conditioned by, created antecedents over which freedom has no direct control" (*GF,* 115).[52] Since his account is quite at variance with John Duns Scotus here, however, what we are tracing is a metaphysical strategy designed to elaborate the Christian tradition rather than a feature of that tradition itself.[53] Metaphysical, because we are concerned with the interaction between creator and creature in a way which reflects the real dependence of creatures upon their creator yet affirms their genuine initiative as well. We have seen that the philosophy which animated *kalam* thinkers would not permit originating action other than from the creator, while Jewish thought often spoke of "making room" for free actors other than God. Aquinas' strategy is to exalt divine activity by identifying its primary effect as the very existence of creatures. As a result, existence is asserted to be "more intimately and profoundly interior to things than anything else" (*ST* 1.8.1), and God's sovereignty is associated primarily and directly with the existing universe. The infelicity remains, of course, that we cannot independently identify *existence,* but if this is asserted to be the "proper effect of the first and most universal cause" (*ST* 1.45.5) and the very node of that dependence which constitutes creaturehood (*ST* 1.45.3), it will not be identifiable in created terms. Similarly, the collaboration between divine grace and human initiative cannot be pictured either, since all divine activity, natural or supernatural, will be understood on the paradigm of creation: as the new life in Christ is called a "new creation."

In what, then, does the "refusal" consist which defines *sin* and which alone accounts for reprobation? Ironically enough, it amounts to that originating action which Mut'azilite and Ash'arite alike associated with free human agency: that is, something outside the influence of divine activity.[54] And what puts sin outside the domain of divine-human interaction is the fact that it is not so much an action as it is a holding back from letting oneself be caught up into the full dynamics of action. What results from such a short circuit is non-action rather than action. And lest this sound bizarre, as though evil were nothing, one has only to dwell on the paradoxical fact of self-deception, the tactic we all employ to put aside those deliberations which affect full-blooded action.[55] By failing to spell out, either to ourselves or to others, our engagements, we allow ourselves to pursue an apparent good to the exclusion of the genuine good we would otherwise acknowledge. We may of course assign reasons to the failure, but these are excuses rather than reasons for acting, so the asymmetry is preserved.[56] And if we think of reasons as causes for acting, then the action *as* an evil action has no cause (*GF,* 114). Ontologically, it is attributable to a failure rather than to an intention, yet a failure for which we are responsible, since we are called upon as free agents to act intelligently rather than heedlessly. And what assures our being responsible for the failure in the case of self-deception, as the very expression implies, is our peripheral awareness of what it is that we are letting go. We can, as it were, sense ourselves failing to engage and so allowing the skewed dynamics of the situation to take over.

The advantage of this Aristotelian-Thomistic analysis of action, then, is that it allows us to see how an agent who attempts to ape the creator and act in such a way as to be the total originator of its action does not so much act as fail to act. Rather than place creature and creator in a competitive situation, such an analysis of created freedom makes it clear that in the agents we know the free action takes place within a matrix of reasons and causes, where the primary cause "produces not only the reality [of the action] but also the modes of emergence"–necessary or contingent (*GF*, 108). Only such a One can so act that its will is efficacious without thereby determining the human action. And the key to this manner of acting lies in God's eternity, for "it is only in the logico-metaphysical simultaneity of the atemporal present that God's knowledge is infallible, [God's] will irresistible, [God's] action efficacious (*GF*, 116). To be the kind of cause which a creator must be, God can only be eternal, and being eternal, there can be no question of "foreknowledge" but only that peculiar form of "simultaneity" which characterizes eternity's relation to temporal process.[57]

It is inevitable that *we* will characterize that relationship by the inherently temporal term 'simultaneity', for our ordinary language for action is inherently tensed. Yet we have seen how one may construct a proper grammar for expressing the relation, even though we will never be able to picture it, so that expressions like "eternity embraces all of time" will remain metaphorical. Yet the point of asserting *simultaneity* is identical with Aquinas' invoking the image of God's *seeing*: the object seen and one's perception of it must needs be simultaneously present, and any complications which may issue from transmission of images in our technological age presume this formal feature of perception as their baseline.[58] If whatever happens happens in the present and happens because

God is present to it, bestowing its very existence, it is God's effective presence which constitutes the present. And the ambiguity here is systematic, for what we experience as *present* is experienced by us in the present which is constitutive of our existing and so bespeaks an immediate dependence on the creating activity of God. For since activity is what is primary, divine knowledge will be ordered to that, and so must be understood on the model of practical knowing. And lest that model seem to evacuate human freedom, we have seen that one analysis of free action is quite compatible with such dependence and that the radical capacity of free agents to refuse the intrinsic orientation of their natures assures that God is not the author of sin, since it alone represents a pure (if paradoxical) origination of the creature.

It should be clear how intimately this account depends on a metaphysics tailored to God as creator and the primacy which such a doctrine presumes for the existing universe, the one which God creates. Coupled with the analysis of created freedom which we have outlined, one can also develop an account of "operative grace" that allows the transforming activity of the creator to be intimately involved in those free actions which merit everlasting life. The conceptual connections will emerge more clearly here if we oppose our account of freedom to one which presumes that all free actions emerge from the will as their uncaused originator. We have seen that this is the presumption of Mut'azilite and Ash'arite alike, as it is the position of Scotus as well, adopted in turn by Molina: the will must be the sheer originator of free actions for them to be free.[59] By definition, then, divine assistance must be external to the workings of will, so that any account will be open to the charge of "semi-Pelagian." (What makes it 'semi' is that divine assistance is recognized to be necessary but remains extrinsic to the action itself.) Molina's "counterfactuals of freedom" not only require envisaging the possible actions of possible individuals but envisage them as free in this manner, and for that reason alone his account has been criticized as "semi-Pelagian," often to the incomprehension of its proponents.[60] So the metaphysics that grants unqualified primacy to *esse* gains correlative support from an analysis of freedom that treats created action within the dynamics of natures oriented to their proper ends. We can only wonder, as Aquinas must have marveled as well, at the serendipity whereby Aristotle's metaphysics can serve so effectively to structure a universe freely caused in a manner which he would presumably have found quite unintelligible—or if not unintelligible, at least so unexpected as to have left him baffled in ways which have baffled many a philosopher since.

7.5 THE PATTERN OF LOVE/FRIENDSHIP AS AN ANALOGY FOR INTERACTION

We have generally avoided the expression 'concurrence' when referring to created agents operating by virtue of the creator's power, for that expression evokes images of parallel actors rowing a boat—an image which the model of creation expressly forbids. And if we strive to remain faithful to "the distinction" of God from the world, we will realize that we are unable to find an image for the interaction of creatures with their creator, since one of the terms is not an object in the world but the source of all that the other is. Yet it is this very fact which suggests a model for their interaction: that of lover and beloved. Expressly eschewed by Aristotle, because gods and human beings would inevitably lack the requisite parity for friendship, it may seem ironic that the very religious traditions which insisted that God is not one of the gods, but rather the source of all-that-is, would propose so intimate a model to structure the relationship between creator and creatures.[61] Yet perhaps the manifest infelicity of causal models (like 'concurrence') forced these traditions to an interpersonal one, where the undeserved and utterly spontaneous character of a free creation would rule out any motive other than love. And if God's love be utterly disinterested, the response of human beings will aspire to return that love in kind—if that be possible.

It is here that the traditions will diverge, in the degree or manner of reciprocity which attends this relationship. Although the scriptures of each avow God's love for humankind, Judaism and Islam will tend to identify the creature as the *lover*, with God as the *beloved*, while Christianity will move either way with more alacrity. Again, what seems to be operative here is less an *a priori* conception of divinity than the manner of self-revelation on the part of God as enshrined in each tradition. Assertions found in the scriptures will be understood in the light of the ways this God characteristically deals with us. Those ways will be documented in the scriptures, of course, but also manifested in the practices of responding to them as well. The triadic relationship of *hallakah* to *haggadah* to ongoing interpretation in Judaism offers a prime example of this path of self-understanding on the part of a community: the spirit with which we are invited to respond to a divine directive (*hallakah*) will be modeled in a narrative of an exemplary figure of the people (*haggadah*) and carefully fashioned to contemporary life by a comparison of similar cases. In Islam, it is normally the example of the Prophet enshrined in traditional *hadith* which offers one a way of capturing the spirit of the warning and guidance which is the Qur'an, while jurisprudents will debate particular applications. In Christianity, the apostolic writers follow the witness of Jesus by entering into an explicit dialogue with "the [Hebrew] scriptures" to transform the covenant with the people into a call to all peoples. The exigencies of that call are enacted in the life, death, and resurrection of Jesus as well as spelled out in some detail in the New Testament writings. The community has also adopted ways of focusing the new relationship with God in Christ by legislating or forbidding certain practices, with various sanctions, as well as articulating the structure of the relationship in doctrinal statements. And as with Judaism and Islam, it is these community practices which divide as well as unite, forming the various groups which purport to follow the way outlined in the respective revelations. So we may expect that a model as rich as that of lover/beloved will be articulated and enacted variously within each tradition as well as between them.

7.5.1 Love of God in Judaism

The title of Georges Vajda's magisterial study, *L'Amour de Dieu dans la théologie juive du moyen age* (Paris: Vrin, 1957), trades on the ambiguity between objective and subjective genitive: 'love of God' can mean either our love for God or God's love for us. As we have already suggested, our daring to speak of love for God will doubtless need to be grounded in God's having first loved us. Otherwise we would hardly presume to venture beyond the idiom of service and servant. On the authority of the rabbinic and medieval periods, Vajda locates the center of Jewish reflection on these matters in Deuteronomy, with its twin perspective: "the love God has for Israel, manifested in the gratuity of election, and the love elicited thereby from Israel for God" (17). Thus Moses: "If [the Lord] set his heart on you and chose you, . . . it was for love of you; . . . you are therefore to keep and observe the commandments . . . that I lay down for you today" (Dt 7:7, 8, 11). Hosea portrays the divine initiative as one of passionate love, echoed in the Lord's promise through Jeremiah: "I have loved you with an everlasting love, so I am constant in my affection for you" (Jer 31:3). Though Jeremiah will go on to remind us how God's constancy will ever be met by Israel's inconstancy, God's initiative has already set the desired pattern for the people's response. The Jewish liturgy will continue to stress the intimate connection of "the election and love of God for Israel, with obedience to the commandments as the privileged path undertaken by Israel in its love for God" (Vajda, 33).

It is understandable that the rabbinic commentary on the Talmud and Midrash would focus on the character of the people's response, resting their understanding of "the love which proceeds from God to humankind" on the firm Deuteronomic foundation of "the love of election with Israel as its exclusive object" (Vajda, 56). What had to concern the rabbis was the wholeheartedness of Israel's response to this love, which they found epitomized in Abraham's willingness to sacrifice his son Isaac—the very paradigm of disinterested love

(48). Using a vocabulary borrowed from temple worship, the rabbis distinguished holocausts from the sacrifices of peace and of expiation: "holocaust corresponds to love, the sacrifice of peace to petition, and the sacrifice of expiation to fear. For holocausts are offered uniquely for the glory of God, while the other two are offered for us" (62). So one can only call God's demand of Abraham to sacrifice his only son, the bearer of all the promises, a holocaust. While God could hardly demand such a sacrifice of every single Jew, the demand does set a pattern for the community whose members may at times be called to so total a response, notably "persecution, martyrdom, and a total rejection of every enticement to assimilate themselves to the gentiles" (66). This is how the rabbis understood God's love for Israel: as calling for a response which strives to be as "disinterested" as God's initial election.

Confrontation with Hellenic philosophy and with Muslim theology regarding divine unity and attributes, as well as with Sufi reflection on the path to proximity with God, all forced Jewish thinkers to assimilate new patterns for their understanding of human beings in relation to God. Yet the new interpretation had also to show that whatever truth "could be found in foreign ideologies was already contained in the traditional Jewish doctrine, which comprised all truth in itself" (72). The notion of love was not exempted. A comparison of the earlier talmudic patterns with those informing Maimonides' reflections on the matter will prove instructive. Where the divine election had formed the foundation and the pattern for a faithful Jew's response, that now seems more of a presupposition than a positive feature. Emphasis shifts to the pervasive action of the source of all existence, and to the need for creatures to respond wholeheartedly with a love which is directed by their understanding yet absorbs their entire lives. Inspired perhaps by the Sufis, Maimonides is not afraid to speak of this love as passionate (*'ishq*): "an excess of love, so that no thought remains that is directed toward anything other than the Beloved" (*Guide* 3.51). Such a love is more than knowledge, yet is only possible in the measure that "the bond between us and Him, [namely] that intellect which overflowed from Him" (3.51) informs our life and action. As we have seen with his presentation of divine providence, it "is constantly watching over those who have obtained this overflow, [and] that individual can never be afflicted with evil of any kind. For he is with God and God is with him" (3.51). The focus of Maimonides is uniquely on our response, while the benevolence of God can be presumed, though knowledge leads to love only when one moves from a general "apprehension of what He is . . . to apprehending those true realities proper to God alone" (3.51). If philosophy can perform this *manuductio* for the learned, observance of the Torah does it for the rest, leading one to "*love* though the opinions [it teaches], while *fear* is achieved by means of all actions prescribed" (3.52).

Maimonides enhances the rabbinic doctrine with a more acutely individual response, for the understanding which attaches a person to the governing will of God will inevitably vary with individuals, as he expressly notes in the concluding paragraph of the *Guide* (3.54). Yet what he obscures is any deliberate divine initiative, and the ultimate perfection of the faithful believer is to "remain permanently in that state of intense pleasure . . . which is achieved through the perfection of the intelligibles that lead to passionate love of Him" (3.51). So while our response to God's benevolence aspires to a "passionate love," Maimonides eschews formulating God's initiating action in such terms. Vajda surmises that this strategy on his part may reflect a philosophical constraint: "to remove from God anything which might resemble a passion" (139). This would cohere with his deliberate recasting of the emanation scheme as an appropriate simile for the action of God, so that the connection of creatures to the creator will be "through the overflow of the intellect that has overflowed from" God (2.12). In this way, divine "grace" would be a constant factor in the created universe; a conception obviously preferable to Maimonides, despite his concern to make room for "belief in the creation of the world in time [so that] all miracles become possible and the Law becomes possible" (2.25).[62]

In any case, we have in Maimonides a philosophical transformation of the biblical and rabbinic patterns, reinterpret-
ing them in line with neoplatonic philosophy. Since he did
not always proceed in this direction, as the example of creation shows, Vajda's surmision may be correct with regard to
Maimonides' treatment of God's love for creatures. For he
did not have the same warrant as the rabbis for eschewing
talk about divine love, especially as that love is manifested
in God's actions on behalf of Israel. If they could plead a
focus on comportment, his scope in the *Guide* is far more
embracing, and his explicit account of divine attributes allows them to be descriptors of God's deeds on our behalf.
We can at best conclude that Maimonides wished to render
the economy of salvation in strict conformity with that of
creation. In that respect, at least, he will be followed by subsequent Jewish tradition, however luxuriant the descriptions
preferred by the Hassidim may be.

7.5.2 Love of God in Islam

Islam can readily be portrayed parallel to the caricature
which Christians have inherited of Judaism: a religion of ex-
ternals, comprised totally by observance of the "five pillars"
of belief in the oneness of God and the prophet Muhammad,
prayer, alms, fasting in Ramadan, and pilgrimage to Mecca.
Once that picture is established, the "extrinsicism" of Islam
is presented as a safeguard for the transcendence of Allah as
well as an explanation of Islam's attractive simplicity; while
those who want more from religion than external observance
are directed to the Sufis, a "branch" of Islam which developed the interior dimensions of the revelation of God in the
Qur'an. Once directed to Sufi practice and teaching, a stu-
dent of Islam will either find the stereotype reinforced for the
exoteric religion while identifying the Sufis as *esoteric* sectarians,
or will rather be brought to wonder about that convenient
bifurcation as well as the intitial stereotype; for it seems that
Sufism is a far more prevalent feature of Islamic life and practice than the expression 'esoteric' would allow. My own expe-

rience reflects the second pattern, following the traditional
thinker who bridged the stereotypic chasm so effectively: al-
Ghazali.

Before examining the fruitful synthesis of Ghazali, it will
help set the record straight to remind ourselves of the rich
teachings regarding love for God in the most literal of Islamic
schools: Hanbalite Islam.[63] In this case it was their single-
minded respect for the language of the Qur'an which resisted
the penchant of the philosophically minded to parse 'love'
in God by 'will', an identification which led them to interpret all Qur'anic references to God's love for creatures as God's
"willing good" to them (Bell, 201). Yet since God's will must
be all-comprehensive, such an identification – on the part of
Mu'tazilite and Ash'arite alike – entailed that God, who "hates
evil" (2.205), could not be said to will it either. Yet, as we
have seen, in some fashion God must will evil since God wills
all that is. So, Ibn Taymīya argued, there must be a point
in the Qur'an's distinguishing 'love' from 'willing' in God. So
if God wills everything, love is reserved for God's "wise purpose [hikma]" (Bell, 70), and the fact that evil may serve good
is comprised under that inscrutable divine wisdom. By negotiating conceptual minefields of this sort, Ibn Taymīya is able
to contend that God does indeed love human beings in creating them: indeed, nothing else could explain God's creation, which "cannot be considered a response to a need existing in [God]; it is rather a natural and logical working out
of the implications of [the divine] attributes – and particularly
the attributes of love" (Bell, 73). Correlatively, the human
response to so altruistic a love must be as selfless as possible,
loving God *not* "for his acts of kindness [but] only, or at least
primarily, for himself, and this despite the fact that his benefi-
cence also requires that he be loved" (Bell, 83).

There are difficulties in the way of affirming a relationship
of love between God and human beings, of course, and the
primary one lies in the presupposition stemming from the
received philosophical tradition that some affinity or similarity is required between lover and beloved. We have seen how,
on one reading of classical Islam, the Qur'anic verse that

"naught is His likeness" (42.11) so prevails over the *hadith*
which says that God created man according to the divine image that any assertion of a similarity between creature and
creator will be suspect.[64] Yet neither Ghazali nor Ibn-Taymīya
shrinks from such an affirmation. Ibn-Taymīya is more cau-
tious, noting that the affinity must lie in the "believer's 'accord' [*muwāfaqa*] in what God commands, through obedience,
and in what [God] loves, by loving it" (Bell, 76). This precondition turns on a pun with the generic term for 'affinity'
or 'similarity' [*munāsaba*], yet it also fulfills the ontological
conditions for such an affinity: that there be "in the beloved
some attribute [*ma'nā*] for the sake of which the lover loves"
the person. That could not be true, of course, of the creature as such before its creator. Ghazali takes a more metaphysical route, relying on a reading of the Qur'anic verse:
"Say: the spirit is an affair [or 'command': *amr*] of my Lord"
(17.85), to postulate a "hidden relationship, which is of an
inward nature and does not appear in a person's outward
form" (Bell, 110). This allows him to insist that the "human
spirit is something divine [*amr rabbānī*], beyond [our] comprehension," so that in loving us God is really loving an image of the divine and may be said to love us without implying
that God be inclined to something that is not God.[65] Moreover, should creatures respond to the divine invitation by removing the veil from their hearts, that same divine love can
bring them into "proximity with their Lord" (ibid.). Thus
Ghazali recognizes both an initial affinity plus the transforming activity of divine love in the creature, so bringing the celebrated "stages" of Sufi teaching under the generic neoplatonic
pattern of emanation and return.

As a result, Ghazali can be said to offer an entire philosophy structured on the relationship of love between creator
and human creatures.[66] The creating activity of God consists
in bestowing existence where there is no reason to do so, with
the result that created beings will move towards what possesses the plenitude of perfection with a desire which is the
expression of their very being, and such a desire we call 'love'
(Siauve, *L'Amour,* 294). So the very being of creatures seeks

to return the love by which they originate, and "the infinity of this desire reveals . . . the infinity of God." From these metaphysical grounds, Ghazali is in a position to argue that the terms used for love which also imply passionate desire, like *'ishq* and *mahabba*, not only may be used for God, but must be, without however any hint of 'penchant' or 'inclination' on the part of God, as though God were in need.[67] This allows him to compare such terms with 'existence' itself, arguing that these key terms must have different meanings when used of God. In the divine attributes of knowledge, will, and power, for example, "the creator in no way resembles creatures; the One who formed language instituted expressions first for creatures, and . . . language uses them in a figurative way to describe the reality of the creator."[68] So there can be affinity or similarity, yet no palpable resemblance. Ghazali may not have had the semantic tools available to him which Aquinas used so adroitly, in distinguishing *manner of signifying* from the *reality signified* in certain privileged expressions whose use proves to be inherently analogous, yet he arrives at a similar conclusion regarding human language pressed into service *in divinis*.

So one can speak of a mutual relation of love between creator and creature in Islam and do so short of the "ontological monism" often associated with later Sufis, notably Ibn al-Arabi.[69] What is open to the faithful servant of Allah is an intentional union of mind and heart, known in the Muslim tradition as "testimonial union" (*wahdat al-shuhūd*). The pivotal witness of this capacity for inner transformation is the Muslim mystic al-Hallaj, whom we know with a particular vivacity thanks to the devotion of the distinguished French Islamicist, Louis Massignon.[70] Hallaj's affronting assertion: "I am the Truth [*Anā'l-Haqq*]," where *al-Haqq* (the Truth) is the preferred Sufi name for God, was regarded as dangerous enough in his own lifetime to account for his death and is often regarded in retrospect as supporting the "existential monism" (*wahdat al-wujūd*) of Ibn al-Arabi. Yet if we are to follow Massignon's cogent and extensive argument, Hallaj was exploiting the resources of an Arabic language whose first-person expression he believed to be susceptible to the "influence of the Spirit" in such a way as to express the divine "indwelling" (*hulūl*) while keeping creator and creature ontologically distinct.[71] In fact, Massignon insists, the statement is not declarative but performative, constituting an "outcry for justice [Qur'an 50:42] announcing the Last Judgment, identifying the present reciter of the *shahāda,* this present Witness, with the *Shahīd al-qidam,* the Eternal Witness" (*Passion* 2.62). However one interprets Hallaj, it is clear from the reconciling work of Ghazali, that one can speak of a transformation of God's faithful servants in Islam which is the fruit of an intentional union of knowledge and of love. So the caricature of Islam can be corrected from the tradition itself, as it is overcome in daily experience among faithful Muslims, whose hospitality alone often testifies to a "testimonial union" with the source of life and nurture.

7.5.3 Love of God in Christianity

"What proves that God loves us is that Christ died for us while we were still sinners" (Rom 5:8) – Paul's words make clear the focus in Christianity: the saving death of Jesus. And the context is supplied by John in Jesus' farewell discourse on the eve of that death: "A man can have no greater love than to lay down his life for his friends. You are my friends. . . ." (15.13–14). Sinners, we are made friends of God, an appellation hitherto reserved to Abraham or to Moses in the Hebrew scriptures and applied to Abraham in the Qur'an as well.[72] Moreover, Jesus' words are performative in character: "I shall not call you servants any more, . . . I call you friends" (15:15). What is set apart in Islam as an advanced stage in the transformation of disciples on the Sufi path is bestowed by Jesus on his own disciples on the threshold of their abandoning him to his fate at the hands of the powers that prevailed in Israel. To be sure, a call is implicit in this elevation: "You did not choose me, no, I chose you; and I commissioned you to go out and to bear fruit, fruit that will last" (15.16). So the title is more an exigency than a status;

in fact it only enhances their own desolation at abandoning him the following day. Yet friends of God we are if Jesus makes us so: such is the legacy of his followers. The author of the first letter of John puts it directly into legacy language: "Think of the love that the Father has lavished on us, by letting us be called God's children; and that is what we are" (1 Jn 3:1). And as legacy it presages destiny: "My dear people, we are already the children of God but what we are to be in the future has not yet been revealed; all we know is, that when it is revealed we shall be like him because we shall see him as he really is" (3:2).

In fact, the metaphors which the New Testament uses are all consciously employed as completions of the Hebrew scriptures, as flesh and blood assertions in the person and actions of Jesus of the promises made to Jeremiah: "I will make a new covenant with the house of Israel" (31:31). In this sense, there is nothing new in Christianity, yet the presence of Jesus with the latent challenge to his followers to clarify who it is that he is, gives those promises a reality which testifies that much more powerfully to their subsequent completion in us: "I have given you an example so that you may copy what I have done to you" (Jn 13:15). And more than an example; a new form of life: "before the world was made, he chose us, chose us in Christ, to be holy and spotless, and to live though love in his presence, determining that we should become his adopted children, through Jesus Christ" (Eph 1:4–5). Paul and John offer the most eloquent articulation of this transformation, employing the Hellenic philosophical schemata already available in Judaic thought of the time. There is no doubt about an ontological transformation, even through this can never be reduced to mere status; it is always an exigency as well. But just as something new happened to humanity when "the Word was made flesh" (Jn 1:14), so are those who seek to follow him empowered to do so by a "new creation" (2 Cor 5:17) in the Spirit of God (Gn 1:2) who, now "living in" the followers of Jesus, will not only "give life to [their] own mortal bodies" but will enable the "entire creation" to realize its purpose (Rom 8:11, 22).

The new covenant promised to Jeremiah then, is understood in Christianity to be of a different order from the first: so much so that Aquinas will identify it "principally [with] the grace itself of the Holy Spirit, which is given to those who believe in Christ" (*ST* 1–2.106.1). 'Grace', as we shall see, will become a quasi-technical term in Christian theology, sometimes eclipsing the inherently relational linkage with the Spirit of Jesus, yet what is relevant here is its affinity with the New Testament affirmations of a new life in Christ. Jesus not only discloses God's love for all creatures, notably his human brothers and sisters, but through his life, death, and resurrection manages to provide the vehicle whereby that love may remake human creatures in his own likeness as Son (Word) of God. So the love which the creator has for creatures is made efficacious for all human beings in Jesus: the Word of God made flesh. That is the ontology which emerges from the gospel narratives as they attempt to capture the effect of his presence in Palestine. What makes the resurrection central, then, is not merely its power to verify but the yet more palpable fact that this new life is thenceforth made available to mere mortals: "they were all astonished and unable to explain what had happened to [the lame man made whole]; . . . the [rulers, elders, and scribes] were astonished at the assurance shown by Peter and John, considering they were uneducated laymen" (Acts 3:10, 4:5, 13). Something new has entered a "creation [that] has been groaning in one great act of giving birth" (Rom 8:23), yet the new is a renewal of the original, for the Word of God who re-creates is the same One who creates. What is new, however, also sheds light on the original, as we have heard from Aquinas, for "the fact of saying that God made all things by His Word excludes the error of those who say that God produced things by necessity" (*ST* 1.32.1.3). What is new in Christianity is the disclosure of that Word as God, and with it the call to all people to become "friends of God."

8

Sin and Redemption

In her monograph, *The Iliad, a Poem of Force* (New York: Politics, 1947), Simone Weil reminds us forcibly of the ethos governing Greek society, and we can say, of pagan society generally: a precarious balancing of forces with a calculated placating of the more powerful among them. If the world is to know something more than a cosmic balance of power, with human aspiration limited to playing an instrumental role in that drama, we will need a vision of a new humanity and the means to implement it. Yet such a vision, promising more to humankind than anything to which it has been accustomed, is at once heady and dangerous. For those who take it to heart may be provoked either to insurrection against the established order or to a form of quiescence in the face of endemic injustice while one awaits deliverance: religion as "the opiate of the people." And if nothing comes of it, such a promise can leave its adherents utterly disillusioned. Hence the posture of those, like Albert Camus, who would prefer the stance of sober atheists in the face of so tantalizing an offer. All of this presumes humanity in place with a history: it is to such human beings that something new is offered, so in this sense the drama of sin and redemption represents a "second moment" in the creator's providential care for creation. The focus of this moment on human beings underscores their special role in creation as the image of divinity, yet given that privileged place, this moment is addressed to all of creation as well.

8.1 TESTIMONY OF REVELATION

On the other hand, it is the same God who both creates and redeems, so we dare not let the language of "second moment" mislead us into thinking of such an offer as inaugurating a second *order* or *dispensation,* independent of the first. Rather, if we wish to speak of "orders" or "dispensations," we will have to acknowledge that the first is launched with a view to the second. Henri de Lubac's landmark deconstruction of baroque Christian theology, *Surnaturel,* showed us just how anthropomorphic a picture governed that theology's insistence on distinct "natural and supernatural orders," whereby creation is deemed a given arrangement into which God intervenes to inaugurate something new. Since we must affirm the oft-told story to represent *our* temporal perspective on God's eternal intent, the language which better respects both that intention and our perspective would speak of a "fresh initiative" or a "fuller disclosure" of God's providential care. In that way, the creator is affirmed to be active throughout, and we will be less tempted to use the metaphor of "intervening" to describe God's action in history. Regarding this tendency of Jewish as well as Christian thinkers to canonize the perspective of "salvation history" into a two-stage theology, Karl Barth issued a characteristically forthright corrective: "the covenant is the goal of creation and creation the way to the covenant."[1] In such a perspective, created reality will not be regarded as something independent of or "over against" its creator, so that divine action must take the form of intervention. For however fixed the laws of retribution and the tendencies to disintegration in human affairs appear to us, God's providential care is exercised throughout. The tenacity of injustice, however, does testify to that stubborn dimension of human affairs to which the fresh initiative must address itself: sin. As we shall see, all three traditions have a keen sense of human recalcitrance in the face of a proffered liberation from those powers which keep us in bondage, so the image of God having to "intervene" in a settled "order" resistant to the purposes of divine providential care is an understandable reading of human experience.

8.1.1 The Jewish Vision: Covenant and Torah

If in the spirit of the Bible we identify covenant with Abraham and Torah with Moses, we will recognize stages in God's disclosure of a new vision to the people whom God "chooses as His own." (This pattern will allow the Jewish followers of Jesus, as exemplified in the writings attributed to both Peter and Paul, to read the earlier stages as preparing for the later ones, as they identify the coming of Jesus as consummating all that went before, with Paul reaching back beyond the giant figure of Moses to the patriarch Abraham for a faith which could dispense with the Torah itself, while John [1:45] identifies Jesus with the prophet promised to Moses [Dt 18:18]. In similar fashion, the Qur'an portrays Moses as the type of Muhammad, who is explicitly promised by Jesus as "a messenger who will come after me, whose name is more highly praised" [61:6].) The people covenanted in Abraham and constituted by the Torah at Sinai will be contrasted to the rest of humanity, epitomized in Noah, with whom God also made a covenant as befitted the frest start in the wake of the deluge (Gn 9:8). Yet that great multitude will not be heard from again except as "the nations," while the covenant which God makes with Noah, which lacks the bilaterality of the Torah, will nonetheless be scrutinized to yield seven norms: six prohibitions against "idolatry, blasphemy, murder, adultery, robbery, and eating a limb torn from a living animal;" and one "positive injunction to establish courts of justice."[2] This reading of the Noahic covenant after the pattern of the Torah offers a possible way for Jews to find a common basis in morality with "the nations," grounded in God's gracious disclosure. Yet the preponderance of Jewish religious thought moves in the opposite direction: seeing in "the nations" a negative image of humanity bereft of the guidance of the Torah and a continuing counterpoint to the chosen people.

So the great gift to Israel is the Torah which completes the covenant providing the people with the operative capacity to respond to God's gracious election and so affirm their proper dignity by their own election of life over death (Dt 30:15). Observance is not enough–not even for the Noahites, according to Maimonides–since one must be responding to a gift from God, and do so in the correct fashion, even to belong to the "righteous of the nations."[3] Nor could our actions be a response, or even more a correct response, without explicit divine instruction. The Torah does represent a fresh initiative on God's part, not merely disclosing the divine will but empowering a particular people to fulfill it in a meritorious fashion by the careful directions it gives. That is how traditional practice presents it as well, introducing young people through the *bar-* or *bat-mitzvah* ritual to the adult privilege of undertaking to observe the Torah. To have been given that way is the glory of Israel, whose people are thereby distinguished from all the other nations of the earth.[4] So while Jewish thought lays more emphasis on a person's choice than it does upon God's grace, the entire transaction is carried out in the light of a gracious gift to this people: the Torah.

Correlatively, God will expect more from this people, as the excoriation of their prophets abundantly testifies. Nor is this unfair, for this people has been given *the* way to salvation; one has only to examine the conduct of "the nations" to see the difference. Maimonides will insist that in the time of Moses "all except a few men were *idolaters*" (1.62), to underscore the fact that God's revelation to Moses of the name "indicative . . . of simple existence and nothing else" was the precondition for the revelation of the Torah as the word of and way to the One God. We shall encounter this scenario in Islam as well, yet while Maimonides' emphasis on the oneness of divinity may corroborate his Islamic milieu, it derives of course from the first commandment of the Torah against idolatry. What preoccupies Maimonides, however, is not the fact itself of false belief so much as the consequences of it in the practices of "the Sabians," which had by his times largely disappeared from the earth, but if we were to experience them

we would "become clear regarding the wisdom manifested
in the details of the practices prescribed in the commandments
concerning the *sacrifices* and the forms of *uncleanness* and other
matters whose reason cannot, to my mind, be easily grasped"
(**3.49**). Again, most are unable to elevate their minds to see
through the enticements of idolatry, yet this people is given
a ready way of doing so by observing "*statutes* whose reason
is hidden from us [yet] everything [in them] serves to keep
people away from *idolatry.*" Such is the gift of the Torah and
the way it grants a wisdom through practice otherwise available
only to a few. And even these may fall short of the accolade
of "wise" if their actions are not explicitly a response to God's
gracious gift.[5]

So while "the nations" may be held to the Noahite commandments, they cannot be expected to behave in a very civi-
lized manner, nor can they be said to be sinners either. For
they have neither the direction of the Torah nor the empower-
ment of the covenant which embraces it. Only members of
God's people can be called "sinners," and they can be in three
distinct ways: ritually, by overlooking a positive prescription
regarding cleanness; legally, by transgressing a commandment;
and interpersonally, by betraying the one who so loved them.[6]
The ultimate image for sin in the Hebrew scriptures is that
of adultery and specifically of "whoring after false gods." The
intimacy of that particular form of betrayal suggests the kind
of relationship which God intends to consummate with Israel
and so supplies the negative image for any one of the people
who refuses such an offer of love. Thus what empowers will
also condemn those who look the other way, while the mass
of humanity has no part in this intercourse nor, it would seem,
in "the world to come." Yet traditional Jewish thought was
largely unwilling to draw so exclusive a conclusion, and re-
turned at this point to the covenant with Noah to assert that
"anyone who conscientiously carries out such instructions is
potentially righteous, and 'All the righteous people of the nations of the world have a share in the world to come.'"[7] Yet
Maimonides has been read as refusing this title to those who
observed the Noahite laws from reason alone, so the issue

remains a disputed one. As logically it might well be, for the full-blooded meaning of 'redemption' for a Jew is intimately connected with fulfilling the covenant which makes this people God's very own, by observing the Torah.

8.1.2 The Christian *Kerygma*: A New Covenant Open to All

Everything in Christianity turns on the person and actions of Jesus, who "became for all who obey him the source of eternal salvation" (Heb 5:9). Jesus' own relation to "the Father" becomes the paradigm for all who respond to the call to follow him: "Father, may they be one in us, as you are in me and I am in you" (Jn 17:21). Before long the tradition articulated this new mode of being in relational terms, which we can see parallel the relation of utter dependence which constitutes a creature. What is new about this life is that it is "in Christ"–"I am the vine, you are the branches" (Jn 15:5) –and Christ himself is the disclosure of the inner life of God, which we would otherwise never have suspected. That life animates the closing words of Jesus' final prayer for his disciples before his death: " . . . so that the love with which you loved me may be in them, and so that I may be in them" (Jn 17.26). John is the most notable witness of this animating relation of Jesus to "the Father," yet the reality of his inner source of strength and serenity is in evidence throughout the synoptics as well. The inference from all this for the Christian is that one's human nature needs both healing and elevation to partake in this unimaginable life. That inference leads to the development of a doctrine of *grace*, usually conceived narratively as counterpoint to "original sin."

Paul sets the plot: "sin entered the world through one man, and through sin death, and thus death has spread through the whole human race because everyone has sinned. [Yet] if it is certain that through one man's fall so many died, it is even more certain that divine grace, coming through the one man, Jesus Christ, came to so many as an abundant free gift" (Rom 5:12, 15). The death to which Paul refers represents our alienation from God, depicted archetypally in the story of Adam and Eve and symbolized in the death that is our certain human fate. So John concludes his gospel by articulating our release from that alienation *as* release from that fate: "these [signs] are recorded so that you may believe that Jesus is the Christ, the Son of God, and that believing this you may have life through his name" (Jn 20:31). So the ultimate parameters of life and death frame this story, which offers an interpretation of the episode recounted in Genesis 3 tailored to the healing and elevation wrought in Christ. What has become the doctrine of *original sin* can be traced to this rhetorical passage of Paul, which also contains the word 'grace' [*charis*], the seed of the complementary doctrine of *grace*. Augustine will orchestrate Paul's fugue into a series of symphonic movements, to be sure, elaborating the theme of *predestination*, which was to be taken up by the Reformers, notably Calvin, with results which all but obscured Paul's contrapuntal movement.

Some have argued that the real culprit, however, was not Augustine but Aquinas, whose articulation of *grace* in Aristotelian terms as an entitative elevation of the person into divine life by way of a created *accident* tends to obscure the inherently relational character of this elevation as we saw it in the New Testament texts. Thomas' distinction between *created* and *uncreated* grace, which identifies the latter with the Holy Spirit and the former with the created effect of that Spirit's indwelling in the person (*ST* 1.43.3), led theologians to focus on the created effect, parsed as an accidental modification of the soul. Aristotle did explicitly connect relations with accidents, insisting that "real relations" will have the effect of modifying one of the *relata* (or terms of the relation).[8] So Aquinas' use of Aristotle did not intentionally suppress the relational character of this new life in Christ, especially since he explicitly identified "uncreated grace" with the very Spirit of Jesus. Yet theologians can be put to quite other uses than the ones intended, and that appears to have been the fate of Aquinas' teaching on grace.[9] Not surprisingly, of course, a perusal of his treatment yields quite another picture. In the section of the *Summa Theologiae* on the trinity of persons in God, Aquinas asserts unequivocally that "the divine person is sent, although it proceeds temporally only according to sanctifying grace." The concern here is an ontological one: the Spirit must so indwell in a creature that the creature can be said to possess it: "the Holy Spirit is possessed by human beings, and dwells within them, in the very gift of sanctifying grace. Hence the very Holy Spirit is given and sent" (1.43.3).

So Aquinas' teaching underscores the relational character of the healing and elevating gift of grace, emphasizing the created modification only to secure the creature's real participation in this new life: "by the gift of sanctifying grace the rational creature is perfected so that it can freely use not only the created gift itself, but also enjoy the very divine person; and so the invisible mission takes place according to the gift of sanctifying grace; and yet the very divine person is given" (*ST* 1.43.3.1). Creatures could freely enjoy the presence of a divine "person" only if they were able to interact after the manner of equals, as Aristotle reminds us. So the created modification of "sanctifying grace" is an enabling gift which allows Jesus' words "I call you not servants but friends" to be efficacious. Yet what is perhaps even more telling from our current perspective is the way in which Aquinas introduces the issue of grace itself: no created nature can "proceed to its act unless it be moved by God" (*ST* 1–2.109.1). The creator is already involved in every action of the creature, as we have seen (*ST* 1.105.5), so it is hardly untoward for that same God to enable creatures to understand and act as "children of God." The dramatic scenario introduced by Paul simply raises the stakes: absent original sin, "the mind of man would not be so much master of its act that it would not need to be moved by God; so much more the free will of man weakened by sin, whereby it is hindered by the corruption of the nature" (*ST* 1–2.109.2.1). So human nature as we experience it bears often tortured witness to being both healed and elevated (*simul justus et peccator*), yet both the healing and the elevation are in the line of divine activity introduced by God's creating action and so "according to the plan of divine providence" (*ST* 1–2.109.1).

Since created human freedom is already acting by the action of God, God's healing and elevating activity in the creature does not raise fresh problems for Aquinas. Only if one presumes creatures to be already constituted as "autonomous" agents does grace conflict with freedom as though it were an "intervention" in human affairs. Once the relational character of being-a-creature has been secured, a fresh relation to the person of the Holy Spirit can be understood according to that same pattern. Aquinas' insistence on a created accidental modification in the creature as the vehicle for so personal a relationship may indeed have come to be misunderstood as distracting from that primary relationality. But the ontological gambit was in fact motivated by a desire to secure the one relating as one among equals and so enable that response of friendship to which Jesus calls his followers.

Some reformers tended to speak more of *faith* than of *grace*, yet parallels abound. Søren Kierkegaard offers a particularly articulate witness in his pseudonymous essay *Sickness unto Death:* "this is one of the most decisive definitions for all Christianity—that the opposite of sin is not virtue but faith."[10] For the author (Anti-Climacus), sin only emerges when one understands oneself to be "before God," where all of the modalities of alienation which he calls *despair* are raised to a higher power than even Socrates could imagine, for whom "sin is ignorance" (Kierkegaard, 87). Yet Kierkegaard has the greatest respect for Socrates; indeed, far more than he could muster for the Hegelians of his day who thought they had "gone beyond Socrates." In fact "no *human being* can come further than" Socrates, for "no man of himself and by himself can declare what sin is, precisely because he is in sin; all his talk about sin is basically a glossing over of sin, an excuse, a sinful watering down. That is why Christianity begins in another way: man has to learn what sin is by a revelation from God" (95). The author goes on to elaborate this difference in terms of *willing* rather than *knowing*, a dimension of human beings which he and others have claimed only came to light under Christian scrutiny.[11] However that may be, the result of S.K.'s analysis echoes that of Judaism "that in the strictest sense the pagan did not sin, for he did not sin before God and all sin is before God. [In fact,] the sin of paganism was essentially despairing ignorance of God, of existing before God . . ." (81). Yet his analysis will differ precisely in the degree of "spirit" (or interiority) required. Hence it hardly suffices to call oneself a Christian; indeed "Christendom [cultural Christianity enshrined in civic patterns] is so far from being what it calls itself that the lives of most men, Christianly understood, are far too spiritless to be called sin in the strictly Christian sense" (104). What is here called "spirit" Aquinas called "grace," yet the parentage is common: the indwelling presence of the Spirit of Jesus.

8.1.3 Islam: Enlightenment
by the Qur'an's Warning and Guidance

Standard Muslim polemics would have it that Islam, like Judaism, has no doctrine of "original sin." That assertion would be consistent as well, for the same catechesis insists that Islam is a "rational religion," meaning that nothing like the entitative elevation associated with Christian doctrines of *grace* and *faith* are required to account for someone's responding to the allure of the Qur'an. Nevertheless, what the Qur'an offers by way of insistent warning and wise guidance is a liberation from the ignorance and barbarism which it identifies with the state of affairs in Arabia before the mission of the Prophet. Called in Arabic *jāhilīya*, the term becomes the widest possible contrast term for what the Qur'an brings to human beings and thus emphasizes the extent to which pagans especially were errant and wandering before the advent of the Qur'an. One could make the customary exceptions for those blessed with "a book," Jews and Christians, but the rest of humanity was mired in ignorance and barbarism. Such contrast terms (like 'gentiles' for Jews) need not be verified in practice to do their job, which is to call attention to the blessings which the Qur'an (or Torah) bestows on those who accept it. What the Qur'an provides is a "straight path [*as-sirat al-mustaqīm*]" (1:6), and thereby offers, supplemented by the sayings of the Prophet (*hadith*), guidance for all aspects of a faithful believer's life. And since the Qur'an comes from God through the Prophet, the guidance it gives is sure. Thus is one who hears and accepts the Qur'an liberated from ignorance and barbarism, and introduced into a community whose patterns of life are God-given and so lead to God's promised rewards. Sufis will be less concerned with rewards and more smitten with the need to respond wholeheartedly to so gracious and loving a gift, while their manner of appropriating the Qur'an will lead them to articulate a veritable "doctrine of grace." For the progressive interiorization of the warning and guidance therein makes them over into "servants of God" so intent on the things of God that little or no ego-self remains. Such is indeed the entire thrust of Sufi teaching regarding the path [*at-tarīqa*] to proximity with God.[12]

So just as the pervasive notion of *jāhilīya* offers an analogue to the Christian doctrine of "original sin," so does the Sufi teaching of progressive interiorization of the Word of God supply a virtual doctrine of grace in Islam. To be sure, there is little explicit talk of entitative elevation, except for the *wahdat al-wujūd* of Ibn al-Arabi and his followers. And if we follow the pattern we noticed in Christianity, where the entitative elevation followed as an ontological corollary of the pivotal focus on Jesus, Islam will not be carried spontaneously in that direction. For the Qur'an insists that Muhammad is "nothing but a warner" (46.9): "Say: I am a mortal man, like all of you" (18:109). Yet the experience of transformation evident in those who follow the Sufi path will require for its articulation something like an entitative elevation of grace, just as tradition will make the Prophet over into "the perfect man."[13] Analogies such as these, drawn more from reflection on actual practice than from more polemically framed expositions of faith, will become even more evident in the final chapter. For that will conclude our reflections on the relation between divine and human freedom in the three traditions by focusing on the face of the God realized in the renewed creation as it is displayed in the covenanted "people of God," the church as the foretaste of the "kingdom of God," and the *umma* or community of believers meant to give flesh and blood to God's Qur'anic word. For now, a closer look at Aquinas' account of grace will help us display his metaphysics of primary and secondary agents, showing how it operates as well in the realm of redemption.[14]

8.2 OPERATING AND COOPERATING GRACE: DYNAMICS OF A NEW CREATION

We have traced the ways in which creatures, and especially free creatures, can be said to move themselves, as secondary agents, always dependent upon the One who bestows their existence. But what are the dynamics of the new creation, to which some free creatures are called and in which they operate with a capacity added to their created natures? The terms in which this question is posed are far more familiar to Christian theologians than to religious thinkers in Judaism or in Islam. And there are good reasons for this, as we shall see, yet we have already noted that the very issue of *grace* is hardly foreign to those traditions. What became specifically associated with Christianity was the "ontological" elaboration of the new situation in which believers found themselves.[15] The outstanding reason for this affinity of Christian theology with metaphysics may well be Thomas Aquinas himself and the effect of his strategic adaptation of the legacy of Greek philosophy to order earlier attempts to use grammar and logic to elucidate the scriptures in the western medieval context. Yet one also suspects that the underlying affinity can be traced to the efforts of the initial centuries of the Christian era to employ Greek metaphysical terms to give clear expression to the nature and person of Jesus. Without that early ecclesial effort, Aquinas' endeavor may have seemed even more alien an affair than it was already suspected of being. Yet we have seen that Jewish and Muslim thinkers as well called upon philosophy to elucidate their scriptures' assertions about a freely created universe and regarded that elaboration as an authentic outworking of their traditions. In a similar fashion, Aquinas' treatment of the "new creation" bestowed upon those who respond to the gospel with faith will model itself on his tradition's elaboration of the nature and person of the Christ.

Christian tradition has often used Augustine's formula to distinguish the new creation in Christ from the first and so to authorize distinct "orders" of *nature* and of *grace:* "the One who without you created you will not justify you without you."[16] Free human response is of the essence of the new creation, for this creation involves a faith-response essentially. Yet note how Aquinas responds to such an authority: "God does not justify us without us, since while we are being justified, we consent to God's justice by a movement of free choice. But that movement is not the cause but the effect of grace. Thus the whole operation belongs to grace" (*ST* 1–2.111.2.2). Note that the human response is not bifurcated into a part initiated by God and another part proper to human beings, but rather all comes from God: the initiative as well as the response which is also properly human. The difference between redemption and creation, then, does not lie in creation's being wholly the work of God, while redemption divides the work between God and creatures, but in creation's being *solely* the work of God and redemption's containing the creature's response as well. We have seen a similar dynamic in discussing the difference which *conservation* adds to *creation:* the activity is the same, but conserving acknowledges that the creature is already in existence. It was to safeguard the insistence that these two activities are the same that I eschewed using the expression *concursus* to express the relationship between a creature's actions and the divine action which sustains them. For that very expression presumes a background picture of "partitioning" the action itself. So we already have a pattern for considering the divine initiative of redemption, in the divine activity of conserving what God creates.

That activity does indeed "operate in every agent," but does so "in such a way that they themselves still exercise their own operations" (1.105.5). And the creator does so (1) as end, for "nothing is good . . . except to the degree that it shares in some likeness to the supreme good which God is"; (2) as agent, since created agents are so ordered that they always "act in dependence on God"; and (3) as the One who preserves creatures in being: since "for all things God is properly the universal cause of *esse* which is innermost in all things, it follows that in all things God works intimately." This classic statement formulates what Lonergan dubbed "the corollary of universal instrumentality" (*GF,* 80–91)–corollary to the "theorem of divine transcendence" (*GF,* 79). We can see how its formulation turns on the background notion of creation as bestowing the very existence of things, for "existence [*esse*] is more intimately and profoundly interior to things than anything else" (1.8.1). And what God's existence in things by grace adds to the "way God exists in everything God creates" (1.8.3) is the intentional intimacy available to "those reasoning creatures [who] are actually knowing or loving [God], or are disposed to do so [by the entitative elevation of grace]." Furthermore, since 'intimacy' is a paradigmatically intentional notion, one can suspect that Aquinas' treatment of God's conserving presence is shaped by his convictions– ontological as well as theological–regarding the manner in which "God is said not only to exist in the [redeemed] rational creature, but also to dwell therein as in [God's] own temple" (1.43.3).

Thus the pattern of revelation, as experienced in the life of the community, supplies Aquinas with a conviction about the intimate presence of God to all creatures and further intimates the personal character of the action of bestowing *esse* which creation is said to be. It is the same God who creates and re-creates, so there need be no "intervention," yet the intentionality of the action is distinct, suggesting the presence of two distinct orders: "since then God is the primary mover absolutely, it is by his motion that all things are turned to him in that general tendency to the good by which everything tends towards likeness to God in its proper mode. . . .

But [God] turns the just to himself as to a special end, to which they tend and to which they desire to cling as to their own good" (1–2.109.6). The special end is the properly intentional one of friendship with God, to which rational creatures are radically open and for which grace disposes them. Yet that new disposition involves a transformation, so it is properly called a "new creation." What Aquinas' treatment underscores, however, is the continuity in interiority: just as the creator must be said to be "active in every agent cause" (*ST.* 1.105.5) from within, in the very act of bestowing *esse,* which is the act of creating and conserving, so the "usual and common course of justification is that when God moves the soul from within, man is turned to God [gradually; though] sometimes God moves the soul so vigorously that it immediately attains a perfection of justice, as was the case in Paul's conversion" (1–2.113.10). So the possibility and the fact of God's moving human agents from within is a simple corollary of the creator-creature relationship. Human freedom is hardly an obstacle to that relationship, for it is constituted by it: As "God moves all things according to the mode proper to each, . . . so [God] moves human beings according to the characteristics of human nature" (1–2.113.3), of which God is the creator. And since "it is proper to human nature to have free choice, so the motion from God towards justice does not take place without a movement of free choice in someone who can exercise free choice." Far from this action being partitioned, however, God "infuses the gift of justifying grace in such a way that at the same time he also moves the free choice to accept the gift of grace." And should one object that God's moving the free choice would seem *ipso facto* to remove its freedom, Aquinas returns to the divine activity constitutive of all creatures: "in moving the will God does not force it, since [God] gives the will its natural leaning" (1.105.4). The very One who bestows the orientation proper to each will to "the good" is "alone the universal good," so can easily move the will without forcing it, since by its very nature the will *is moved* to whatever it apprehends as good.

Such is the logic of Aquinas' analysis. No "mechanics" are given, of course, so the manner of movement remains mysterious. Yet its propriety can hardly be gainsaid. He will specify, with regard to the movements of grace, an ordering more perspicuous than any available for natural things. He will distinguish between grace as a transforming *quality* in the very essence of the [human] soul (1–2.110.4), "so that of themselves [redeemed persons] tend to movements . . . towards obtaining the eternal good" (1–2.110.2); and grace as "the divine *assistance* [*auxilium*] by which God moves us to will and do good." The first is transforming of persons themselves, and hence spoken of as "habitual gift implanted in us by God," while the second is transitory. Yet two moments can be discerned in each, one *operative* and the other *cooperative*, depending upon whether the full dynamics of willing, including specification, are brought into play or not. So *operative* grace, be it a transitory assist or a transforming habitual gift, has the effect of establishing the intention of the end, which initiates the process of deliberation issuing in a free human act.[17] *Cooperative* grace regards the entire process of deliberating about the means according to the specification of the end, once it has been established, as well as the performance of the actions involved. Taken as the natural outworking of the transforming habitual gift, cooperative grace will constitute the life-long process of *sanctification,* the complement to *justification.* Yet since that same process will involve crisis as well, particular cooperative divine assistances may also be needed. Such is indeed the experience of persons who set out to live a life of friendship with God. Yet the attempt to match Aquinas' analysis with specific experiences may also be wrong-headed, as it addresses the very structure of willing, which is not always available to us.[18] What is quite startling, however, is the manner in which so analytic a treatment can illuminate our own experience; a feature which contributes to making Aquinas' recasting of Aristotle an attractive alternative to the stark "libertarian" scenario of "could do otherwise," which seems quite incapable of authentic self-ascription.

8.3 THE SURD OF SIN

The questions which arise in the wake of so powerful an analysis have rather to do with what the tradition has called "predestination." If it is always possible for God to move the human will, and to do so without coercing it, why are not all persons saved? What appears to stand as an absolute limit to God's gracious power is what we have called human *refusal*. Yet since it is a non-action rather than an action, it cannot be a part of God's intent. So predestination and reprobation are not parallel activities of God, as though one could speak of *positive* and *negative* predestination. As Lonergan puts it: "sin is a cause of punishment in a way in which merit is not a cause of glory" (*GF*, 114). Yet the "objective falsity" which is sin is not itself caused, so has no part in a "divine plan." What remains unintelligible because it is irrational is the way we can "remove ourselves from the ordering of the divine intellect" (*ST* 1.17.1), when that ordering takes in all there is. Fingarette's attempt to formulate "self-deception" offers one fascinating model, Kierkegaard's presentation by Anti-Climacus of defiant despair another. What both acknowledge is that we are at the limits of rational analysis, yet *what* is described is hardly alien to us. It is not the fact of sin which eludes us but its explanation; just as we often find it so difficult to acknowledge our own complicity. Such is the stuff of self-deception, which offers us a clue to the unintelligibility peculiar to sin. So the modal questions – why could not God see to it that all are saved? – are quite beside the point, in the face of the radical human capacity for refusal. Nor need we have recourse to an autonomous "libertarian" conception of human freedom to appreciate the limits of divine power; Aquinas' analysis of created freedom leaves room for that peculiar non-action of the person which amounts to one's "withdrawing oneself from the ordering of divine understanding": that "absolute objective falsity" which represents *autonomy* in Aquinas' scheme.

Something like this is certainly required to safeguard what Maritain called "the divine innocence": that God would not

intend the reprobation of anyone. Later controversies surrounding *sufficient* and *efficacious* grace raised the question in
yet other terms: everyone receives grace sufficient for salvation, but what they do with it is their responsibility; the "predestined" receive grace efficacious to salvation, assuring that
they will cooperate with it.[19] The obvious question to be put
to such a scheme is: why doesn't everyone receive that "extra
amount" which will prove efficacious? We should be able to
see by now how such a scheme represents an *ad hoc* proposal
to conciliate the scriptural assertion that "God wants all to
be saved" with "many are called but few are chosen." For the
background doctrine of creation which is elaborated in all three
traditions belies a picture of such a divinity parceling out
"amounts" of grace. Rather, all creatures are subject to the
"ordering of divine understanding," each kind according to
its nature. What singles out rational creatures is their capacity for actions of ultimate irrationality: not only to "fall short
of the good which is appropriate [to their] own nature" (1–
2.109.2.2), but to act in such a way as to refuse that very good,
and so remove themselves from the dynamics of authentic
acting: the "ordering of divine understanding."

Reprobation cannot be part of "the divine design" (*GF,* 114),
nor is it implied by *predestination* as though it were its contrary. Reprobation represents the inescapable effect of "actions"
which contradict that divine providence in the way in which
only free creatures are capable of doing, while "predestination" refers to that providence as it envisages "the planned
sending of a rational creature to the end which is eternal
life" (*ST* 1.23.1). So everything which Aquinas says about predestination will be subject to his grammatical constraints on
providence-talk: "God's knowledge of future things is more
properly called 'providence' than 'pre-vidence'" (De ver 2.12).
So discussions of "predestination" which focus on the prefix,
like the notorious queries as to whether creatures are predestined *ante praevisa merita* [before their merits are foreseen],
offer one more example of being misled by surface grammar.
Our analysis, on the other hand, retains the controlling context of the practical knowing which an eternal creator has of

its doings, while allowing for the failure – indeed tragic failure – of creatures who are otherwise "in God's hands." Such a possibility is open only to rational creatures, who can "fall short of the good by themselves, just as they could fall away into non-being by themselves, if they were not conserved in being by God" (*ST* 1–2.109.2.2). And since "falling short of the good which is appropriate [to their] nature" represents, in rational creatures, a refusal to become what one is called to become, there can be no other outcome than reprobation. While no creature can cancel God's conserving providential care and so bring about its own "fall into non-being," creatures able to cooperate with God's elevating action in their regard to an intentional union of knowing and loving – to friendship with God – are able to effect the intentional analogue of reducing themselves to non-being, which is reprobation. So this concluding section on sin completes the previous analysis of the elevation due to grace by underscoring the special effects of divine providence (or predestination) in rational creatures. There is a strong continuity in Aquinas' presentation between the action of the creating and redeeming God; the discontinuity regards what is peculiar to that sector of creation endowed with freedom. Yet it is not that the creator needs to "withdraw itself" to leave room for human freedom, for human freedom can be analyzed fruitfully as created freedom. It is rather that rational creatures, at the limit, are able to withdraw themselves from a divine hegemony that need never be conceived as threatening their freedom. The only ultimate threat to such creatures as we are, then, remains ourselves.

9

The God Realized in Renewed Creation

We have presented three elaborated accounts of creation as the necessary context for a proper understanding of the interaction of God and human beings, where the God in question is creator of all that is, including rational creatures like human beings. Yet it proved impossible to consider any tradition's account of creation apart from its appropriation of the revelation proper to it. For the affirmation of creation does not conclude an argument to ultimate origins so much as assert the utter dependence of all-that-is on the One from whom all originates and is held in being. So the "doctrine of creation" as it is articulated in these three traditions will be comprised of three components: a *source* (identified with God), the *word* revealing that source as the One from whom all-that-is freely emanates, and the *community* in which that revelatory word is received and through which it is articulated, elucidated, and celebrated. In Judaism, it is the one God ("Hear, O Israel, God your God is one"), who first called Abraham and later liberated his descendants through Isaac and Jacob from slavery in Egypt. Yet that care and those exploits would be unavailable to us except through the accounts offered in the Hebrew scriptures, which serve the community out of which they emerged as a guide directing its actions as well as the liturgical context through which those saving events can become shaping ones for that same community. Similarly for Christians, who profess their faith "in one God, the Father almighty, creator of heaven and earth," accessible to them by that very name "in one Lord, Jesus Christ, the only

Son of God, eternally begotten of the Father" (who is also presented as "the Word who was with God in the beginning and is God" [Jn 1:1]), and who profess all of this in the context of "the one, holy, catholic and apostolic church" animated by "the Holy Spirit, the Lord, the giver of life" (Nicene Creed). And the pattern is, if anything, even clearer in Islam, where the uncreated word of God, the Qur'an, is freely given by the "Lord of the worlds" to the prophet Muhammad with a view to forming that community (*umma*) in which human beings can accomplish the proper response to this divine "warning and guide": Islam.

9.1 ANALOGIES AMONG THE TRADITIONS

What seems crucial to the pattern is that no one of the three components is available without the others: the God who is presented in each is a God who reveals God's own self, and yet that "revelation" can only be appropriated by those who came after the founding figures within the community which they were enjoined to form. Because the "revelation" is delivered in each case in words, however, there is the temptation (in each tradition) to make that Word central, so that it absorbs all the attention—even at the risk of detracting from the One whom it intends to reveal! And the most effective antidote to that tendency is, of course, to remind those who hear the word that they do so profitably and efficaciously only in the community formed by it. So any attempt to separate *word* from *community* risks an "idolatry of the word," which effectively substitutes that word for its *source,* which is also the source of all-that-is. Such is the experience of each of these communities; the correlative tendency on the part of those who do not hear the word as something to which one is called to submit, but rather encounter it simply as text, will be as reductive as the earlier one was idolatrous. The word alone, as it were, has not even the ability to convey its message, to say nothing of convert its hearers—whatever exalted claims may be made by those who believe in it regarding its intrinsic intelligibility and power. What such claims overlook, quite understandably on the part of faithful who tend to take the living context of their lives for granted, is the community which gives that word its efficacy by elucidating and celebrating it, thereby displaying its formative power. So the order from our side is: without community no word can be heard to lead us to a creator of all.

The desire to place religious and theological discussions about the divine-human interaction into the context of creation has not yielded an independent criterion for adjudicating that discourse, but it has reminded us forcibly of the inseparability of these three components. Just as we were unable to come up with a depiction of the source-of-all that was independent of its revelatory activity, so we cannot pretend to speak of "revelation" except in the context of the communities which have appropriated it. The search for the context of creation proved in reality to be a reminder that one cannot speak of the revelatory *word* or the *community* which appropriates it without acknowledging their *source*. And correlatively, our attempt to characterize that source as "bestowing *existing*" on things, where *existing* (or *esse*) is not itself independently characterizable, could not but sound circular. For *what* the source-of-all bestows on creatures to bring them forth without any presupposition will not be *something* in the world but rather that relation to the creator which constitutes them in being. In other words, the "distinction of essence from *existing [esse]*" is contested precisely because it does not mark a "division within the world."[1] Rather, what it marks is the corollary in the created universe of "the distinction" of creator from creatures; it is the sign of that relationship which (in Aquinas' terms) constitutes the creature: "creation in the creature is none other than a relation to the creator as the origin of its existence" (*ST* 1.45.3).[2] One more reminder that we would not rise to the notion of a free creator of the universe without that same creator's free revelation, and since "revelation" requires a response, there could be none such without a receptive and responding community.

Furthermore, if we are to speak of creatures as related to the One from whom they derive their existence, and related by a free act of that One, then the "bestowal of *existing*" can hardly be an impersonal act. It is indeed an act whose manner remains utterly opaque to us, since there can be no process involved; for if there were, then we would not be speaking of an utter origination in which nothing whatsoever is presupposed. Yet the God who reveals God's very self in granting the scriptures to human beings, as at least a "warning and a guide," might be expected through that "revelation" to indicate something of what that God is like: what it is to be One who freely creates and desires that humans become part of that original free intent. For whatever else is involved in offering humankind a "revelation," human well-being is certainly intended, and is linked to attuning themselves with the creator's original purposes. And that attunement will take the form of a community of faithful whose efforts over time give an appropriate cultural form to the response called for by the divine initiative on their behalf. It is this community which will receive children into its midst, educate and form them in the diverse ways of responding, as well as elaborate the community's response in intellectual and artistic ways that display the creativity originally given to human beings by the creator. So the vision, promises, and new possibilities which are opened to us by the prospect of knowing and responding properly to the One from whom we have received all that we are, are articulated in the community animated by those same promises and vision. Only such a community, shaped in response to the word, will facilitate an appropriate response within us and in our actions. For the vision and the promises speak of a world quite beyond what we might conjure up for ourselves, and yet which elicits from us a response at least implicitly commensurate with its horizons. That is to say, however tepid our personal response, we know that something much more is called for.

We have tried to show that, while "the distinction" of creator from creatures cannot mark a division in the world, it nonetheless may be reflected there, notably in the structure of created freedom. The orientation of rational creatures to their God-given end is not itself something *chosen*, so that freedom is not exhausted by "free choice." Yet that very analysis of human freedom is ever threatened by conversation partners who profess themselves unable to understand how God's orienting the will to its proper end could leave it free at all. The relation of created spiritual creatures to the creator can only be conceived properly if one keeps "the distinction" to the fore. Like the distinction between a thing and its *existing*, "the distinction" of creator from creatures manifests itself "on the margin of reason, . . . at the intersection of reason and faith."[3] We may adapt Aquinas' prescient statement about the knowledge of divine truinity being "'necessary' for us to have the right idea of creation, to wit that God did not produce things of necessity" (*ST* 1.32.1.3). While that perhaps was the sole perspective deemed philosophically respectable in his time, philosophers of religion in our time have great difficulty with "the distinction," entailing as it does a radical unknowing on the part of human beings and an inescapable recourse to analogous discourse regarding divinity. Then we may be in a position to see the appositeness of a triune conception of the divine unity for different yet related reasons, for it appears increasingly to be the case that an intellectual "distinction" which is not strictly speaking *conceptual*—that is, cannot be formulated as a division in the world—is only sustainable in a *community* which has so appropriated the revealing *word* as to create a viable margin of reason, a strategic point of intersection of faith and reason, where inquirers can stand to affirm what they apprehend.

    Aquinas went on to make his point about the "necessity" of knowledge of divine triunity succinctly: "when we say that in God there is a procession of love, we show that God produced creatures not out of need, nor for any other extrinsic reason, but on account of the love of God's own goodness" (*ST* 1.32.1.3). In short, knowing that the divine goodness is inherently generative in itself, as it were, obviates any need on God's part to originate a universe in order that divinity might be complete, as Hegel and others well before him liked to put it. But there is even more to it than that. One might argue that, given the inherent generativity of divine goodness, it would be "natural" for it to go on to originate a universe as well, so that the very account which seems to argue so persuasively for a free creation can also suggest the very opposite, thus requiring the proponent of a free creation to offer reasons why such a God would *not* have created.[4] Yet Aquinas' construction is telling: *not* that "God produced creatures . . . on account of . . . God's own goodness," but "on account *of the love of* God's own goodness." The "Word by which God made all things" is indeed a *"procession* of love" and so inherent to divinity, yet the act of creating by that Word is a free act of love. How can we know that? Only because we have been told that the God whose very essence is to-exist so exists as to be inherently knowing and loving. Avicenna's "necessary being" can be shown to be adequately "distinct" from the universe in its lacking the "composition" of essence and *existing* which characterizes creatures—in its utter simpleness, yet that "simpleness" offers no reason for creating. So for Avicenna, origination had to be "necessary emanation," an activity "natural" to this One. An alternative will hardly emerge, as Aquinas avers, unless one can offer reasons which are not necessitating, and the best such ones are, of course, love. For if 'free' were to mean merely 'arbitrary', his philosophical opponents would have won the day: such could hardly befit divinity; necessary emanation proves the only position possible to sustain intellectually.

The alternative position we have been expounding, as the fruit of reflection on the three traditions' assertions that God is the free author of all-that-is, will be seen to require a perspective on the inner life of God which is either implicitly or explicitly trinitarian. For the freedom asserted cannot be arbitrary, if only for the fact that the "names of God" culled from the diverse revelatory traditions culminate in a God of wisdom and love.[5] Moreover, divine wisdom and love need to be reflected in the world as well, and we have seen that each of the traditions exhibits the threefold pattern of transcendent source, revealing word (wisdom), and nourishing community (love). So the triune structure of God is not merely a matter for theologians' speculation or polemical debate; it can be found reflected in the communal and personal patterns of accepting and responding to that God's call. Adapting Nicholas Lash's contention to our interfaith perspective, we can say that "the doctrine of God's Trinity provides the pattern within which [the] principal tendencies to self-destruction [of each tradition are] held in check through the corrective operation of the other [dimensions available to each]."[6] That pattern, we have seen, is the threefold one of source, word, and community; where each of the dimensions needs to be present to counter these religions' inevitable march to alienation (where the transcendent source overcomes all created initiative), fundamentalism (when the word is read univocally and used as a club), and chauvinism (where this group and its interests eclipse all others).

If these observations strike one as "imperialistic" in tone or even in substance, it is worth remarking that the view of God's trinity presented here is not what one would read in standard Christian presentations. Nor does it falsify or dilute those presentations in the interest of interfaith consensus about God. What it seeks to do, rather, is to exploit the insistence of Karl Rahner that the ways in which Christians have come to know this God, through the Word's becoming flesh and the Spirit's enlivening the community of faithful, are essentially related to the triune differentiation within God.[7] Not, of course, that God *needs* to accomplish that effective self-revelation to be God, but that the One to whom those who respond to such initiatives are related *is* the very God whom Christians believe to be triune. It is not simply that we would otherwise never have come to such conclusions about God, that the "doctrine of the trinity" is a retrospective formulation of the *grammar* of Christian practice, but that *what* is so formulated represents the structure of that practice in such a way that God's inner life finds expression in God's ways with us and our response to those ways. It is especially through the work of Nicholas Lash, culminating in his *Easter in Ordinary,* that we can begin to mine such an understanding of Karl Rahner's rule of inquiry in matters trinitarian.[8] I am moved to extend Lash's explorations of the way in which the doctrine of God's trinity provides the "pattern of Christian pedagogy," using them to help discover similar patterns in

Jewish and Muslim life, by his own insistence that "the function of the Christian doctrine of God . . . is to enable us,
in every area of our ordinary human existence and experience,
to live in relation to God."⁹ For one could certainly argue that
such is the function of the doctrine of God, however expounded, in the other two traditions as well.

And while it is true that neither Judaism nor Islam has
such a highly developed *doctrinal* dimension as Christianity,
it is also the case that current understandings of *doctrine* in
Christianity, which locate its "*primary* function [as] regula-
tive rather than descriptive," help us to understand how the
patterns of life displayed in doctrines of particular communities might be reflected in other faiths as well.¹⁰ If we can
find analogies among the ways in which faithful of these three
traditions live in relation to God, then we may also expect
that the patterns developed so explicitly within the Christian
tradition will be found, if implicitly and inchoately, in Judaism and Islam as well. This expectation, however, need carry
no theological implications, as though it were to embody a
particular view on the relations among religious faiths, and
especially of the relationship of other religions to Christian-
ity.¹¹ It is simply that, in the challenge to formulate the meaning of the person of Jesus, Christianity was impelled to spell
out the patterns of living in relation to God which Jesus embodied in his own person and which his spirit empowered
others to live as well. It was these very patterns which offered
the clues assembled over four centuries to culminate in the
doctrinal statements of divine triunity. Without presuming
that formulation to offer, as such, the grammar for Jewish
or Muslim life in relation to God, we may nonetheless find
analogies which indicate sufficient similarities to bridge what
have long been seen as incompatible and even polemically antithetical doctrines of God.

9.2 PRELIMINARY RULES OF DISCOURSE
IN DIVINIS

Before setting out on that task, however, we need to remind ourselves of the structure of this inquiry and its loca-

tion in the recent history of Western reflection on divinity. Taking the three traditions that avow the free creation of the universe, we began explicitly with the accounts which each of them offers of the relationship between creator and creatures. The ostensible goal was to illustrate the fruitfulness of such a comparative study for philosophical theology. The implicit polemic has been twofold: against a settled mode of theological inquiry which remains Eurocentric and confined to residual questions of inter-Christian debate; and against some recent philosophical enthusiasms for exploring theological topics which uncritically presume notions of God which are less than adequate to the task and do so largely because they see no need of becoming literate in the history of theological refinements.[12] If the first is preoccupied with its own history, the aggressive innocence of history in the second dooms it to presume a god tailored to philosophers' considerations by the forces of modernity. And while this "'God' of modern theism was born of a deliberate decision to *break* with the Jewish and Christian traditions of 'authorized' usage, it is surely evident that modern philosophical uses of the word stand in traditions which are every bit as particular (and hence contestable) as" those original traditions.[13] So the consideration of the three Abrahamic traditions and their parallel developments has been offered as a way of assuring ourselves that the God of whom we are speaking is rooted other than in our own "intuitions" (or even predilections), since one need not consult Freud to remind oneself that the "God" of whom we spontaneously speak will invariably represent not a little of projection and of the *Zeitgeist*.

Hence our concern to reiterate "the distinction" of God from the world, such that God is not *a* being, much less "*a* person," even though each tradition's scriptures and subsequent theological reflection will firmly endorse *personal* language as that most appropriate for God and God's actions.[14] Judaism and Islam make this point central to the articulation of their faith in *one* God. It is in their insistence on God's oneness, as we have seen, that both rabbis and 'ulamā rise to a proto-philosophical discourse: the doctrine of God's unity is nearly equivalent to the *doctrine* of God, that is, to the grammatical stipulations needed to avoid idolatry. Christianity did not need to underscore this point in its catechesis precisely because, in assimilating the Hebrew scriptures, it could incorporate these elaborations of Judaism as its own. For the rabbis were not adding anything to the scriptures; they were articulating the grammar of divinity woven into their very fabric. In a similar fashion, the originating context and the subsequent missionary zeal of Islam led to focusing on *tawhīd* (the doctrine of divine unity) as a way of forging the "warning and guidance" of the Qur'an into a pointed antithesis to the polytheism (or idolatry) surrounding the *umma*. And once again, their experience should be illuminating for us. Christian theologians today wonder aloud, with Karl Rahner, at the order of teaching theology (settled since Aquinas) which invariably placed a consideration of the "one God" before that of the "triune God."[15] And their wonderment is usually derogatory, pointing to a preoccupation with establishing God's existence and unique nature which has tended to render subsequent elaboration of God's triunity as a kind of afterthought and a change in theological fashions, an irrelevancy. Moreover, linked to a baroque Thomism which divided philosophy from theology in a manner alien to Thomas himself, the pedagogical ordering also intimated that it was not only possible but desirable to treat of God first by reason and then by faith, as though one might be led to believe in the God of Abraham, Isaac, Jacob, and Jesus in that stepwise fashion. And while all these subsequent infelicities have indeed plagued Catholic theology, the strategy of proceeding first to establish "the distinction" of God from the world seems quite separable from such fall-out.

For what if the characteristic language of the scriptures—Hebrew, Christian, and Muslim—adopts a mode which could lead people to believe that God was indeed part of the world, despite the insistence on its free creation? Are we to brand Maimonides' efforts at the outset of the *Guide* to "deconstruct" the anthropomorphic language of the Hebrew scriptures as the idle speculations of a philosopher? Or must we not admit that the narrative quality of these scriptures, in which God is sometimes depicted as an actor within the story, can be misleading regarding the nature of the God who is so portrayed? And while the structure of the Qur'an is not so pervasively narrative, its outspokenly paranetic quality, together with its vivid descriptions of God's response to human doings, elicited a similar reaction among the various schools of *tafsīr* (or commentary). Some explicitly "grammatical" efforts must be made, it seems, to insist that our God does not belong to the world which God creates. Thus the triunity of the Christian God will logically and pedagogically presuppose an established "set of protocols against idolatry." In fact, in the absence of some such "grammatical" treatment of divinity, discussion of the "divine names" (or "attributes"), gleaned from scripture yet available in human discourse, will almost certainly be misconstrued as offering "an outline description of God."[16] This has certainly been the history of such reflection in all three traditions. So a philosophical theology rooted in the scriptures, and in no wise presuming a step-wise process of learning about divinity, first from philosophy and only then from theology, could still insist on establishing "the distinction" of God from the world as a necessary preliminary to elucidating the grammar of living in relation to such a One. And if one were writing, as Aquinas was, in an intellectual climate in which Jewish and Muslim reflection on God's *oneness* set the parameters of discourse, then focusing on God's oneness would also serve to establish the ground rules for a shared discourse. What came later—discussion of God's triunity—would not then be an addition to such considerations, but their inner elaboration. And we want now to show that while such an elaboration is indeed peculiar to Christianity, the patterns which it explicitly discloses are not exclusively Christian property.

9.3 ANALOGOUS PATTERNS IN JUDAISM, CHRISTIANITY, AND ISLAM

The threefold pattern which we have proposed, of *source, word,* and *community,* will prove to be indispensable in negotiating the ambiguities which arise in speaking of "revelation," as has already been suggested. Since each tradition speaks of a revealing *word* and since words convey messages to us, each tradition has been tempted to identify that revelation with the revealing *word*. The tenacity of this temptation is best illustrated in Christianity, where the *word* is expressly said to be "made flesh" in Jesus, yet various strands of the tradition have insisted on locating that revealing word in the New Testament instead. The temptation is certainly a natural one, since 'word' implies 'text', yet it remains a temptation since no text can wear "revelation" on its face. Equally natural will be the propensities of each of these communities to exalt the revealing word, endowing it with healing properties and even with "inimitability," as in the Islamic doctrine of *i'jāz al-Quran*.[17] Yet further reflection shows that it is precisely the vitality of these texts in the communities which they shape, and which form people to be nourished by them, that contributes to their extraordinary power. There is an operative mutual inclusion of *word* in *community* which participants in the community would quite naturally overlook because they take it for granted. The word is in fact revealing because it lives in a community of worship and of human interaction which it animates. Likewise, the word itself refers to its divine source and is constantly employed in returning thanks to that source for granting humankind this access to the life and work of God. "Revelation," in short, requires such a threefold structure to be what it claims to be.

9.3.1 Judaism: A Divine Community

It is notorious that one can converse at length about Judaism without mentioning God. There seems to be such a rich tradition of response to the Lord's initial call that the varieties of that response can exhaust the conversation. Mistaken by Christians as "legalism," especially in the wake of Luther's canonizing the opposition of *law* to *gospel*, this preoccupation with oral as well as written Torah, along with patterns of observance, has served to define Judaism in a world dominated by either Christian or Muslim polities. And perhaps that is all that needs to be said to explain the single-minded focus on the dimension of *word*. For the dominant religious groups acknowledged the God of Abraham, Isaac, and Jacob to be theirs as well, while the dimension of *community*, as is so often the case, was articulated in living rather than in words. Yet the tenor of the prayer book suggests a reciprocity between the creator and this community, especially in the celebration of *shabbat*, introduced by the recitation of the Song of Songs, followed by an invitatory:

> "Observe and Remember," in a single command, the One God announced to us.

The Lord is One, and his name is One, for fame, for glory and for praise to which the congregation responds:

> Come, my friend, to meet the bride; let us welcome the Sabbath.[18]

If the sabbath affords a ritual reenactment of creation, it does so explicitly invoking the One who has "chosen us and hallowed us above all nations, and graciously given us the holy Sabbath as a heritage" (278). The very One who orders and regulates the universe has "loved the house of Israel with everlasting love" (258). So the observance of this holy day renews the spousal bond between the "Lord our God, King of the Universe" and the people Israel. And such bonds are only sustained, we know quite well, by constantly being renewed.

It is not a large step from here to consider "the performance of the commandments as necessary for the divine welfare," a theurgical view which Moshe Idel traces back from kabbalist theory to early rabbinic reflections on community practice.[19] He uses the term 'theurgy' (or 'theurgical') "to refer to operations intended to influence the Divinity, mostly in its own inner state or dynamics" (157), and that in three schematic ways: augmenting the divine power or glory, drawing down the divine presence [*shekhinah*], or helping to maintain the

universe. While the kabbalists linked this theurgical activity
to a theosophic scheme of *sephirot,* earlier sources as well as
some later hassidic writers had no need of such a superstruc-
ture to consider "theurgical activity as the main raison d'etre
of the commandments" (166). Rooted in an active understanding of covenant, "the performance of the divine will via
the commandments [becomes] the means by which man par-
ticipates in the divine process" (166). And actively so, by adding to or detracting from the divine power, insofar as Israel
acts in accord with or counter to "the will of heaven" (158–
59). In the rabbinic *Berakhot,* a blessing rite calls upon the
divine mercy to conquer the divine anger, thus attributing to
the act of blessing power "to cause the overflowing of mercy"
(164). It follows that "according to talmudic-midrashic
thought, one of the basic repercussions of the fulfillment of
the commandments is the indwelling of the divine presence
[*shekhinah*] among the Jewish people" (166). Finally, "the
receiving of the Torah by the people of Israel is presented by
the Talmud as a prerequisite for the existence of the universe:

> The Holy One, blessed be he, made a condition with the Crea-
> tion, saying: "If Israel receive my Torah, good; if not, I shall re-
> turn you to chaos."[20]

So a select set of rational creatures – Israel – is empowered by
the originating covenant with rituals "which alone are able
to sustain the dynamic bond between God and man" (167).

Thus, Israel not only has privileged access to the divinity
but is empowered to enter into the "inner life" of God to influence the relation among the divine attributes and even aug-
ment or diminish divine power and glory. And if later, "in
the theology of Ashkenazic Hasidism, the glory is usually
separated from the Creator" (160), so that "the glory is the
recipient and beneficiary of the worship, whereas the higher
entity [God as *'Eiyn Sof* or eternal] remains recondite" (162),
such a process of making distinctions "within" divinity only
contributes to our thesis. For we are not yet subjected to
an elaborate emanation scheme of *sephirot,* threatening to attentuate "the distinction" of creator from creatures, but well

within the Hebrew insistence on that "infinite qualitative difference." What seems to be at work, however, is a linking of certain actions of the community with the divinity through the Torah, which specifies the shape of that activity. That very *theurgical* capacity to influence divinity is made possible through the revelation of the commandments [*mitzvot*], yet it is their observance by the community which not only sustains that people as God's people but also renews the bonds between creator and creatures, thus conserving the universe itself. So the covenant between God and Israel displays *in actu* the inter-relation among the divine *source,* the revealed *word,* and the chosen *community.* And in some inchoate yet effective manner these interactions resonate in the divinity itself.

9.3.2 Christianity: Irenaeus and the Early Response to Heterodoxy

While it may seem redundant to introduce a Christian example for the thesis that the response to God in each of the traditions displays a threefold structure which itself indicates something of the revealing God, an early Christian witness could help to make apparent its plausibility. Well before the initial elaborations of a trinitarian theology in the late fourth century, Irenaeus of Lyons (130–202) was faced with the Gnostic challenge, which was driving a wedge between creation and redemption. Whether in its Valentinian form, whereby material creation results from the defect in divinity, or in Marcion's outright dualism, there can be no "economy" relating creation and redemption.[21] If the demiurge of Valentinus "is the indirect fruit of [God's] inner process, there is simply no relationship between the Marcionite Good, Transcendent God who was completely unknown before the advent of Jesus Christ, and the Just or Evil Creator God known through the Old Testament" (10–11). Faced with so radical a challenge to the faith, yet one operating in the name of the Christian scriptures, Irenaeus needed to establish a unitary yet differentiated divine "economy" to articulate the indivisible oneness of the creating and redeeming God, for the Gnostic

"Good God . . . is absolutely transmundane and his nature is alien to the universe which he neither created nor governs" (21). Whether human beings be essentially divine (as in Valentinus) or the "products of an inferior God" (as in Marcion), the status of Father as creator and of Son as redeemer is completely undermined: "the Valentinian Christ can only serve as an occasion of salvation by reminding divine beings of their birthright, while the Marcionite Christ can come only as an unheralded novelty sent to foreigners by One who is not their Father" (24)!

Irenaeus' response to this subverting of the scriptures as understood and transmitted from generation to generation in the young community of Christians took the form of showing, from creed and from practice, that a single "economy" comprising creation and redemption reflected a similar differentiation *within* God, so that neither internal fissure nor external competitor threatened the essential unity of God and of God's plan for all creatures. In a later theological jargon, Irenaeus' strategy exemplified Karl Rahner's contention that *immanent* and *economic* ought not be separated from one another; yet it is fair to say that the witness of Irenaeus predated any such distinction and for that very reason is of value to us. In one way, of course, his defense of tradition would appear hardly to require any work at all, for the threefold structure of the apostolic creed spoke eloquently of unity where the Gnostics introduced opposition. Yet the manner in which that one God operates in history demanded a presentation faithful to the emerging Christian consensus of divine triunity. And this is precisely what Irenaeus supplied: "the creator God was for him triune in the very act of creation" (54). He elaborated this conviction with the metaphor of God's "two hands," animated by "the deep-seated belief in a God who freely desires to impart himself to non-divine beings, to enter into communion with that which is not himself, so share and self-communicate himself in love" (57). God stands in need of no intermediate being, such as angels, to carry out the divine purposes, "for with him were always present the Word and Wisdom, the Son and the Spirit" (*AH*

4.20.1)–God's "two hands" (59). Their presence assures us that God need not have created, "for it is by them and in them that [God] made all things, freely and in total independence" (*AH* 4.20.1). Moreover, the image of Son and Spirit as "God's two hands" emphasizes that creation is a self-communication of divinity itself: "the Father conveys *himself* through *his* hands" (60). While this will only be completed in the gift of the Son and Spirit, it is that gift which animates creation, as that "divinely-initiated process that is dominated and suffused by the attraction of this greater grace to which it is related as to its own completion" (65).

Yet these are not two activities of God, for "the creator of the world is truly the Word of God" (*AH* 5.18.3) and it is "through the vivifying power of the Holy Spirit, the second hand of the Father, [that] the church makes manifest in its members the original design of the creator" (89). So the unity of God's purpose is assured in that the one God as *source* creates in the *Word,* and this pattern is discernible through the eyes of faith nourished in the *community* of the faithful. None of these three components can be split off, as the Gnostics try to do, or collapsed one into the other. The single *economy* of creation-redemption requires such an articulation of the one God from whom all-that-is originates. Otherwise we might presume with many philosophers that the universe was either itself divine or emanated necessarily from the One; or we might fall prey to the diverse dualisms of the Gnostics. Irenaeus offers us an account of the threefold unity implicit in the divine activity of redeeming and creating, and does so two centuries before the "high trinitarian" formulations of the Cappadocians and the Council of Constantinople (381). What distinguished his treatment from roughly contemporary Greek apologists, like Justin Martyr, was his insistence that creation was a faith-assertion, which allowed him to exploit his scheme of a single *economy* of creation and salvation. Perhaps the claims of the Gnostics that they were interpreting the evangelical faith, suggested that approach. In any case, it allowed us to present him as an early Christian analogue to the Jewish and Muslim treatments, which also adumbrate a threefold structure to the divine call and consequent human response.

9.3.3 Islam: An Uncreated Qur'an Calls Forth a Communal Response to Allah

The prospect of finding vestigial traces of a triune divinity in Islam may strike one as foolhardy, given the outright polemic against such a notion, beginning with the Qur'an itself:

They surely disbelieve who say: Lo! Allah is the third of three; when there is no God save the One God. (5:73)

O People of the Scripture! Do not exaggerate in your religion nor utter aught concerning Allah save the truth.
The Messiah, Jesus son of Mary, was only a messenger of Allah, and His word which He conveyed unto Mary, and a spirit from
Him. (4:171)

Besides the manifest idolatry implied by suggesting there could be more than one God and the pretense of Christians to elevate their prophet to divine rank, there is the preposterous claim that this same Jesus could be God's *son*. The sura *Mary* takes the lead, but parallels abound:

It hardly befits the majesty of Allah that He should take unto
Himself a son.
Glory be to Him! When He decrees a thing, He says unto it
only Be! and it is. (19:35)

The Originator of the heavens and the earth!
How can He have a child, when there is for Him no consort,
when He created all things and is Aware of all things? (6:102)

The words capitalized in this translation mark the recognized "names of God," attributes of divinity canonically authorized since they appear in the Qur'an.[22] Those attributes which have to do with God's relations with creatures serve to bolster the feature of free and effortless creation. And even to entertain the thought of such a One "having a son" seems blasphemous, not simply in that children are the result of intercourse be-

tween a man and a woman, but that men need sons to carry
on their patrimony and God has no needs whatsoever:

> They say: Allah has taken (unto Him) a son – Glorified be He!
> He has no needs! His is all that is in the heavens and all that
> is in the earth. (10:69)

Yet these considerations certainly soften one's initial im-
pressions regarding our proposal, since it is now clear just
how polemical is the Qur'anic treatment of God's triunity.
If the gospel of John were one's source rather than the simple
words of the baptismal formula – Father, Son, and Holy Spirit
– we would be presented with the following paean:

> In the beginning was the Word: the Word was with God and
> the Word was God. (1:1)

'Word' hardly connotes consorting with another to bring it
forth; and *God's word* is precisely how the Qur'an is presented
to humankind. Moreover, John's insistence that this Word
"was with God from the beginning" as that "through [which]
all things came to be" (1:2) testifies to the later *sunna* teaching that the Qur'an is at once uncreated and the pattern
according to which the universe is ordered.[23] And as the history of Christian developments manifests, John's more "spiritual" presentation served to "demythologize" reflection on
Jesus' words of address to "the Father," which helped to canonize the baptismal formula of faith in God as "Father, Son,
and Holy Spirit."[24] So much so, indeed, that no Christian
who employs the "sign of the cross" even suspects there to
have been a mother! Something powerful has been at work
in the tradition giving that language such a novel twist, but
that is precisely what traditions do with the words of scripture.
 So the Qur'an plays a role in Islam as exalted as that of Jesus in an orthodox Christianity which espouses the high Chris-
tology of Chalcedon: God's word made flesh becomes God's
Word made Arabic.[25] Not only is the Qur'an deemed to be
"inimitable" (*i'jāz*) in principle; it is also considered to be un-
translatable: a rendition of the Qur'an into a language other
than Arabic is *not* the Qur'an, but (as Arberry's version an-

nounces in its title) "the Qur'an interpreted." It is no matter
that Muhammad worked no miracles, for the Qur'an itself
is the miracle of Islam. Those who focus on the Qur'an as
God's eternal *word* put it this way: God is, *ab aeterno;* the word
is one of His attributes, subsisting in Him; God is eternal
as to the word, the word subsists in Him just as knowledge
subsists in Him and power subsists in him. . . . It is wrong
to say that the word is God identically, or partially, or anything other than God."[26] The terms employed here are not
unfamiliar to early Christian discussions of "the Word" referred
to in John 1, and the mention of attributes alerts one to the
ways in which Muslim-Christian debates over the trinity naturally enough conflated that issue with Islamic debate over the
reality or not of attributes in God.[27] But for all that the Qur'an,
so exalted, is deemed to be "God witnessing to Himself, real,
unique," Massignon nonetheless queries: "Is that the only
fruit which the faithful can glean from reading the Qur'an?
Is it not the life principle of the Islamic Community [*umma*]?"
(3.141).

And the answer, of course, must be *yes:* Muhāsibi "considers the Qur'an to be above all a supernatural source of prayer,
teaching the soul how to converse with God, . . . a foretaste
of eternal life."[28] We have already seen how the Qur'an is not
so much read as recited in the Muslim community, so that
verses chanted and heard in a recurring fashion have the effect of shaping lives by offering spontaneous phrases with
which to guide action. And quite consciously so, since the
term *qur'an* means 'a reciting', and so it was delivered to Muhammad, who was then told often enough to *recite* what he
heard.[29] Western writers cannot resist the expression "sacra-
mental" when remarking on the role which recitation of the
Qur'an plays in Muslim life, for "reciting of the sacred words
is itself a participation in God's speech."[30] So the central Sufi
discipline of interiority, *dhikr* (or "recollection"), represents
an organic outgrowth of Muslim life and practice, where the
preferred expressions for such active recollecting of the divine
invariably include one of the "names of God," the Qur'an's
way of presenting the myriad aspects of the divine, canon-

ized as "Allah's ninety-nine beautiful names."[31] So the internal dynamic of the Qur'an, as God's living word recited and recollected, guides the individual Muslim to prayer and converse with God, and does so within a community which is bonded by a daily pattern of common prayer in a shared language. It is in this way that the Qur'an becomes the life principle of the Muslim community, the *umma,* which is in turn the vehicle of the Qur'an's enduring presence in the world.

Nothing is quite so fascinating and repelling to modern Western consciousness as the bonding and power of the *umma.* Fascinating in that it creates a world in which Muslims know their proper roles: as God bestows a *qur'an* to a wayward humanity through Muhammad, that same Qur'an shapes a community in which those who receive it are given direction, and through which the rest of humanity will be made aware of that God-given Qur'an. Repelling for the same reasons, for there seems as a result to be so little room to move, so little "individual freedom." In theory and in practice the *umma* represents that classical community which is decidedly more than the sum of its individual members and to which they instinctively turn for inspiration and guidance. Protestant Christians in the West have often regarded Catholicism with the same fascination and repulsion, for the self-understanding of the Catholic church is of a community constituted by the Spirit of Jesus and unwilling to present itself as "the church of your choice." So it can emerge as a palpable presence in literature, for example, in a way impossible to Protestantism, whose origins in the principle of individual interpretation have been transmuted into one of individual choice. Of such stuff consumers, not heros, are made. Yet Catholics, faced with the *umma,* are incapable of understanding how it can hold together without a "teaching authority" (*magisterium*). The principle of consensus (*ijmāʿ*) can be traced to a *hadith* in which Muhammad declared: "My community [*umma*] will never agree upon an error," yet what distinguishes it is its outworking in practice.[32] For Islam prides itself on tolerance and can in fact tolerate many different varieties of practice – the major division into Sunni and Shiʿite Islam offering the most

striking example. Yet tolerance has its limits, and the history
of Islam is studded with bloody battles in which one doctrinal view—say, the uncreated character of the Qur'an—ex-
tirpated its opposite. Moreover, certain paradigmatic figures
like Ghazali continue to dominate the landscape.[33] So Islamic
consensus functions more like the informal social structures
which fascinate anthropologists than the contractual modes
which political scientists study. Hence while Pakistani reformers like Muhammad Iqbal have campaigned to open the "gates
of *ijmā*'" to new voices for a fresh consensus, and his com-
patriot Fazlur Rahman finds the prospects dim, one may nonetheless discern such efforts bearing fruit in some sectors of
the Islamic world, despite the fact that no corporate body
or person can be styled the gatekeeper.[34] One also suspects,
however, that other factors are present to attentuate what
western observers cannot help but feel to be the "tyranny of
the majority." The threefold structure of *source*, *word*, and *community* is doubtless operative in Islam as well.

What the *umma* lacks in authoritative structures seems to
be supplied, where it is supplied, by the transforming presence of persons who embody a life in communion with God
which reflects the harmonies of the Qur'an. So a propensity
of the *umma* and its informal processes of *ijmā*' to become
suffocating can be corrected by a direct appeal to the one *source*.
Friendship with God [*walāya*], while at first blush apparently
antithetical to the severe doctrine of divine unity [*tawhīd*],
became the animating goal of Sufi interior ascesis. Initiated
by God, who "leads human beings from darkness to light as
their *friend*," the possibility of becoming God's friend in return became the Sufi reading of the doctrine of divine unity:
understanding "*tawhīd* not primarily as propositional against
the idols, but as experience of the unitive state in which the
self, by *fana*' [annihilation], passed out of selfhood into divine oneness."[35] Nor is this an individual task, however personal the transformation may be. The context is always that
of master/disciple [*pir/murid*], so that the *umma* finds expression in even the most intimate of communication with God.[36]
The presence of Sufi fraternities is widespread in both Sunni

and Shi'ite Islam, though less evident than Western monastic endeavors, since the network is less formal, following the Muslim dictum that Islam is a religion without monks. Yet the attraction of holy men and women, as evidenced in pilgrimages to their tombs, is a pervasive feature of Islam, especially in the Asian subcontinent and among Shi'ites. So in practice the consensus [*ijmā'*] of the community is not felt as an impersonal "majority rule," but as a cross-hatching of sustaining interpersonal networks among people who wish to live in wholehearted response to the gift of the Qur'an.

9.4 SUMMARY

It is the trinitarian structure of God's saving action which can serve as an operative pattern to correct the principal tendencies to self-destruction endemic to each of the three traditions which we have been considering.[37] Judaism and Islam do not articulate this pattern into the divinity itself, although each of them finds in the interaction of *source*, revealing *word*, and liberating *community* something proper to the God whom they worship. And each uses those dimensions creatively over against one another to offset a less-than-liberating reception of that divine initiative. The Christian propensity to elaborate a doctrine of divine triunity, with the sophisticated theological apparatus required to be consistent with the confession of one God, has tended to create a chasm between Christians and the other two Abrahamic traditions regarding the doctrine of God. Moreover, within Christian theology itself, two divergent attitudes toward trinitarian theology have been evident in modern times, perhaps in function of one another. One has insisted on the exclusive propriety of such a teaching, limiting it utterly to a series of statements about the relations *within* divinity, insisting that the divine operations in the created universe (*ad extra*) had always to be located in the nature of God and so could never be revelatory of God's trinitarian character. Karl Rahner's observation that such an axiom went a long way to rendering the trinitarian faith and teaching otiose, by relegating it to the arena of recondite theological discussions, has stimulated fresh approaches to the central mystery of the Christian faith by various theologians.[38] His counter-axiom that the immanent trinity *is* the economic trinity has suggested the propriety of finding traces of divine triunity in creation—a practice popular with twelfth-century Christian thinkers but virtually abandoned subsequently. It is that lead which we have explored in this chapter, focusing on the revelational encounter as a place where the character of God would need to make itself manifest. The scheme suggested, of *source*, *word*, and *community*, was inspired by the recent work of Nicholas Lash and adapted expressly to the three traditions which avow the free creation of the universe. It has been offered as a way of showing how traditions contain their own resources for fertility and adaptation, identifying a pattern which appears to be operative in each. Readers may take issue with these contentions or develop them in new ways. The essay is clearly exploratory and in that sense appropriate for the final chapter of this exploration into comparative philosophical theology.

Notes

INTRODUCTION

1. Robert Sokolowski develops this use of "the distinction" in *The God of Faith and Reason* (Notre Dame, Ind.: University of Notre Dame Press, 1982).

2. I am indebted to Alasdair MacIntyre here, whose clearest rendition of this perspective can be found in *Three Rival Versions of Moral Enquiry* (Notre Dame, Ind.: University of Notre Dame Press, 1990).

3. The medieval setting has been explored in a symposium volume edited by David Burrell and Bernard McGinn: *God and Creation* (Notre Dame, Ind.: University of Notre Dame Press, 1990).

1. THE CONTEXT: CREATION

1. Moses Maimonides: *The Guide of the Perplexed*, trans. Shlomo Pines (Chicago: University of Chicago Press, 1963) 2.25.

2. Kathryn Tanner develops this point eloquently in *God and Creation in Christian Theology* (Oxford: Blackwell, 1988).

3. Josef Pieper, *The Silence of St. Thomas* (New York: Pantheon, 1957): "The Negative Element in the Philosophy of St. Thomas," 47–67.

4. A recent and eloquent example is Jon Levenson, *Creation and the Persistence of Evil* (New York: Harper and Row, 1988). Hereafter references to this work will be cited by page number in the text.

5. Or they had a different conception of exegesis: see Lenn Evan Goodman's work on "Saadiah Gaon's Interpretive Technique in Translating the Book of Job," in *Translation of Scripture* (*Jewish Quarterly Review* supplementary vol., 1990), 47–76, which eluci-

dates the method which Maimonides employed as a practical foundation in reading scripture; see also Seymour Feldman's "'In the Beginning God Created': A Philosophical Midrash," in David Burrell and Bernard McGinn, eds., *God and Creation* (above Introduction, n. 3), 3–26 for medieval Jewish exegesis.

6. J. L. Austin, in *How to Do Things with Words* (Cambridge, Mass.: Harvard University Press, 1962) notes that we need sometimes to put expressions to use in unusual environments, and part of the virtuosity of some expressions is their ability to "play away from home." These observations offer a gentle and prescient entré into the domain of analogous usage.

7. There is a debate regarding the need for one or fifty-three unmoved movers: Joseph Owens, "The Reality of the Aristotelian Separate Movers," *Review of Metaphysics* 3 (1950): 319–37.

8. See David Braine, *The Reality of Time and the Existence of God* (Oxford: Clarendon Press, 1988). For a brief resumé, see my review in *Faith and Philosophy* 7 (1990): 361–64. Barry Miller takes a different tack, arguing that a coherent understanding of *existing* demands an explanation of a different type from any available explanatory paradigm: *From Existence to God* (London: Routledge, 1991).

9. The protagonists in this debate are principally John Wippel, whose discussion (with reply to Joseph Owens) may be found in *Metaphysical Themes in Thomas Aquinas* (Washington, D.C.: Catholic University of America Press, 1984), 107–32, and Joseph Owens, "Stages and Distinction in *De ente:* A Rejoinder," *Thomist* 45 (1981): 99–123. See also Owens' earlier "Quiddity and Real Distinction in St. Thomas Aquinas," *Medieval Studies* 27 (1965): 1–22, esp. 19–22.

10. My treatment here will follow the outlines of Jon D. Levenson's challenging work: *Creation and the Persistence of Evil*, which resumes the current as well as some rabbinic commentaries.

11. *The Hirsch Siddur* (New York: Feldheim, 1978), 273. I am indebted to Pierre Lenhardt for these liturgical connections: see his *Evangile et tradition d'Israel* (Paris: Cerf, 1990).

12. *Church Dogmatics,* vol. 3: *The Doctrine of Creation* (Edinburgh: T & T Clark, 1958) 50. We shall explore the parallel which Barth draws between the eternal begetting of the Word of God in God and the gratuity of creation in chapter 9. Astute readers will wonder whether the begetting of the Word in God is a free act and so can offer a paradigm within divinity for free creation.

13. *Physics* 2.9 (200a34).

14. Thomas J. O'Shaughnessy, S.J., *Creation and the Teaching of the Qur'an* (Rome: Biblical Institute Press, 1985), esp. 1–10; see also the review by A. H. Johns in *Abr-Nahrain* [Leiden] 25 (1987): 156–61.

15. For a classical commentary on these names, see David Burrell and Nazih Daher's translation: *Al-Ghazali on the Ninety-nine Beautiful Names of God* (Cambridge: Islamic Texts Society/Notre Dame, Ind.: University of Notre Dame Press, 1991), under the relevant names.

16. Or so Louis Gardet contends in *EI²* 3, 663; the remarks about *Khalīq* are dependent upon Roger Arnaldez' account in *EI²* 4, 980–88.

17. And the community functions through its exemplary individuals: one can consider Maimonides' deliberate "deconstruction" of the language of the Torah (in part 1 of the *Guide*) as one attempt to show how the scriptures reveal the logic of perfection. See Lenn Evan Goodman, *Rambam: Readings in the Philosophy of Moses Maimonides* (New York: Viking, 1975), 52–118.

2. ON CHARACTERIZING THE CREATOR

1. The allusion here is to the neoplatonic scheme, in which *intellect* is an emanation from the One; Maimonides is using the Torah's assertions regarding creation as a wedge to propose an alternative metaphysical scheme.

2. For Maimonides' appropriation of this distinction, see Alexander Altmann, "Essence and Existence in Maimonides," in *Studies in Religious Philosophy and Mysticism* (London: Routledge and Kegan Paul, 1969), 108–27.

3. See the elucidating remarks by Nicholas Lash, "Production and Prospect: Reflections on Christian Hope and Original Sin," in Ernan McMullin, ed., *Evolution and Creation* (Notre Dame, Ind.: University of Notre Dame Press, 1985), 273–89.

4. For a more complete narrative of this matter, see my *Knowing the Unknowable God* (Notre Dame, Ind.: University of Notre Dame Press, 1986); and for a more careful treatment of Avicenna, see my "Essence and Existence: Avicenna and Greek Philosophy," *Mélanges de l'Institut Dominicain d'Etudes Orientales* 17 (1986): 53–66. Fazlur Rahman's "Essence and Existence in Avicenna" is now a classic source for correcting misunderstandings: Richard Hunt

et al., eds., *Mediaeval and Renaissance Studies* 4 (London: Warburg Institute, 1958), 1–16.

5. A careful analysis of questions 3 to 13 of the first part of the *Summa* can be found in my *Aquinas: God and Action* (Notre Dame, Ind.: University of Notre Dame Press, 1979).

6. Although attempts have been made to reduce Aquinas' account of divine simpleness and its consequences to Plotinus' "unconditioned" One, as in Nicholas Wolterstorff's "Suffering Love," in Thomas Morris, ed., *Philosophy and the Christian Faith* (Notre Dame, Ind.: University of Notre Dame Press, 1988), 217–23, the weight of scholarship tends toward endorsing the novelty of Aquinas' account precisely in the primacy he accords to *esse*. For a balanced account of sources and appropriation see Wayne Hankey, "Aquinas' First Principle: Being or Unity?" in *Dionysius* 4 (1980): 133–72.

7. In what follows I am indebted to W. Norris Clarke, S.J., "Action as the Self-Revelation of Being: A Central Theme in the Thought of St. Thomas," in Linus J. Thro, ed., *History of Philosophy in the Making* (Washington, D.C.: Catholic University of America Press, 1981), 63–80.

8. See the discussion by Armand Maurer in his second edition of *On Being and Essence* (Toronto: Pontifical Institute of Medieval Studies, 1968), 14–15, regarding translating this term. For a recent example of incomprehension of this central move of Aquinas, see Christopher Hughes, *On a Complex Theory of a Simple God* (Ithaca, N.Y.: Cornell University Press, 1989), 27–28, 83.

9. See James Ross, *Portraying Analogy* (Cambridge: Cambridge University Press, 1982), for a careful semantic treatment of analogous discourse and my earlier historical-analytic treatment: *Analogy and Philosophical Language* (New Haven: Yale University Press, 1973). My review of Ross in *New Scholasticism* 59 (1985): 347–57 tries to depict the sophistication of his work.

10. For a series of essays probing this contention in the specific form in which Etienne Gilson espoused it, see *Dieu et l'être* (Paris: Etudes Augustiniennes, 1978), especially Pierre Hadot, "Dieu comme acte d'être dans le néoplatonisme" (57–63), for neoplatonic precursors to Aquinas' identification of the One with *esse*.

11. *Al-Shifā'* 1.16 (Cairo, 1960), p. 38, line 12 (*La Métaphysique du Shifā'*. trans. G. C. Anawati [Paris: Vrin, 1978] 114).

12. For a brief presentation of this approach, which attempts to avoid the obvious difficulty of there being things which do not exist, see Alvin Plantinga, "Actualism and Possible Worlds," in Mi-

chael J. Loux, ed., *The Possible and the Actual* (Ithaca, N.Y.: Cornell University Press, 1979), 253–73. The price to be paid, among others, is that "existence is essential to each object, and necessarily so, for . . . every object has existence in each world in which it exists" (261). This strategy returns us to Avicenna's infelicitous terminology of *existence* as "accident," yet does so unabashedly, since his celebrated distinction is eliminated as well.

13. This was, of course, al-Ghazali's criticism of Avicenna's propounding a necessary emanation scheme *as* a Muslim philosopher (cf. *Averroës' Tahāfut al-Tahāfut*, ed. and trans. Simon Van den Bergh [Cambridge: Cambridge University Press, 1978] "Fourth Discussion," 156–79) and it would be my criticism of Plantinga's account of creation *as* a Christian philosopher in *Does God Have a Nature?* (Milwaukee: Marquette University Press, 1980).

14. The testimony of Jacques Maritain is perhaps instructive here. In treating of God's knowledge of creatures in a late reflection (*God and the Permission of Evil,* trans. Joseph Evans [Milwaukee: Bruce, 1956]) he warns us against transferring to God a theory similar to that of Descartes, albeit its inverse: "we must be careful not to imagine that in the divine 'science [i.e., knowledge] of vision'– where the creative will is linked with intelligence–God would attain or would properly speaking know only His own essence and His own ideas, which would be as it were *models* of the things produced in being by the creative will . . . in such a way that things would supposedly be known only because they would resemble the models in question, at which alone the divine knowledge would stop" (70).

15. For a more detailed treatment of this, see my *Knowing the Unknowable God,* 97–99; and for a full-scale treatment of the issues and their philosophical implications, see James Ross, "God, Creator of Kinds and Possibilities: *Requiescant universalia ante res,*" in Robert Audi and William Wainwright, eds., *Rationality, Religious Belief, and Moral Commitment* (Ithaca, N.Y.: Cornell University Press, 1986), 315–34.

16. Aquinas had no direct access to al-Ghazali's work, except through a translation of the intended introduction to his criticism of the Muslim philosophers al-Farabi and Ibn-Sina, in which he laid out their thought so fairly that his translators assumed he was one of them (*Maqāsid al-falāsifā* [Cairo, 1936]); Ghazali's objections can be found in Van den Bergh (n. 13 above) "Second Discussion" (69–74) and "Third Discussion" (117–21).

17. For a fuller treatment of this, see my *Knowing the Unknowable God*, 67–70, 89–91.

3. ON CHARACTERIZING CREATION

1. Paul Helm so criticizes James Ross in *Eternal God* (Oxford: Clarendon Press, 1988), 165–69.

2. This observation offers a way of reading Peter Winch's provocative essay "Ceasing to Exist," in *Proceedings of the British Academy* 68 (1982): 329–53, on which Normal Malcolm comments: "On 'Ceasing to Exist'," in R. Gaita, ed., *Value and Understanding* (London: Routledge, 1990). For Winch makes his point about the oddity of something simply ceasing to exist over against the background of a presumed continuity of context. That oddity is precisely what creation celebrates in a positive way.

3. As J. L. Ackrill renders *De interpretatione* 4: "The present investigation deals with the statement-making sentence . . ." (17a6).

4. A classic Thomistic statement of this position is that of Joseph de Finance in *Etre et agir dans la philosophie de S. Thomas*, 2nd ed. (Rome: Università Gregoriana, 1960). An insightful treatment in the analytic vein has been developed over the years by Barry Miller, most succinctly in his recent *From Existence to God* (ch. 1, n. 8), 75–78: "existence is . . . a real property . . . , though not an Aristotelian accident" (77–78), so not a characterizing feature. See also "'Exists' and Existence," *Review of Metaphysics* 40 (1986): 237–70.

5. Cf. Robert M. Adams, "Actualism and Thisness," in *Synthese* 49 (1981): 3–41, reprinted in his *Virtue of Faith and Other Essays* (Ithaca, N.Y.: Cornell University Press, 1988), and Alvin Plantinga, "Actualism and Possible Worlds," *Theoria* 42 (139–60), reprinted in Michael J. Loux, ed., *The Possible and the Actual* (above, ch. 2, n. 12), 253–73.

6. *La Metaphysique du Shifa*, trans. G. C. Anawati (above, ch. 2, n. 11) 78.

7. Cf. Linda Zagzebski, "Individual Essence and the Creation," in Thomas Morris, ed., *Divine and Human Action* (Ithaca, N.Y.: Cornell University Press, 1988), 119–43, where she asserts that "these essences include only purely conceptual properties" (142) and that "God chooses among [them] those he wishes to exemplify" (143). Making the link with divine ideas as "exemplars," she can then say that "the exemplar of a thing is just what makes it

intelligible. It is each object's way of imitating the divine essence" (143).

8. See Barry Miller's careful arguments in *From Existence to God*, ch. 3: "The inconceivability of future individuals," 40–63.

9. Alternatively, the notion of existence is altered from that of *coming-to-be* to a "property . . . essential to each object; . . . every object has existence in each world in which it exists" (Alvin Plantinga, "Actualism and Possible Worlds," 261), where "existing-in-a-[possible]-world" simply takes on the meaning of "self-identity," or "being the object that it is." Then the valence of *coming-to-be [in reality]*, which we have associated with *existing* is transferred to "actualizing," with the consequences noted.

10. See my contribution to the festschrift for George Lindbeck: "Aquinas and Scotus: Contrary Patterns for Philosophical Theology," in Bruce Marshall, ed., *Theology in Dialogue* (Notre Dame, Ind.: University of Notre Dame Press, 1990).

11. James Ross, "God, Creator of Kinds and Possibilities: *Requiescant universalia ante res*," in Audi and Wainwright, eds., *Rationality, Religious Belief, and Moral Commitment* (above, ch. 2, n. 15), 315–34; and "The Crash of Modal Metaphysics," *Review of Metaphysics* 43 (1989): 251–79.

12. References to Aquinas' treatment may be found in my *Knowing the Unknowable God*, 97–98.

13. Christopher Hughes, *On a Complex Theory of a Simple God* (above, ch. 2, n. 8), 27.

4. ON CHARACTERIZING THE RELATION: JEWS, CHRISTIANS, AND MUSLIMS

1. On the question, see David Braine, *The Reality of Time and the Existence of God* (above, ch. 1, n. 8), ch. V, esp. 123–29; and Barry Miller, "'Exists' and Existence," *Review of Metaphysics* 40 (1986): 237–70.

2. That 'exists' is not a formal predicate is shown by Barry Miller in *From Existence to God* (above, ch. 3, n. 4), 195.

3. Van den Bergh's edition of Averroës' *Tahāfut al-Tahāfut* [The incoherence of the Incoherence] contains within it the entire work of Ghazali's which it criticizes and offers the best English rendition of that work (Cambridge: Cambridge University Press, 1954). For Aquinas' acquaintance with *kalām*, see Louis Gardet, "St. Thomas et ses Prédécesseurs Arabes," in *St. Thomas Aquinas (1274–1974)*

Commemorative Studies I (Toronto: Pontifical Institute of Mediaeval Studies, 1974), 419–48.

4. Roger Arnaldez has argued that Islamic thought is inherently *voluntarist,* even when presenting a straightforwardly intellectualist position: "Intellectualism et volontarisme dans la pensée Musulmane," *1274 – Année charnière – Mutations et continuités* (Paris: Editions du centre nationale de la recherche scientifique, 1977), 121–29; so the opposition may be more than any single thinker could bridge.

5. Roger Arnaldez, "Trouvailes philosophiques dans le commentaire coranique de Fakhr al-Din al-Rāzī," *Etudes philosophiques et litteraires* [Rabat] (1968), 11–24.

6. Daniel Gimaret, *Théories de l'acte humain en théologie musulmane* (Paris: Vrin, 1980), 130–33; Marie-Louise Siauve, *L'Amour de Dieu chez Gazālī* (Paris: Vrin, 1986), 140.

7. For a comprehensive *tour d'horizon* of this milieu, see Joel Kraemer's *Philosophy in the Renaissance of Islam* (Leiden: Brill, 1986).

8. Richard Frank, "The Origin of the Arabic Philosophical Term *anniya,*" *Cahiers de Byrsa* (Musée Lavigerie) 6 (1956): 181–201.

9. Alfred Ivry, *Al-Kindi's Metaphysics* (Albany: State University of New York Press, 1974); Jean Jolivet, *L'intellect selon Kindi* (Leiden: Brill, 1971).

10. Ibrahim Madkour, *La Place d'al Farabi dans l'ecole philosophique musulmane* (Paris: Librairie de Amerique et d'Orient, 1934); Richard Walzer, *Al-Farabi on the Perfect State* (Oxford: Clarendon Press, 1985).

11. On Aquinas' use of the *Liber de causis* and other neoplatonic writings, see Richard Taylor, "Thomas Aquinas and *Plotiniana Arabica,*" to appear in *Journal of the History of Philosophy.*

12. Georges Vajda, "Les notes d'Avicenne sur *la Théologie d'Aristote,*" *Révue Thomiste* 59 (1951): 346–406.

13. See Louis Gardet, *Le Pensée réligieuse d'Avicenne* (Paris: Vrin, 1951), 185–96.

14. The most reliable English translation of this work is found in *Averroës' Tahāfut al-Tahāfūt,* translated by Simon Van den Bergh (n. 3 above).

15. See ibid.

16. Averroës' reflections of the relations between what is apprehended by reason and what is apprehended by faith in response to revelation have been much debated. An earlier work by Leon Gauthier: *Ibn Rochd* (Paris: Presses Universitaires de France, 1948) ought to be supplemented by Roger Arnaldez: "La pensée réligieuse

d'Averroës: le doctrine de la création dans la *Tahāfut*," *Studia Islamica* (1957), 99–114, and Charles Butterworth, "Religion et philosophie dans la pensée d'Averroës," *Annuaire d'Ecole Pratique des Hautes Etudes* (Vième) 86 (1977–78): 387–89, as well as Jean Jolivet, "Divergences entre les métaphysiques d'Ibn Rushd et d'Aristote," *Arabica* 29 (1982): 225–45.

17. See Arnaldez' reference in note 16, as well as Barry Kogan, *Averroës and the Metaphysics of Causation* (Albany, N.Y.: State University of New York Press, 1985), and Oliver Leaman, *Averroës and His Philosophy* (Oxford: Clarendon Press, 1988).

18. For an assessment of the controversy surrounding Maimonides' "true position" in this debate, see Tamar Rudavsky, "Creation and Time in Maimonides and Gersonides," in David Burrell and Bernard McGinn, eds., *God and Creation* (above, Introduction, n. 3), 122–46, esp. 127–31.

19. Current Maimonides interpretation owes considerable impetus to Leo Strauss' introduction to Shlomo Pines' translation: *The Guide of the Perplexed* (Chicago: University of Chicago Press, 1963), xi–cxxiv, as the articles cited in Tamar Rudavsky's study (above, n. 18) will illustrate for this topic.

20. Seymour Feldman, "Abravanel on Maimonides' Critique of the Kalām Arguments for Creation," *Maimonidean Studies* 1 (1990): 5–25, esp. 18, n. 35; for a comprehensive philosophical discussion of the entire question, see Feldman's "The Theory of Eternal Creation in Hasdai Crescas and Some of His Predecessors," *Viator* 11 (1980): 289–320.

21. *Guide* 2.21; *Tahāfut al-Tahāfut*, Discussion 11, VDB 263–65.

22. For Abravanel, see Feldman (above, n. 20); for the ambiguities in diverse uses of the expression 'creation', see William Dunphy, "Maimonides and Aquinas on Creation: A Critique of Their Historians," *Graceful Reason: Essays in Ancient and Medieval Philosophy presented to Joseph Owens, C.Ss.R.*, ed. Lloyd P. Gerson (Toronto: Pontifical Institute of Medieval Studies, 1983), 361–79.

23. *Al-Shifā': al-Illāhiyāt* 8.6 (Anawati trans., vol. 2:96–97).

24. It is the contention of Levi ben Gershon that the conundrum of divine knowledge of the future free actions of creatures forced Maimonides to the position he took on all divine attributes. Whether or not that be the case, his more "metaphysical" reasons for asserting that God's manner of being wise or benevolent is totally different from ours (1.51–60) receive striking confirmation when he comes to treat of the modalities of divine knowing under providence. See Norbert Max Samuelson, trans. and ed., *Gersonides*

on God's Knowledge (Toronto: Pontifical Institute of Medieval Studies, 1977), 232.

25. Cf. Samuelson (ibid.) and my "Maimonides, Aquinas and Gersonides on Providence and Evil," *Religious Studies* 20 (1984): 335–51. Linda Zagzebski's "individual essences [which] include only purely conceptual properties [and so] are knowable [by God] prior to their exemplification in an actual being" ("Individual Essence and the Creation," in Thomas Morris, ed., *Divine and Human Action* [Ithaca, N.Y.: Cornell University Press, 1988], 142) reflect a similar strategy for knowing individuals. The original context is Avicenna: *al-Shifā: al-Ilāhiyyāt* 8.6 (Anawati trans., vol. 2:98–100).

26. See Thomas Weinandy's illuminating historical-conceptual account of the journey to a clear formulation, entitled *Does God Change?* (Still River, Mass.: St. Bede's Publications, 1985).

27. Sebastian Moore utilizes the work of Bernard Lonergan to great avail in his "God Suffered," *Downside Review* 27 (1959): 122–40.

28. See his praise of Socrates in *Sickness unto Death*, ed. and trans. Howard and Edna Hong (Princeton, N.J.: Princeton University Press, 1980), 92. Socrates raises the question in Plato's *Euthyphro*.

29. For an illuminating discussion of the effect of such a metaphysical perspective on one's understanding of divine freedom, see Roger Arnaldez, "Intellectualisme et voluntarisme dans la pensée musulmane," in *1274–Année charnière–mutation et continuités* (Paris: Editions du centre national de la récherche scientifique, 1977), 121–29.

30. James Ross, "God, Creator of Kinds and Possibilities: Requiescant universalia ante res," in Robert Audi and William Wainwright, eds., *Rationality, Religious Belief, and Moral Commitment* (above, ch. 3, n. 11), 315–34.

31. See my *Knowing the Unknowable God*, 67–70.

32. For Philo, see Harry A. Wolfson, *The Philosophy of the Kalam* (Cambridge, Mass.: Harvard University Press, 1976), 729; for Maimonides, this is implied by his insistence that "all things in the universe are the result of [divine] design" (2.19).

33. This is the position argued persuasively by Marie-Louise Siauve in *L'Amour de Dieu chez Gazālī* (above, n. 6).

5. GOD'S ACTING IN THE WORLD GOD CREATES

1. One thinks of G. E. Wright's influential *God Who Acts* (London: SCM, 1952) as a paradigm of a recent phase in biblical

theology, currently criticized for its epistemological presuppositions but not for the overall characterization of divinity it espouses.

2. For a comprehensive treatment of the tradition of "naming God" in Islam, see Daniel Gimaret, *Les Noms de Dieu en Islam* (Paris: Cerf, 1988).

3. Alfred Freddoso, "God's General Concurrence with Secondary Causes: Why Conservation Is Not Enough," in *Philosophical Perspectives* 5 (1991): 553–85.

4. See Alred Freddoso, "Medieval Aristotelianism and the Case against Secondary Causation in Nature," in Thomas Morris, ed., *Divine and Human Action* (above, ch. 5, n. 25), 74–118.

5. Daniel Gimaret, *Théories de l'acte humain en théologie musulmane* (above, ch. 4, n. 6), 80.

6. Gimaret reproduces the critique of 'Abd al-Jabbār in ibid., 251–52, 301.

7. *Metaphysics* 9.6 (1048a25–b36). See David Braine's extension of this method to principles of the generality demanded by philosophical theology, in his *Reality of Time and the Existence of God* (above, ch. 1, n. 8), 275–65.

8. For a blatant example, see Richard Swinburne, *Coherence of Theism* (Oxford: Oxford University Press, 1979): "By a 'God' [a theist] understands something like a 'person without a body (i.e., a spirit) who is eternal, free, able to do anything, knows everything, is perfectly good. . . .'" (p.1).

9. This is obvious from the ordinary use of Christian faithful, who would certainly subscribe to the Qur'an's insistence that "He – exalted be the glory of the Lord! – has taken neither wife nor son" (72:3); cf. David Braine, *Reality of Time and the Existence of God*, 330–33.

10. Bernard J. Lonergan, *Grace and Freedom* (London: Darton, Longman, and Todd, 1971), 80–91, 120–27.

11. See Richard Bernstein, *Beyond Objectivism and Relativism* (Philadelphia: University of Pennsylvania Press, 1983), and in another key, George Steiner, *Real Presences* (Chicago: University of Chicago, 1989).

12. *Al-Shifā: al-Ilāhiyyāt* 8.6 (Anawati trans., vol. 2: 98–100).

6. CREATURES ACTING IN A CREATED WORLD

1. Maritain, *God and the Permission of Evil,* trans. Joseph Evans (Milwaukee: Bruce, 1956); for a summary of the *de auxiliis* con-

troversy, see Alfred Freddoso's introduction to his translation of Luis de Molina, *On Divine Foreknowledge: Part IV of the Concordia* (Ithaca, N.Y.: Cornell University Press, 1988).

2. For "the individual" as cultural construct, see Alasdair MacIntyre, *Whose Justice? Which Rationality?* (Notre Dame, Ind.: University of Notre Dame Press, 1988), 339.

3. W. Montgomery Watt, *Free Will and Predestination in Early Islam* (London: Luzac, 1948).

4. For a summary account of their teaching on human acts, see Richard Frank, "The Autonomy of the Human Agent in the Teaching of 'Abd al-Jabbar," *Le Museon* [Louvain-la-Neuve] 95 (1982): 232–55.

5. Ibid., 323.

6. Maritain (n. 1 above): "The fundamental certitude . . . is the *absolute innocence of God*" (3).

7. Frank (n. 4), 324.

8. Daniel Gimaret, *Théories de l'acte humain* (above, ch. 4, n. 6), 7–11. The key Arabic terms are *fā'il* (agent) and *hāliq* (creator), and if the only genuine agent is a creator, then creatures and *not* God must be *creators* of their action if they are to be held accountable.

9. It has become customary to refer to *kalām* as "theology," yet the term is in quotes here because what may be called "Islamic theology" cannot be said to "seek to penetrate rationally into the mysteries of God and His creation," as it has come to mean in Western thought. See the introductory remarks of Richard Frank in his astute monograph on the metaphysics of early Mu'tazilite *kalām: The Metaphysics of Created Being according to Abū l-Hudayl al-'Allāf* (Leiden: Nederlands Historich-Archaeologisch Institut in het Nabije Oosten, 1966), esp. 5–6.

10. Daniel Gimaret, *La Doctrine d'al-Ash'ari* (Paris: Cerf, 1990), 372–87; Richard McCarthy, *The Theology of al-Ash'ari* (Beyrouth: Imprimérie Catholique, 1953).

11. Cf. EI² article '*kasb*' by Louis Gardet (IV:690–94), as well as the studies by M. Schwartz: "'Acquisition' (*kasb*) in Early Kalām," in S. M. Stern and A. Hourani, eds., *Islamic Philosophy and the Classical Tradition* (Columbia: University of South Carolina Press, 1972), 355–87; and "The Qādī 'Abd al-Jabbār's refutation of the Ash'arite doctrine of 'Acquisition' (*kasb*)," *Israel Oriental Studies* 6 (1976): 229–63.

12. Gimaret, *Théories*, 67, 68.

13. Richard Frank, "Moral Obligation in Classical Muslim Theology," *Journal of Religious Ethics* 11 (1983): 210; 228 n. 19.

14. Dorothy Sayers, in her durable essay *The Mind of the Maker* (Grand Rapids, Mich.: Eerdmanns, 1963) proposes and develops it only to find it wanting in the end; I would be more tolerant, but one ought to give special respect to the reflective work of a creative writer.

15. Gimaret, *La Doctrine d'al-Ash'ari*, 371 n. 1.

16. Gimaret, *Théories*, 71.

17. Gimaret, *La Doctrine d'al-Ash'ari*, 92–118.

18. Gimaret, *Théories*, 251–52, 301.

19. Gimaret, *La Doctrine d'al-Ash'ari*, 305–7.

20. Alter, *The Art of Biblical Narrative* (New York: Basic Books, 1981).

21. Hans Frei's challenge to historicist biblical criticism to attend to the character of biblical texts in their "narrative realism" has had considerable effect in Christian theological circles. See *The Eclipse of Biblical Narrative* (New Haven: Yale University Press, 1974). For an appreciation, see Frank McConnell, ed., *The Bible and the Narrative Tradition* (New York: Oxford University Press, 1986).

22. See relevant passages in the Genesis *targum*, in Roger Le-Déault, trans. and ed., *Targum de Pentateuche* (Paris: Cerf, 1978).

23. For a sensitive reading of the Joseph sura, see Anthony Johns, "Joseph in the Qur'an: Dramatic Dialogue, Human Emotion and Prophetic Wisdom," *Islamochristiana* [Rome] 7 (1981) 29–55; and for the oral/aural dimensions of the Qur'an, see William Graham, *Beyond the Written Word: Oral Aspects of Scripture in the History of Religion* (Cambridge: Cambridge University Press, 1987), 79–115; Frederick Denny, "Exegesis and Recitation," in *Transitions and Transformations in the History of Religions: Essays in Honor of Joseph M. Kitagawa* (Leiden: Brill, 1980), 91–123; "Qur'an Recitation: A Tradition of Oral Performance and Transmission," *Oral Tradition* 4/1–2 (1989): 5–26; and Gerald Bruns, "The Mystical Hermeneutics of al-Ghazali," in *Hermeneutics Ancient and Modern: Studies in the History and Theory of Interpretation* (New Haven: Yale University Press, 1991).

24. For a representative survey of others, see Lenn Evan Goodman, "Determinism and Freedom in Spinoza, Maimonides, and Aristotle: A Retrospective Study," in Ferdinand Schoeman, ed., *Responsibility, Character, and the Emotions* (Cambridge: Cambridge University Press, 1987), 107–64, esp. 114–17, 145–53; Menachem Kellner, "Gersonides, Providence, and the Rabbinic Tradition," *Journal of the American Academy of Religion* 42 (1974): 673–85; and Norbert Samuelson, "The Problem of Free Will in Maimonides,

Gersonides, and Aquinas," *Central Conference of American Rabbis* [CCAR] *Journal* 17 (1970): 2–20.

25. See my "Reading the *Confessions* of Augustine: An Exercise in Theological Understanding," *Journal of Religion* 50 (1970): 327–51; reprinted in my *Exercises in Religious Understanding* (Notre Dame, Ind.: University of Notre Dame Press, 1974), 11–41.

26. Jean Porter, in her recent *Recovery of Virtue* (Louisville: Westminster/John Knox, 1991) notes how, for Aristotle and Aquinas, "the goal of acting virtuously is not the sort of goal that lends itself to means/ends analysis" (159), but only because the means are integral to the end.

27. I am indebted here to Alasdair MacIntyre's *Whose Justice? Which Rationality?* (n. 2 above), where his narrative of the movement from Aristotle to Aquinas through Augustine manages to do justice to each protagonist in turn.

28. The other citations in the *ST* can be found in 1-2.9.4, and 1.82.4.3. Each consists in a consistent application of the means/end scheme, coupled with the need for an initial moment.

29. On this feature of willing, see Yves R. Simon, *Freedom of Choice,* ed. Peter Wolff (New York: Fordham University Press, 1969). He also uses the term "comprehensive good" for the *ur*-object of willing.

30. Kierkegaard has catalogued this radical freedom as "despair of defiance" in *Sickness Unto Death,* trans. Howard and Edna Hong (above, ch. 4, n. 28), 57–74; in *The Brothers Karamazov,* Dostoevsky has Ivan "turn in the ticket": "It isn't that I reject God; I am simply returning Him most respectfully the ticket that would entitle me to a seat" (bk. 5, ch. 4: "Rebellion").

31. For a sketch of the dynamics, see Mary T. Clark, "Willing Freely according to Thomas Aquinas," in Ruth Link-Salinger et al., eds., *A Straight Path* (Washington, D.C.: Catholic University of America Press, 1988), 49–56; Alan Donaghan, "Thomas Aquinas on Human Action," in Norman Kretzmann et al., eds., *Cambridge History of Late Medieval Philosophy* (Cambridge: Cambridge University Press, 1982), 45–79.

32. I am indebted to Joseph Incandela for these observations on the communal dimension of sin; see his Ph.D. dissertation: "Aquinas' Lost Legacy: God's Practical Knowledge and Situated Human Freedom" (Princeton University, 1986).

33. Three distinct views of human freedom can be gleaned from Scotus, represented by the work of (1) Lawrence Roberts, in "John

Duns Scotus and the Concept of Human Freedom," in *Deus et Homo ad mentem I. Duns Scotus* (Rome: Societas Internationalis Scotistica, 1972), 317–25; (2) Douglas Langston, *God's Willing Knowledge* (University Park, Pa.: Pennsylvania State University Press, 1986), and (3) William Frank, "Duns Scotus' Concept of Willing Freely: What Divine Freedom beyond Choice Teaches Us," *Franciscan Studies* 42 (1982) 68–89.

34. The illuminating and irenic article by Patrick Lee, "The Relation between Intellect and Will in Free Choice according to Aquinas and Scotus," *Thomist* 49 (1985): 321–40, concludes with these words. His laudable intent to reduce caricature and polarization need not extend, however, to asserting that "they agree on how intellect and will are related in the act of choice" (340), as Joseph Incandela's article ("Duns Scotus and the Experience of Human Freedom," *Thomist* 56 [1992]: 229–56) demonstrates: what is intrinsic and constitutive for Aquinas is extrinsic or (at best) coordinate for Scotus (Lee, 322–26).

35. I am indebted to Joseph Incandela for this observation. On the condemnations of 1277, see Roland Hissette, *Enquête sur les 219 articles condamnés à Paris le 7 mars 1277* (Louvain: Publications Universitaires, 1977).

36. Patrick Lee (n. 34), 341.

37. William Frank, "Duns Scotus on Autonomous Freedom and Divine Co-Causality," in *Medieval Philosophy and Theology* 2 (1992): 142–64.

38. Patrick Lee (n. 34), 322–26, citing C. Balic, "Une question inédite de J. Duns Scot sur la volonté," *Récherches de Théologie Ancienne et Mediévale* 3 (1931): 191–208, at 203; see Frank (n. 37), where "co-causality" is distinguished from instrumentality.

7. ON THE RELATIONS BETWEEN THE TWO ACTORS

1. My *Knowing the Unknowable God: Ibn Sina, Maimonides, Aquinas* (above, ch. 2, n. 4), proffers a plausible narrative of that "collaboration."

2. Robert Sokolowski, *The God of Faith and Reason* (Notre Dame, Ind.: University of Notre Dame Press, 1982), 124–30.

3. The most astute scrutiny of this condition is that of Yves Simon: "Order in Analogical Sets," *New Scholasticism* 34 (1960): 1–41; cf. my *Analogy and Philosophical Language* (New Haven: Yale University Press, 1973), 202–8.

4. This is the point which Ghazali saw in his critique of "the philosophers" in Islam, yet applied it only to the activity of God and not to that of creatures, unless Lenn Goodman's reading is to be accepted: "Did al-Ghazali deny Causality?" *Studia Islamica* 47 (1978): 83–120. But see Michael Marmura, "Al-Ghazali on Bodily Resurrection and Causality in *Tahafut* and the *Iqtisad*," *Aligarh Journal of Islamic Thought* (1989), 46–75.

5. See David Novak's treatment, "Self-Contraction of the Godhead in Kabbalistic Theology," in Lenn Evan Goodman, ed., *Neoplatonism and Jewish Thought* (Albany: State University of New York Press, 1992), 299–318.

6. My argument here is beholden to David Braine's careful elaboration of these points in *The Reality of Time and the Existence of God* (above, ch. 1, n. 8), 265–87, 293–96.

7. As Christopher Hughes presumes *existing* must be, thus keeping him from understanding the key terms in Aquinas' argument for divine simpleness or the relation of participation which is creation, in *On a Complex Theory of a Simple God* (Ithaca, N.Y.: Cornell University Press, 1989), 83, 27. Hughes' arguments present a useful foil to mine: how one might proceed to parse Aquinas without a hint of the role which creation plays in his ontology.

8. This section is derived majorly from Aquinas' treatment of divine knowing in *ST* 1.14.

9. A useful essay on this topic by Herbert McCabe, "The Involvement of God," has been reprinted in his *God Matters* (London: Chapman, 1987), 39–51.

10. See my elaboration of this strategy, plus a defense of its "grammatical" character, in *Knowing the Unknowable God* and *Aquinas: God and Action*.

11. Ian Richard Netton's *Allah Transcendent* (London: Routledge, 1989) offers a structuralist reading of the canonical Muslim *falasifa* as well as their *Ishraqi* (or "Eastern") counterparts, Suhrawardi and Ibn Arabi, in terms of competing paradigms for God: that of *Qur'anic Creator* or of *Islamic Transcendence*.

12. It will be useful to contrast the following with William Hasker's struggle to understand accounts of "God's timelessness" in his *God, Time, and Knowledge* (Ithaca, N.Y.: Cornell University Press, 1989), chs. 9 and 10. Rather than reach for the dialectical strategy of Aquinas, he suggests a principle which he takes to be the most general of the "metaphysical reasons" which have motivated and supported the theory of timelessness: "Wherever pos-

sible, we should subordinate ontological categories to God rather than subsuming God under the categories" (178). Ghazali would heartily agree, but Aquinas would find him begging the question, for one's *God* will be shaped inescapably by metaphysical categories, which Hasker adopts from a hymn of John Mason that he takes to articulate "God's ontological self-sufficiency and independence from the world" (189)!

13. Such is the contention of Charles Hartshorne and Schubert Ogden, to name the two most influential contenders for a new philosophical theology inspired by the work of Alfred North Whitehead, which has come to be called "process theology."

14. So Hasker (n. 12 above), whose fair canvas of views concludes: "In the final analysis, then, I am convinced that the Neoplatonic-Augustinian metaphysics is intimately involved in the doctrine of divine timelessness, which cannot and probably should not survive without it" (183).

15. Which is how theologians have employed the phrase "classical theism;" see my note on the controversy: "Does Process Theology Rest on a Mistake?" *Theological Studies* 43 (1982): 125–35.

16. This is the burden of Kathryn Tanner's perceptive study, *God and Creation in Christian Theology*, as well as Robert Sokolowski's *God of Faith and Reason*, which argues in these terms for "the distinction" of God from the world.

17. I have attempted this phenomenologically in *Aquinas: God and Action*, 87–88.

18. Most of the debate triggered by Norman Kretzmann and Eleonore Stump's seminal essay, "Eternity" (*Journal of Philosophy* 78 [1981]: 429–58) has turned on their use of 'duration' to characterize eternity: see Paul Fitzgerald, "Stump and Kretzmann on Time and Eternity," *Journal of Philosophy* 82 (1985): 260–69.

19. For a structural analysis of *ST* 1.3–11, which argues that the "formal features" of *goodness, limitlessness, unchangeableness*, and *oneness* are themselves logically equivalent to Aquinas' presentation of divine *simpleness*, see my *Aquinas: God and Action*, ch. 2.

20. Aquinas' proof can be found in a single paragraph of *De ente et essentia* 4 ¶7, while David Braine's requires an entire monograph: *The Reality of Time and the Existence of God*.

21. In an especially fair presentation, Hasker (note 12) finds it intelligible to say that God is "timelessly eternal" (145), but finds the assertion intertwined with "an abstruse metaphysic that holds little appeal for most contemporary philosophers" (186). We shall

see that his major objection – regarding God's knowledge of temporal realities (169) – relies on a speculative model.

22. Richard Swinburne is certainly correct that an "eternalist" must "maintain that many words are being used in highly analogical senses" in characterizing divinity (*Coherence of Theism* [above, ch. 5, n. 8], 221–22), but my contention would be that analogy goes with a creator, while the "temporalist" avoids employing language analogously only by making divinity a part of the world.

23. Barry Miller, *From Existence to God* (London: Routledge, 1992) ch. 3, esp. 42.

24. See the objection of Robert M. Adams in James Tomberlin and Peter van Inwangen, eds., *Alvin Plantinga* (Dordrecht: Reidel, 1985) 231–32, with Plantinga's reply, 372–79.

25. *De interpretatione,* ch. 9, 19a23–38; *Guide* 3.20.

26. See my discussion of Aquinas' use of the metaphor of vision in God's knowing of future contingents, in "Maimonides, Aquinas and Gersonides on Providence and Evil," *Religious Studies* 20 (1986) 335–51, esp. 346–48.

27. See Alfred Freddoso's introduction to his translation of Luis de Molina: *On Divine Foreknowledge* (Ithaca, N.Y.: Cornell University Press, 1988).

28. On the question of God's intentions, construed eternally, see Barry Miller, "Future Individuals and Haecceitism," *Review of Metaphysics* 20 (1986): 237–70.

29. David Braine reminded me that "formal features" of divinity are just that and cannot be considered to be "properties," in the current sense of the term, which would then be said of God; cf. *Reality of Time,* 170–73.

30. On Aquinas' use of a visual example which likens providence to a far-seeing lookout, see my "Maimonides, Aquinas and Gersonides on Providence and Evil," esp. 347.

31. The *contemporaneity,* of course, will have to be interpreted according to a grammar like that offered by Kretzmann and Stump in "Eternity" (n. 18): their proposal is called "ET-simultaneity," and I have been attempting here to remove the infelicitous image of "duration" from their proposal.

32. Which explains why William Hasker, who cannot countenance an eternal divinity, argues so effectively that God cannot know "the future"; see *God, Time, and Knowledge,* ch. 3.

33. See Thomas Flint, "Two Accounts of Providence," in Thomas Morris, ed., *Divine and Human Action,* 147–81, esp. 175

and 179, where he presumes, in reading Aquinas, that the creator's action "externally determines" a created free agent.

34. Plantinga in Tomberlin and van Inwangen, eds., *Alvin Plantinga* (note 24), 372–79.

35. In another context, see my note: "Does Process Theology Rest on a Mistake," *Theological Studies* 43 (1982): 125–35, where the crucial omission in that debate is also that of creation.

36. The contrast with Scotus is clearly delineated in Simo Knuuttila's "Being *qua* Being in Thomas Aquinas and John Duns Scotus," in his *Logic of Being* (Dordrecht: Reidel, 1986), 201–22, esp. 210–11; for a more synoptic view, see my "Aquinas and Scotus: Contrary Patterns for Philosophical Theology," in Bruce D. Marshall, ed., *Theology and Dialogue: Essays in Conversation with George Lindbeck* (above, ch. 3, n. 10), 105–29.

37. G. K. Chesterton is said to have quipped that St. Thomas was intent on "showing the independence of dependent things."

38. For this as a description of Scotus' position on the matter, see Knuuttila (n. 36) 209–10.

39. I am indebted to personal communication of Douglas Langston for the felicitous phrase: "Without doubt, Scotus as a logician and a metaphysician emphasizes possibility and sees actuality as a subset of possibility." The description certainly fits a current "school" of philosophical theologians inspired by the work of Alvin Plantinga.

40. This is clearly the case with Flint (n. 33) and Freddoso (n. 27).

41. Linda Zagzebski, "Individual Essence and the Creation," in Thomas Morris, ed., *Divine and Human Action* (above, ch. 4, n. 25), 142.

42. On the incapacity of such *haecceities* to do that job, see Barry Miller, "Future Individuals and Haecceitism" (above, n. 28).

43. *ST* 1.15, replete with references to classic *loci* in Augustine's works.

44. Arnaldez, "Intellectualism et voluntarisme dans la pensée musulmane," in *1274–Année charnière* (above, ch. 4, n. 29), 125.

45. Ross argues against a position which he calls "exemplarism," which would have "God create from a universal domain the divine exemplars," on the grounds that "it is inconsistent to say that God works from a domain of kinds and individuals . . . lying outside his will, determined by his nature," in the essay which Linda Zagzebski has in mind: "God, Creator of Kinds and Possibilities: *Re-*

quiescant universalia ante res," in Robert Audi and William Wainwright, eds., *Rationality, Religious Belief, and Moral Commitment* (above, ch. 3, n. 11), 315; yet he exempts Aquinas from "exemplarism" since for Aquinas "there are *rationes* for whatever God can do, but exemplars only for what he makes" (315, n. 1).

46. "Of things which neither are nor will be nor were, God has not practical knowledge except in the sense that he could have had. Hence with regard to them there is in God no Idea in the sense of exemplar, but only in the sense of intelligible nature [*ratio*]" (*ST* 1.15.3.2).

47. Besides the article cited above, see Ross's "The Crash of Modal Metaphysics," *Review of Metaphysics* 43 (1989): 251–79; and (among others) Barry Miller's "In Defense of the Predicate 'Exists'," *Mind* 84 (1975): 338–54, esp. 349: "['exists' is] unlike wisdom and every other property in that its possession by an individual is a necessary condition of that individual's being individuated." The article is expanded in his recent *From Existence to God* (London: Routledge, 1991).

48. Aquinas makes oblique reference to Avicenna in *ST* 1.14.11, while Maimonides identifies Ibn Sina's position as that of Aristotle (*Guide*, 3.17); for Avicenna, see Anawati vol 2: 358, line 14 to 362, line 14.

49. This citation from Aquinas occurs in an inquiry into truth and falsity: free agents alone can elicit "absolute objective falsity" by their capacity to work a paradoxical self-removal from that ordering which is the primary intent of the creator. Cf. Lonergan, *Grace and Freedom*, 111.

50. As Kierkegaard's Anti-Climacus puts it in *Sickness unto Death:* "this is one of the most decisive definitions for all Christianity— that the opposite of sin is not virtue but faith," (above, ch. 4, n. 28), 82.

51. This is Bernard Lonergan's argument against *premotio physica* in *GF,* 71, 144.

52. See the elaboration of this notion of freedom in the dissertation by Joseph Incandela, "Aquinas' Lost Legacy: God's Practical Knowledge and Situated Human Freedom" (Princeton University, 1986).

53. But I have argued that Aquinas offers the more faithful rendition of that tradition, in "Aquinas and Scotus: Contrary Patterns" (n. 36).

54. Lonergan offers a pattern for Aquinas' handling what seems

to be a contradiction here, since nothing can be outside the influence of divine activity. He locates Aquinas' treatment of God's "willing to allow [evil] to happen" (*ST* 1.19.9.3) as part of a "three-lane highway: . . . what God wills to happen, what He wills not to happen, and what He permits to happen" (*GF*, 110).

55. The paradoxical features of *self-deception* are nicely unraveled by Herbert Fingarette: *Self-Deception* (New York: Humanities Press, 1969).

56. On the difference between excuses and reasons for acting, see Julius Kovesi, *Moral Notions* (London: Routledge and Kegan Paul, 1967).

57. On the form which such "simultaneity" must take, see the article by Norman Kretzmann and Eleonore Stump, "Eternity" (above, n. 18).

58. See my "Maimonides, Aquinas and Gersonides . . . " (n. 30) for this reading of Aquinas.

59. See Lonergan, *GF*, 115, and the discussion by Joseph Incandela, "Duns Scotus and the Experience of Human Freedom" (*Thomist* 56 [1992]: 229–56), which offers a fair and competent review of the literature as well.

60. See the discussion in Freddoso's introduction to his translation of Luis de Molina (n. 27), and the short notice by John Wright in *Theological Studies* 50 (1989): 615.

61. Aristotle, *Nicomachean Ethics* 8.7 (1159a7).

62. The tone of the language employed by David Hartman, a contemporary expositor of Maimonides, is illustrative: "One can distinguish between the subjective *appropriation* of the constant, natural, divine overflow that one experiences at rare moments, and a conception of grace which implies a miraculous and unpredictable [sic!] act of divine will" (*Maimonides: Torah and Philosophical Quest* [Philadelphia: Jewish Publication Society, 1976], 257 n. 12).

63. Joseph Norment Bell has carefully sifted the evidence into illuminating categories in his *Love Theory in Later Hanbalite Islam* (Albany: State University of New York Press, 1979).

64. See the discussion by Roger Arnaldez (n. 44).

65. *Ihya'* 36 (IV, 328), M-L Siauve, *Livre de l'amour* (Paris: Vrin, 1986) 155, also 157 n.1.

66. I am much indebted here to M-L Siauve, *L'Amour de Dieu chez Ghazālī* (above, ch. 4, n. 6).

67. *Ihya'* IV, 327; Siauve, *Livre*, 153–54.

68. Ibid., I have rendered three terms of Ghazali by 'figurative':

'metaphor' [isti'āra], 'allegory' [tajawwaz], and 'transposition' [naql].

69. Yet more recent Islamicists in the West have questioned this characterization: cf. Annemarie Schimmel, *Mystical Dimensions of Islam* (Chapel Hill: University of North Carolina Press, 1975), 267–74, and William Chittick's *Sufi Path of Knowledge* (Albany: State University of New York Press, 1989), esp. ch. 3: "Ontology."

70. Massignon's four-volume *Passion of al-Hallaj* has been painstakingly edited and translated by Herbert Mason (Princeton: Princeton University Press, 1982), whose poetic précis of the story, *The Death of al-Hallaj* (Notre Dame, Ind.: University of Notre Dame Press, 1979) offers a moving portrait of the person and teaching of al-Hallaj.

71. *Passion* 2.57–62, where Massignon contrasts the accounts of Hallaj and Ibn al-Arabi. On the two forms of *union,* see also Annemarie Schimmel, *Mystical Dimensions of Islam,* 267. She renders *hulūl* by 'indwelling' (144) and by 'incarnation' (73); the first being considered orthodox, the second "heretical."

72. Biblical references to Abraham as God's friend: Gn 18:17, 2 Chr 20:7, Is 41:8, Wis 7:27, Jas 2:23; and Moses: Ex 33:11. For the commentary tradition on Qur'an 4:125, see Bell (n. 63), 159–62.

8. SIN AND REDEMPTION

1. *Church Dogmatics* 3.1, p. 97.

2. See the discussion of these matters in Oliver Leaman's *Introduction to Medieval Islamic Philosophy* (Cambridge: Cambridge University Press, 1985), 148–53, citation at 149.

3. In the *Mishneh Torah* [*Melakim* VIII, II] Maimonides insists that if a gentile "observes [the seven Noahite laws] because of his own conclusions based on reason, then he is not a resident-alien and is not one of the righteous of the nations of the world," so placing the meritorious valence on the side of recognizing their divine origin (see discussion in Leaman, and bibliography at 150 n. 41).

4. Maimonides concludes his discussion of the perfection of human beings (and concludes the *Guide* itself) by noting that observance of the Torah offers a shortcut to anyone who would achieve perfection "through assimilation to [God's] actions" (3.54 *ad fin*) – see Menachem Kellner's argument in *Maimonides on Human Perfection* (Atlanta: Scholars Press, 1990).

5. Since this reading of Maimonides is disputed, my sentence is qualified—see Leaman, 150.

6. These three levels of *sin* are elucidated by Paul Ricoeur in his classic *Symbolism of Evil,* trans. Emerson Buchanan (New York: Harper and Row, 1967).

7. *Sanhedrin* 13:2, 105a, as cited in Leaman, 149 n. 37.

8. On the vexing question of relations, see Mark Henninger, *Relations: Medieval Theories* (New York: Oxford University Press, 1989).

9. This sketch of the reception of Aquinas is largely gleaned from Henri de Lubac's *Surnaturel* (Paris: Aubier, 1946).

10. Published in Copenhagen in 1849 as "A Christian Psychological Exposition for Upbuilding and Awakening," by Anti-Climacus, trans. by Howard and Edna Hong (Princeton, N.J.: Princeton University Press, 1980), 82.

11. See Alasdair MacIntyre's treatment of Augustine and *willing* in *Whose Justice?* (above, ch. 6, n. 2).

12. See the central chapter, "The Path," in Annemarie Schimmel's *Mystical Dimensions* (above, ch. 7, n. 69), 98–186.

13. See Annemarie Schimmel's *Mystical Dimensions,* 213–27; as well as her *And Muhammad is His Messenger* (Chapel Hill: University of North Carolina Press, 1985).

14. I was encouraged to add this section by the extensive comments of my colleague Joseph Wawrykow, to whose pregnant suggestions I am much indebted.

15. For a useful elucidation of the term 'ontological' in this context, see Cornelius Ernst's introduction to vol. 30 of the Blackfriars edition of *ST* 1.2.106–114: *The Gospel of Grace* (New York: McGraw-Hill, 1972), xix–xxi. I shall use this translation and his guiding notes throughout.

16. *Sermo* 169 *Patrologia Latina* vol. 38:923 (cited in second objection to *ST* 1–2.111.2).

17. I am indebted to a personal communication from Joseph Wawrykow for these precisions. A classic example is given in Augustine's highly constructed recollection of his moment of conversion: "I could see the chaste beauty of Continence in all her serene, unsullied joy, as she modestly beckoned me to cross over and to hesitate no more" (*Confessions* 8.11). Whatever made him see *continence* as beauty and joy would move his heart without coercing it.

18. See Aquinas' sensitive response to the query "whether one can know that one has grace?" (1–2.112.5): the pathways of de-

sire are far less evident to us than the reaches of understanding.

19. For two "classic" versions, see H. Lennerz, *De gratia redemptoris* (Rome: Pontificia Universitas Gregoriana, 1949), 344–91; and Reginald Garrigou-Lagrange, *La Prédestination des saints et la grace* (Paris: Desclée, 1936), 95–100, which correlates the later terms, 'sufficient' and 'efficacious' grace with Aquinas' use of 'antecedent' and 'consequent' divine will.

9. THE GOD REALIZED IN RENEWED CREATION

1. Nicholas Lash, *Easter in Ordinary* (Notre Dame, Ind.: University of Notre Dame Press, 1990), 244.

2. See Joseph Owens' rejoinder to John Wippel: "Stages and Distinction in *de Ente*," *Thomist* 45 (1981), 99–123.

3. Sokolowski, *God of Faith and Reason*, 39.

4. Norman Kretzmann, "A General Problem of Creation: Why Would God Create Anything at All?" in Scott MacDonald, ed., *Being and Goodness* (Ithaca, N.Y.: Cornell University Press, 1991), 208–28.

5. Eric Ormsby's landmark study, *Theodicy in Islamic Thought* (Princeton, N.J.: Princeton University Press, 1984) traces the Qur'anic commentary tradition to the summary conclusion that "divine wisdom is the ultimate justification for things as they are" (264).

6. *Easter in Ordinary*, 265–66.

7. In theological parlance, "the Trinity of the economy of salvation *is* the immanent Trinity and vice versa" (87), found in Rahner's "Remarks on the Dogmatic Treatise 'De Trinitate,'" *Theological Investigations* 4 (Baltimore: Helicon, 1966): 77–102.

8. See also Lash's earlier "Considering the Trinity," in *Modern Theology* 2 (1986): 183–96.

9. *Easter*, 271; "Pattern of Christian Pedagogy" is the title of his crucial chapter 16.

10. *Easter*, 260; the approach alluded to is developed by George Lindbeck in *The Nature of Doctrine* (Philadelphia: Westminster, 1984), against the general background of Ludwig Wittgenstein's aphorism: "theology as grammar" (*Philosophical Investigations* #373: "Grammar tells us what kind of object anything is."

11. It is essential to say this, since the current discussion of these matters has introduced a jejune typology of "exclusive" or "inclusive" views: cf. Gavin D'Costa, *Theology and Religious Pluralism* (New

York: Blackwell, 1986), 80; and my presentation could be read as "inclusive."

12. The first tendency was "located" by Karl Rahner's bold essay in re-periodizing the history of Christianity, "Towards a Fundamental Interpretation of Vatican II," *Theological Studies* 40 (1979): 716–27. The second can be illustrated by any of the essays in Thomas or in Richard Swinburne's *Coherence of Theism* (above, ch. 5, n. 8).

13. Lash, *Easter,* 264; cf. also "Considering the Trinity," 185.

14. See Lash's discussion of this point in "Considering the Trinity," 195 n. 29.

15. Rahner, "Remarks on the Dogmatic Treatise," 83–87.

16. Both quotations are from Lash, "Considering the Trinity," 187.

17. See the article by G. E. von Grunebaum in *EI²* 3.1018–20.

18. *Daily Prayer Book,* trans. Philip Birnbaum (New York: Hebrew Publishing Company, 1977) 222ff., refrain at 246.

19. Moshe Idel, *Kabbalah: New Perspectives* (New Haven: Yale University Press, 1988) 161.

20. *Kabbalah,* 171, the citation is from 'Avodah Zarah 3a.

21. I am indebted, in this summary of Irenaeus, to the master's essay of John D. Leonard: "Creator and Creature in the Theology of St. Irenaeus" (1973), St. Vladimir's Orthodox Theological Seminary, Crestwood, Tuckahoe: N.Y. 10707. (Pronouns have usually been reduced to lower case in citations.) Irenaeus' *Adversus Haereses* (=*AH*) is volume 1 in the Ante-Nicene Fathers series.

22. See the translation by David Burrell and Nazih Daher: *Al-Ghazālī on the Ninety-nine Beautiful Names of God* (Cambridge: Islamic Texts Society, 1992), for a classical presentation of the Muslim doctrine of God.

23. Al-Ash'ari made this an axial point in his polemic against the Mu'tazilites: see Daniel Gimaret, *La Doctrine d'al-Ash'ari* (Paris: Cerf, 1990), ch. 8: "Parole de Dieu," esp. 310–15; but also see A. T. Welch's article in *EI²* 5.426.

24. Catherine Mowry LaCugna, "The Baptismal Formula, Feminist Objections, and Trinitarian Theology," *Journal of Ecumenical Studies* 26 (1989): 235–50.

25. Wilfrid Cantwell Smith has noted how the Muslim appellation "peoples of the book" may mislead Christians into thinking that the relevant analogy links the Qur'an with the Bible, whereas

"the parallel is to the Christian doctrine that Jesus Christ is the Word of God" (*Questions of Religious Diversity* [New York: Crossroad, 1982], 24).

26. Ibn Kullab, from Basra, whose chief ideas were taken up by al-Ash'ari – cited by Louis Massignon, *Passion of al-Hallaj*, trans. Herbert Mason (Princeton, N.J.: Princeton University Press, 1982), 3:140.

27. Michel Allard, *Le Problème des attributs divins* (Beyrouth: Imprimérie Catholique, 1965).

28. Massignon, *Passion*, 3:143; for Muhāsibi (781–857), see Massignon's article in *SEI*, 410.

29. The famous *'kul'* suras; see ch. 6, n. 23, notably William Graham, *Beyond the Written Word*, ch. 8: "Muslim Scripture as Spoken Word."

30. Frederick Denny, *Introduction to Islam* (New York: Macmillan, 1985), 160.

31. Annemarie Schimmel, *Mystical Dimensions*, 167–78, esp. 177–78.

32. See the article by M. Bernand in *EI²* 3.1023–26.

33. Ignaz Goldziher's assessment of Wahhabism offers a signal illustration of *ijmā'* in practice: "For orthodox Islam, since the twelfth century, Ghazāli has been the final authority. [Since] the Wahhabis advance against Ghazāli the doctrines of the man whom the ruling theology rejected: Ibn Taymīya . . . , they must be regarded as heterodox and condemned as such" (245) – *Introduction to Islamic Law and Theology*, trans. Andras and Ruth Hamori (Princeton, N.J.: Princeton University Press, 1981). A sounding of Islam worldwide would, I believe, corroborate this judgment.

34. Fazlur Rahman, *Islam*, 2nd ed. (Chicago: University of Chicago Press, 1979), 72–78, 239–40.

35. Roger Arnaldez, "Prophétie et sainteté en Islam," in A.-T. Khoury and M. Weigels, eds., *Weg in der Zufunft* (Leiden: Brill, 1975), 229–57, first citation at 253; second is from Kenneth Cragg, "Sainthood and Spirituality in Islam," *Studia Missionalia* 35 (1986): 179–98, at 190.

36. Martin Lings' account of his encounter with Shaikh Ahmad al-'Alawī, *A Sufi Saint of the Twentieth Century* (London: George Allen and Unwin, 1961) details the relationships involved.

37. I am here extending Nicholas Lash's observation (in *Easter*, 266) to all three traditions.

38. Notably Catherine Mowry LaCugna, "The Relational God: Aquinas and Beyond," *Theological Studies* 46 (1985): 647–63; and *God for Us: Trinity and the Christian Life* (San Francisco: Harper-Collins, 1992).

Index to Key Arabic Terms

Index

Weil, Simone, 141
Weinandy, Thomas, 194 n.26
Welch, A. T., 209 n.23
Whitehead, Alfred North, 201
    n.13
Will: as autonomous in Scotus,
    88; divine, 45–46; human,
    90
Winch, Peter, 190 n.2

Wippel, John, 186 n.9, 208 n.2
Wittgenstein, Ludwig, 208 n.10
Wolfson, Harry A., 194 n.32
Wolterstorff, Nicholas, 188 n.6
Wright, G. E., 194 n.1
Wright, John, 205 n.60

Zagzebski, Linda, 115, 116, 190
    n.7, 194 n.25, 203 n.45

About the Author

David B. Burrell, C.S.C., received his Ph.D. from Yale University. He is the Theodore M. Hesburgh Professor of Philosophy and Theology at the University of Notre Dame. He has received numerous awards, such as the Woodrow Wilson and Fulbright fellowships, and has been a visiting professor at many universities, including National Major Seminary, Dhaka, Bangladesh; Hebrew University, Jerusalem; and Princeton Theological Seminary. He is the author of *Knowing the Unknowable God* (Notre Dame Press, 1986), coeditor of *God and Creation* (Notre Dame Press, 1990), and coauthor of *Voices from Jerusalem* (Paulist, 1992).